D1556726

Astonishing Britain

Astonishing Britain

Anthony Burton

DAVID & CHARLES
Newton Abbot   London

Page 2: The Pineapple at Dunmore,
built as a summer-house *(Landmark Trust)*

British Library Cataloguing in Publication Data
Burton, Anthony, *1934–*
　　Astonishing Britain
　　1.　Great Britain. Description & travel
　　I.　Title
　　914.1'04858

ISBN 0–7153–9469–X

Typeset in 11/13pt Cheltenham Light by
ABM Typographics Ltd, Hull
and printed in Portugal by Resopal
for David & Charles plc
Brunel House　Newton Abbot　Devon

Contents

Introduction

WHEN I wrote the forerunner of this book, *The Shell Book of Curious Britain* in 1981 I ended with these words:

> I have no doubt at all that after the book is published I shall find a new and amazing site which I had never known of before. Even as I write, someone, somewhere, is perhaps providing a new wonder – painting a bizarre mural on a terrace end or constructing a maze. Elsewhere someone is rediscovering a long-forgotten wonder, perhaps an eighteenth-century folly that the rest of us had ignored.

The prophecy came true: I did discover more curious delights, and readers wrote to me with details of their favourites as well. New oddities are still being added, so that Britain sometimes seems, like Alice's Wonderland, to be getting 'curiouser and curiouser'. It would be curiouser still if planners did not reject so many wonderfully bizarre designs and schemes. A huge man built out of brick, intended for Leeds, was never built; a shark nose-diving into a house roof in Oxford was greeted with complaints and rejection by the authorities – yet still it dives (see p41). It is apparently acceptable to cover the country with four-square office blocks of stultifying dullness, but unacceptable to erect a structure whose only justification might be that it is attractive and makes for a touch of fun and amusement.

This book is firmly on the side of the off-beat and the unconventional, the odd and the eccentric. But what is meant by 'unusual'? What is unusual to me might be perfectly conventional to anyone else, just as the oddly name occupation 'saggar maker's bottom knocker' seems extraordinarily funny to outsiders, but is no more than a plain definition of an essential occupation in the potteries. The first chapter looks at those strange standing stones of prehistory, which can seem so baffling to us today. Yet once they must have been a part of everyday experience. A great stone circle such as Stonehenge might well have inspired awe and reverence, but to those who built it or came to it for rituals it was not something strange – no stranger than we should regard a great medieval cathedral. But, in complete contrast, are 'follies', objects set up for no 'practical' purpose whatsoever – other than to stop passers-by in their tracks, while they stare

The impressive Wallace
Tower in Stirling
(Anthony Burton)

Once the tower of a
windmill in Dumfries, this is
now a museum and
camera obscura
(Anthony Burton)

at them in astonishment. Many follies are all the more bizarre simply because they do not look like anything else – they are purely original creations, realisations of their builders' fantasies. Other buildings are equally surprising, not because they look like nothing at all but because they look very much like something, but that something turns out to be totally misleading. Most people recognise St Pancras Station in London as one of the great examples of Victorian Gothic architecture. But just imagine not knowing that behind the pinnacles and arches lurks something as commonplace as a railway station. How remarkable it would seem, even more so than it does now that the shock has worn off. My one regret in writing this book is that there was no opportunity to look further afield, for Bombay boasts a station that out-Pancrases St Pancras. It is, however, only a fleeting regret, for really there is no shortage of similarly extravagant buildings to enjoy in Britain.

Oddity can reach to all aspects of human life. We live in an age which places a high priority on standardisation and regulation. Houses, for example, must conform to certain rules. This is fine when the rules are designed to cover such matters as safety, but too often they can be used to produce mere conformity, for the sake of conformity. It can be, and indeed is, claimed that such rules prevent the construction of eyesores, although when such claims are put forward by those bodies which actively encourage the construction of tower blocks they need not be taken so seriously. But what is an eyesore? To some the mock-Gothic so beloved of Victorian builders is simply hideous; for others the Gothic cottage is a home of character and individuality. Certainly some of the bizarre buildings that are discussed in this book would never get past the local planning committee nowadays. Many people find this rather regrettable, and as there is a limited stock of 'houses of character' – there are far fewer than one is led to believe by the claims of estate agents – people look to other buildings. Chapels, village schools, disused railway stations, barns and mills: all have been converted into homes by enthusiastic owners looking for something different. Such schemes often prove very successful, achieving effects of great exuberance which high costs and rigid rules make all but impossible in the more ordinary house.

In an earlier age this same exuberance extended to the homes of domestic animals. Many a horse or dog enjoyed better accommodation than those who tended them. And even death failed to provide an end to this world of curiosity, for dotted around the country are many strange and bizarre tombs and epitaphs. Did anyone, for example, ever receive a grander, yet more unlikely, monument than that put up at Stirling to William Wallace, who defeated the English at the Battle of Stirling in 1297? The monument was a little while coming – it was finished in 1869 – but what a structure it is. From a distance it looks like a rotten tooth sticking up from a swollen gum, but viewed close up, it appears as a pseudo-medieval tower, over 200ft (61m) high, strongly reminiscent of the work of Mervyn Peake. But what is one to make of the decoration? Why does a stone rope

curl itself around doors and windows and disappear into holes in the walls? It might make sense in a monument to a great sailor, but it makes no sense on a Stirling hill-top. It is wholly, but delightfully, illogical. Scotland, in fact, is a happy hunting ground for those in search of oddities, and they even come in pairs. At Dumfries, a monument to Old Mortality, in which the surgeon, John Sinclair, takes his rest while his faithful horse munches alongside him, is contained within a pretty little classical rotunda. Next to it is a circular tower which also has a classical air, but which serves no obvious function. At one time, however, it was a windmill and now is home to a small museum that houses the perennially fascinating device, a camera obscura.

So the list can be continued into events as well as permanent structures. It seems that on almost any day in the year, someone, somewhere, is reviving some strange custom. Old traditions are untidy anachronisms to some, living links with the past to others. I once took a Swedish friend down to my local for a pint, where we were greeted by the sight of a troop of Morris men. It was difficult to tell whether he was delighted or merely astonished. He had never, he declared, seen anything so bizarre. What, then, would he have made of the Coconut Dancers of Bacup, those stout Lancashire men who black their faces, don outlandish costumes and then proceed to clog dance through the streets?

Perhaps the best news for those who feel that anything which adds individuality and colour to streets which are all too often dominated by advertisements and signs for national and multi-national companies has to be a good thing, is that there has been a great revival in activity in recent years. Murals spring up everywhere, some inspired by local themes, others touching the surreal. A railway bridge has been painted in a most realistic style in London's Camden Town, depicting men painting a railway bridge in London's Camden Town. And that traditional source of puzzlement and wonder, the maze, is making a welcome return.

With such a wealth of material how does one select what to include in a book? There are no rules here, other than the totally pragmatic, and doubtless egocentric one, that what I found interesting and amusing was included. What failed to excite me was left out. I can do no more than hope that readers will share my enjoyment of some of the myriad of strange objects and places which help to bring such rich diversity to the British landscape.

GAZETTEER

These are brief notes on a selection of other locations arranged inside columns to accompany their respective chapters. Inclusion of buildings etc should not be taken as an indication that they are open to the public. Those marked NT and NTS are the properties of the National Trust and National Trust for Scotland respectively.

A full list of Landmark Trust properties is obtainable from The Landmark Trust, Shottesbrooke, Maidenhead, Berkshire SL6 3SW.

Standing Stones and Other Mysteries

W IND and rain have carved stones into many strange and grotesque shapes and they have been given equally fanciful names: the Cheesewring on Bodmin Moor in Cornwall does look something like a pile of round cheeses, and Brimham Rocks in Yorkshire has a craggy outcrop that looks remarkably like a dancing bear when seen from the right angle. Other names, however, say more about the anonymous namers' imaginations than about the shapes themselves. But it is unwise to be too scornful. The well-known isolated sea stack in Orkney, the Old Man of Hoy, originally did stand on two legs, until the waves carried one away. The sea is, indeed, responsible for many fantastic shapes, such as Durdle Door which strides out into the water from the cliffs of Dorset. But among the most popular of all natural formations are those rocks which appear to have got themselves into impossible positions and are only staying in place by a miracle. The Norber stones on the southern edge of Ingleborough are huge dark boulders precariously balanced on white limestone plinths, like oversized teed-up golf balls awaiting some giant's driver. Even more precarious is the Logan Rock, near the tip of Cornwall, which can be moved by a hard push. It is not, however, about to topple over, any more than it was in 1851 when the novelist Wilkie Collins came to the area and shouted to his friends with glee: 'You have treated eighty-five tons of granite like a child's cradle!' But fascinating though such stones are, they can all be explained away. The

Ashburton, Devon The stones of Buckland Beacon are inscribed with the Ten Commandments.

Brynberian, Dyfed Pentre Ifan cromlech, arguably the most impressive prehistoric monument in Wales, 1 mile (1.6km) north of village.

Castlerigg, Cumbria (1½ miles (2.5km) east of Keswick) Stone circle with stone rectangle inside (NT).

Dorstone, Hereford & Worcester Arthur's Stone is a Neolithic tomb, one of the many legendary resting places of King Arthur.

Elton, Derbyshire Nine Stones; the name is misleading since only four ancient stones remain on the site on Harthill Moor, SK226 626.

Grange in Borrowdale, Cumbria The Bowder Stone is a massive boulder, estimated to weigh 2,000 tons, improbably balanced on one corner.

Henley-on-Thames, Oxfordshire Park Place, a private house near Marsh Lock, has a

Wilkie Collins and friend enjoying a visit to Cornwall's Logan Rock, which the novelist noted rocked 'like a child's cradle' *(Bodleian Library, Oxford: Gough Adds Cornwall 8.5 opp p.189)*

Norbers, for example, are simply blocks of gritstone that were carried down the mountain in the last glaciation and finally came to rest on a bed of limestone. Over the centuries, the limestone eroded until it reached a point where the dark stone above kept off the weather. Fantasies, sadly perhaps, seldom stand up to careful scrutiny: giants never had jolly games on the slopes of a Yorkshire hillside. Things are a little different, however, when one turns to the stones set in the landscape by man.

Not so far from the rocking Logan Rock is another odd stone, Men-an-Tol, or the stone with a hole, looking not unlike a petrified doughnut set on end, with other standing stones associated with it. Archaeologists have their theories to explain the stones: to some the circle was the entrance to a Neolithic grave, while to others the stones are Bronze Age 'monuments', although monuments to what is seldom explained. Evidence to support either view is, to say the least, somewhat scanty – and this is one of the great appeals of ancient stones. Where no logical explanation for the mystery can be proved, the way is open to the individual to promote the illogical. Our forebears had their own responses to ancient stones. In legend after legend they are described as the work of the devil – although equally the stones can have magical healing properties. Men-an-Tol is also known as the Devil's Eye and it does indeed have a long tradition of healing. Naked boys and girls were passed through the hole three times

The natural rock arch of Durdle Door on the Dorset coast *(Anthony Burton)*

and each time they had to be pulled away towards the east. This, it was claimed, was an infallible cure for diseases such as rickets. We now know that rickets is a disease associated with poor diet, so how could dragging a naked child through a hole in a stone effect its cure? Did it, in fact, ever work at all? We simply do not know the answer to such questions. Rheumatism could also be cured, or so legend says, if the sufferer crawled nine times through the hole in the direction of the rising sun. Sceptics might argue that any chronic rheumatic who could manage to crawl through the hole once, let alone nine times, was not so chronically ill as he supposed. Possibly so, yet the stories have lasted literally for millennia. The question that comes to mind is whether the stories are, in fact, derived from an experience of healing, or whether the stories of miracle cures have grown up to explain the otherwise inexplicable presence of such strange structures.

Stones with holes in them were often endowed with special powers. Odin's Stone was said to be especially potent. Special powers could be obtained by visiting the stone at nine consecutive full moons and crawling around it nine times on bare knees on each occasion (nine is a much

miniature Stonehenge in the garden which can be glimpsed from the river.

Leckhampton, Gloucestershire Devil's Chimney, a tall pinnacle on the escarpment to the south of Cheltenham.

Little Salkeld, Cumbria (4 miles (6.5km) north east of Penrith) Long Meg and her daughters – a stone circle in a dramatic setting, NY57 37.

Llanagllgo, Anglesey, Gwynedd Lligwy cromlech is a burial site capped by an immense stone which may have been in use since Neolithic times. Nearby is the Iron Age settlement of Din Lligwy.

Lybster, Highlands Hill o' Many Stanes, an extraordinary ancient site on a minor road off the A9 4 miles (6.5km) north of the village.

Merrivale, Devon Stone row said to have mystical properties 1 mile (1.6km) east of the village, just south of Princetown Road.

Morvah, Cornwall The starting point for a hunt for some ancient stones: Lanyon Quoit (NT) SW430 337, Chun Quoit SW402 339, Men-an-Tol and Men Screfys SW43 35.

Priestweston, Shropshire 1 mile (1.6km) to the north-east is Mitchell's Fold. A stone circle high up the mountainside.

Rudston, Humberside A monolithic stone stands within the churchyard.

favoured magical number). Young lovers would become betrothed by holding hands through the stone and swearing undying fidelity. Odin's Stone has now vanished, destroyed because the farmer on whose land it stood had no time for superstition and was tired of couples stomping through his fields to declare their love. The locals retaliated by burning down his house – it is not generally considered wise to tamper with magic stones. Originally Odin's Stone stood at Stenness in Orkney where it had many companions, the Stenness stones and the Ring of Brodgar among them, which happily still remain. What an extraordinary sight they are on the moor, especially the Ring of Brodgar. This is a henge monument, a class 2 henge monument to be precise, that is one with a circular bank and ditch with two entrances. Inside the circle is the great ring of stones, over 110yd (100m) in diameter, with nearly half of the original sixty stones still standing, each rising to a height of about 6½ft (2m). It is dramatic, exciting, strange, and inevitably one is left wondering why they were erected. Why was so much effort put into the ring's creation? The obvious answer is that it has some religious significance, but that provides no clue as to the purpose of the carefully arranged pattern.

One thing that many archaeologists are agreed upon is that many, if not all, stone circles have some sort of astronomical significance. Professor Alexander Thom has argued this case most convincingly, showing how the circles can be used for the calculation of seasonal changes and the like. The alignments are often connected with astonishingly accurate measurements. What this theory does not explain, however, is why such

The ancient stones of Men-an-Tol are supposed to have healing powers
(Derek Pratt)

The brooding stones of Orkney's Ring of Brodgar
(Anthony Burton)

calculations were needed in the first place. True, an agricultural society needs to know when to plant and when to harvest, but scarcely with that sort of precision. No farmer lays down rigid rules that the corn must go in, say, at 4.30 next Wednesday afternoon or all will be lost. Accurate dating of phenomena such as the equinoxes and phases of the moon would, however, be required in a society that believed that the movement of the heavens had a practical importance in determining the course of their lives. If gods need to be propitiated by specific actions at specific times, then it might well be thought crucial that the timing should be accurate. Those who had the job of timing would be important members of society, and the time-keeping mechanism itself might also be considered of sufficient importance to merit a place in the temple structure. So there are

two parts to the possible explanation. The stones are giant calculators, which only the priests would use: ordinary members of the society could not and would not meddle in the business of enumeration and calculation. Also, because the stones have religious significance, there would have been food offerings, and sacrifices do seem to have been made at Stenness.

Popular mythology about stone circles often describes the stones as petrified human beings. Cornwall boasts Nine Maidens (the occurrence of nine again) and Merry Maidens. In both cases, the maidens were stunned into perpetual stony immobility as punishment for dancing on the Sabbath. Similar stories are told of The Hurlers, not one but three stone circles, their centres aligned. Each is over 100ft (30m) in diameter and they seem

Castlerigg stone circle may be one of the oldest in Britain, but its significance has long since been forgotten *(Cumbria Libraries)*

originally to have each held twenty-five to thirty stones, although the most that survive are the seventeen stones of the centre circle. They have all been carefully positioned and to ensure that they stayed put each was sunk several feet into the ground. It is not difficult to guess what legend has to say about them. The first record dates from the sixteenth century: the historian William Camden wrote that the locals gave the stones their popular name 'being by devout and godly error perswaded that they had been men sometimes transformed into stone for profaning the Lord's Day with hurling the ball'. This story is corroborated by the various petrified maidens of other circles, but it is not the only legend associated with The Hurlers. It was claimed at one time that no one could count the stones. The only way you could get an accurate count was to get a huge basketful of buns and count those. Then one bun had to be placed on each of the stones in the circles. When every stone was topped by a bun, all that remained was to count the buns in the basket, subtract that number from the original one, and the calculation was complete. Just another old legend, you might suppose, but where did it originate? And, even more interestingly, why does the same tale crop up at other stone circles in other parts of the country, as at the Rollright Stones in Oxfordshire? The legend as it relates to the Rollright Stones has an elaboration for even the bun-counting did not prove infallible, because as the would-be counters went around the circle placing their buns, so the Devil would walk behind taking them off again. The Rollright Stones have one of the most elaborate of all legends associated with them. They consist of a stone circle known as the King's Men, a group of five stones huddled together – the Whispering Knights – and a large single stone – the King's Stone. The Knights were, in fact, a dolmen or open burial chamber, the cap-stone having at some time fallen off the supporting stones. The groups are contemporary with each other, dating from around 2000 to 1800BC. Many of the stories surrounding the stones have familiar themes: the King's Men cannot be counted, for example, without resorting to the old penny buns. Other tales concern movement: legend has it that at midnight the stones get up and dance, and on certain special nights they also wander off to a nearby stream for a drink, having worked up a thirst from the dancing, no doubt. Yet although the stones spend a good deal of time roaming and skipping about the countryside, they take a dim view of any mere human trying to shift them. It is said that a farmer decided that the cap-stone from the Whispering Knights was ideal for bridging a stream that ran across his land – the same stream from which the stones were said to drink. Dragging the stone to the site proved an incredibly difficult job. Some stories tell that a mere six horses were used, while others describe how fifty beasts were necessary, and a third variation relates that the horses dropped dead from the effort. And once the stone was in place, it refused to stay put. Every morning it had left the brook and was found lying in the grass. Eventually the farmer gave up the struggle and took the stone back, and for the return journey one horse moved it with ease.

The Rollright Stones, in legend a king's army petrified by a witch (Anthony Burton)

With so many stories about the activities of these energetic stones, it is not surprising to find that, in legend, they are given animal, and even human, origins. The best-known story concerns a king who was marching his army through the land, when he was stopped by a witch with these words:

> Seven long strides shalt thou take.
> If Long Compton thou canst see,
> King of England thou shalt be.

As Long Compton was close at hand, it seemed a reasonable offer, so the king duly strode forward with this reply:

> Stick, stock, stone,
> As King of England I shall be known.

St Cleer, Cornwall (3 miles (5km) north of Liskeard) Trethevy Quoit, one of the most impressive ancient monuments in Cornwall, SX260 688.

Stanton Drew, Avon Three stone circles which, though not as impressive as Stonehenge or Avebury, actually cover a greater area.

Shebbear, Devon The Devil's Boulder on the village green is turned over each 5 November by local bell-ringers.

Uffington, Oxfordshire Wayland's Smithy. This long barrow can be found near the famous White Horse. Tradition says that a traveller who leaves an unshod horse and a coin here will find his horse miraculously shod.

Weston Rhyn, Shropshire A somewhat unconvincing miniature Stonehenge, built in the 1830s to provide a view from Quinton House.

Wolverhampton, West Midlands The Bargain Stone stands in St Peter's Collegiate churchyard. A handshake through a hole in the stone was considered a binding contract.

When he had taken his seven strides, however, he found to his dismay that a large mound of earth – known as the Archdruid's Barrow, although it is neither a barrow nor anything to do with the Druids – blocked his view. He was not, it would seem, a man well versed in the ways of witches, who are generally recognised as unreliable in such matters. So it proved on this occasion, for the witch added this incantation to her original offer:

> As Long Compton thou canst not see,
> King of England thou shalt not be.
> Rise up stick, and stand still stone,
> For King of England thou shalt be none.
> Thou and thy men hoar stones shall be
> And myself an elder tree.

So the king was turned to stone, with his men standing in a circle and his knights huddled together in eternal conference.

So here we have mystery compounded: the previously familiar elements of astronomy and fertility seem to be of minor importance, while in their place are stories of activity. If the theory is that such stones have some relationship to old forgotten beliefs, then what can all this signify? Many people have numerous different theories ranging from spacemen arriving in flying saucers to set up the stones to the idea that the stones are some kind of battery, storing a special sort of power. The spacemen stories can be discounted for the present, not because they are obviously untrue but because there is no way of testing them – and anyway, if one decides that spacemen did, indeed, erect the stones we are still no nearer to an understanding of their purpose than we are if we decide they were erected by early man. But what of the idea of the stone circle as a place where some sort of force is concentrated? There are, after all, many forces which were unknown and unrecognised until modern times. We accept the notion of an invisible electro-magnetic field because we can see its effect on, for example, a simple bar magnet. It has been suggested that just as there are forces which were unrecognised by the ancients, so too there were forces which they knew about but which we have subsequently lost from sight. A number of theorists have suggested ways in which the forces of the stones can be tested.

Being something of a sceptic, I am by no means eager to adopt such notions; being also trained as a scientist, I am a great believer in the experimental method. A pendulum test is easily carried out, and on one occasion I determined to try it at the Rollright Stones. I carried the experiment one stage further by tape-recording the exercise for the local radio station. As any pendulum should behave like any other pendulum, and as it was autumn, I took with me a conker on the end of a piece of string. The listeners received the story as it happened, and could make of it what they liked. My humble conker went berserk whenever it was brought near one of the King's Men in the circle, and if the listeners were surprised,

I was even more astonished. I would not suggest that such a simple test proves anything, although since making it myself I have been less inclined to scoff at all theories that speak of the power of the stones.

There is, it seems, no end to the stories associated with stone circles. One of the most impressive collections of stones in Britain is at Callanish on the Hebridean island of Lewis. It is the sheer complexity of the site which is so overwhelming: a circle of standing stones with one massive stone at the centre, with wide avenues of stones running away to the four points of the compass. In the fables, a great white cow came out of the sea to provide endless supplies of milk for the impoverished islanders, provided that none took more than a single pailful. Inevitably, one greedy woman sneaked back for more, but with no success. In revenge, she substituted a sieve for the bucket on her next visit, and milked the magic cow dry. It never returned to the stone circle of Callanish. Those who believe that legends are something more than simple tales for simple people might well link this story with the theory that the stones are great astronomical calculators. All the elements are there: the white cow that comes at night symbolises the moon, the milking symbolises the milky

The ancient stones of Callanish: was this an ancient astronomical calculator? *(Crown copyright, reproduced by permission of the Scottish Development Department)*

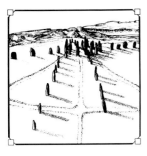

way and there is a ritual that if correctly performed brings plenty but which otherwise leads to disaster. The beauty of these stories is that there are as many interpretations as there are stories.

When it comes to the great prehistoric monuments, to Stonehenge, say, or Avebury, such ideas seem almost paltry in relation to the magnificence of the sites themselves. Whether those who claim to feel the power of the stones are indulging in self-delusion or not, our forebears took them seriously. Christian churches were often built close to the important sites, such as Avebury. The number of demonic stories may be no mere accident, but a continuation of the notion that ancient sites have an association with pagan religions, which they certainly have. So we have the Devil's Jumps on the South Downs, which are, in fact, a group of massive Bronze Age bell barrows or burial mounds; or the Devil's Arrows at Boroughbridge – tall stones said to have been fired at the locals by the Devil in a fit of pique. The Devil was, it seems, much given to irritation, but his planned revenges generally went astray. In fact, almost all of his endeavours proved fruitless. Perhaps the oddest story of all is the one that describes Satan winging his way over Cornwall carrying a huge boulder with which he hoped to block the entrance to Hell in order to deal with a serious problem of overcrowding. He was over Cornwall when he met his great enemy St Michael, and in the engagement between them the stone was dropped. In time it was used for building what was to become the Angel Inn in the town of Hell Stone or, as we know it today, Helston.

Occasionally an ancient monument can be seen that is so vast and so apparently devoid of rational explanations that only two options are available: either to invent an irrational explanation or simply to abandon the attempt altogether. Silbury Hill in Wiltshire is just such a monument. It is a great earth mound, covering over 5 acres and rising to a height of nearly 131ft (40m). It has been dated to around 2500BC and experts have estimated that it took 18 million man hours to construct. To put that in modern terms, if you took a thousand navvies, armed with buckets and spades and working a standard thirty-five-hour week, they would need ten years to complete the job. It was clearly an immense – and immensely important – labour, and we do not have even the least idea what it is. Tradition has it that King Sil lies buried here, clad in gold, but excavations, whether by treasure hunters or archaeologists have found nothing. Popular theories include the notion that it was a giant sundial – somewhat excessively large, one might think. It has also been described as an earth goddess. Everyone is free to reach his or her own conclusion. Some, however, are content to accept the mound for what it is – one of the world's great unsolved mysteries.

With other ancient monuments, one is on surer ground. The barrows and cromlechs and burial chambers might look odd, but they become comprehensible once their purpose is known. Near Silbury Hill, West Kennet long barrow can be found. This is a Neolithic or New Stone Age burial chamber, covered by a 330ft (100m) long mound and closed off at

The Cerne Abbas Giant: it comes as no surprise to discover that this hill figure is generally thought of as a fertility symbol *(Royal Commission on the Historical Monuments of England)*.

the end by massive stones. Excavation has revealed multiple burials extending over centuries. But knowing what it is makes it no less impressive, and does nothing to change the stories of a ghostly priest with a ghostly hound who arrives just before dawn on Midsummer's Day. Similarly, the round barrows that are a feature of the chalky downland of southern England seem just as strange in the landscape after they have been identified as round barrows as they did when they were known as mounds like landed flying saucers.

Hill figures should be the easiest ancient monuments to explain. They are, after all, representational. We can see what they are; what we cannot see, however, is why they were made. The Uffington White Horse, which has given its name to the Vale of the White Horse, is a beautiful, sinuous creature which was created when the turf on the hillside was cut to reveal the white chalk underneath. It is found next to an Iron Age hill fort, so there is a tendency to date it to that period – and similar designs were known to exist at that time. What is most remarkable is its survival. If left untended,

the grass would cover it, so it needs to be cleared and this is traditionally done every seven years. If the dating is accurate, generation after generation must have tended the White Horse, which may well be approaching its 300th grooming. Tradition associates the figure with St George – who never visited England – and the dragon, although there is no record that he ever met his fiery opponent. Westbury White Horse in Wiltshire may well be equally old, but as it was completely remodelled by a well-meaning but inept person in the eighteenth century, all that remains now is a conventional horse with what appears to be a beak.

Of the human figures, only two are ancient: the Cerne Abbas giant and the Long Man of Wilmington. It comes as no surprise to learn that the 200ft (60m) high figure at Cerne Abbas is generally regarded as a fertility symbol, since the gentleman is notably well endowed with a huge phallus. The fertility symbolism has lasted to the present day, with maypole dancing in a small enclosure near the figure and the story that women who wish to conceive have only to spend a night in the giant's company. The Long Man on the Downs above Wilmington is altogether more mysterious. An even bigger figure, 230ft (70m) high, he appears in simple outline to be holding a long staff or wand in each hand. He may once have been, like the Cerne Abbas giant, a more obviously masculine figure, but he was restored with unrecorded alterations by the Victorians. Again, no one knows when, why or by whom he was built, but one thing is significant: the site is packed with ancient remains. Neolithic man came to the area of Wilmington to mine flint for axes; and there is a long barrow burial mound from the same period as well as the more familiar round barrows of the later Bronze Age. The idea that the Long Man is a figure of religious significance is reinforced by the setting and by the care with which he was constructed, set into a rectangle with a precise 2:1 ratio of the sides. The sense of meaningful antiquity in the area is reinforced for those walking east on the South Downs Way, for across the valley on the hill above Jevington are piles of antique stones. Alas, all is not always what it seems. These 'ancient rocks' started life as decoration on Barclays Bank, Eastbourne, and were placed above Jevington to create a picturesque effect.

There are a number of convincing stone circles to be seen in Britain, although none is finer than the Druid's Circle, an imitation Stonehenge which now stands in a clearing in a pine forest at Ilton in Yorkshire. The fact that there is absolutely no connection between the building of Stonehenge and the Druids, who appeared in Britain many centuries after the great stone site was completed, has never deterred the true romantic. William Danby's work was not, however, a matter of satisfying a personal whim, for he used it to provide work for the local unemployed. It helped the poor, provided and provides harmless amusement, but is generally referred to as a folly – which leads us on to the next chapter.

Follies

THE notion suggested by the name 'folly' is inevitably one of 'foolish-ness', of a building erected out of a desire to satisfy some absurd dream or even out of blind stupidity. Many of the stories that go with follies seem to support this view. The Wentworth Woodhouse Estate and neighbouring Wentworth Castle, near Sheffield, are a happy hunting ground for folly finders, with strange structures in a rich variety of styles, one of which comes complete with an interesting story. In the 1780s the Marquess of Rockingham of Wentworth Woodhouse began to boast of his prowess as driver of a coach-and-four. He could, he declared, drive a carriage through the eye of a needle – at which point a fellow guest suggested that he put his money where his mouth was. A wager was made, which might have seemed good fun over the port, but presumably began to look less amusing to the Marquess at breakfast-time. What was to be done if he was not to accept humiliating defeat? The solution to his problem can still be seen: he built 'The Eye of the Needle', a slender, tall pyramid with an arch at the foot, just wide enough for a careful driver to manoeuvre a carriage through the space. Now this certainly sounds foolish: a foolish boast followed by a foolish bet, finally resolved by the foolish expense of building a foolish monument. But is the story true, or is it merely a later addition invented by those who cannot accept the notion of the arch existing for no other reason than to make the landscape more attractive and interesting? For there is another definition of the word 'folly', the French *folie* meaning 'delight'. Perhaps actual follies are both foolish and delightful, and the Wentworth follies certainly show both aspects.

The story of the Wentworth follies certainly began in rivalries and jealousies. In 1695 William Wentworth left his estate to Thomas Watson, at which point a furious Thomas Wentworth, who had expected to be heir, began to build his own house, Wentworth Castle. He at once began embellishing his new home: a sham castle was built, Steeple Lodge was built near the entrance disguised as a church and various odd buildings were erected in the park, from a copy of Chichester's market cross to a

Edinburgh, Lothian
Calton Hill has a number of monuments including an acropolis that was never completed because the money ran out.
Enville, Staffordshire (5 miles (8km) west of Stourbridge) There is a triple-arch eye-catcher in the park at Enville Hall.
Eversden, Cambridgeshire (6 miles (9.6km) north of Royston) A sham castle by Sanderson Miller graces the view from Wimpole Hall.
Geddington, Northamptonshire Boughton House has a rare, portable folly; an exotic Chinese-style tent is still given occasional outings.
Gunnersbury Park, London, W3 Sham ruin and tower in the grounds laid out by William Kent.
Hagley Park, Hereford and Worcester (2 miles (3.2km) south of Stourbridge) The grounds contain a sham castle, obelisk and classical temple.
Hedsor, Buckinghamshire (3 miles (5km) south-west of Beaconsfield) A huge mock castle, also known as Lord Boston's Folly, lies immediately to the north of the B476, near the priory.
Helmsley, North Yorkshire Some 2½ miles (4km) north-west of the town is Rievaulx Terrace, a grass terrace decorated with temples (NT).

Chinese temple. Not to be outdone, Thomas Watson, later Marquess of Rockingham, began his own building programme. The earliest of these is a 100ft (30m) pyramid known as the Hoober Stand. There is no mystery about the structure for the builder has left an inscription, telling precisely why it was built:

1748. this Pyramidal Building was Erected by his Majesty's most Dutiful Subject, Thomas, Marquess of Rockingham in Grateful Respect to the Preserver of our Religion, Laws and Libertys, King George the Second, Who by the Blessing of God having Subdued a most Unnatural Rebellion in Britain, anno 1746 Maintains the Balance of Power, and Settles a Just, and Honourable Peace in Europe. 1748.

The column, then, is no more than a memorial to the victors of the '45 rebellion. It seems, however, to have given the marquis a taste for monument construction. In 1778, he built a more conventional column, in the Doric style, which stands 50ft (15m) higher than Hoober Stand. This was built not to celebrate a victory but a defeat – that of Admiral Keppel at the Battle of Ushant. After the battle, the Admiral was court-martialled, but he was able to demonstrate that much of the fault for the defeat lay in the wretched state of the fleet, which had been starved of funds for essential repairs. The blame was, for once, fixed where it belonged – on Lord Sandwich, who had pocketed the funds. So one might say that the column celebrates a victory after all – a victory for justice.

The motives in this case are plain, but the rival builders were doing no more than reflecting the taste of the age for such buildings. To understand how it all began, one has to look back to an art movement that was born and flourished in the eighteenth century. At the beginning of the century, the highest praise a writer could bestow on a landscape was 'useful'. Daniel Defoe in his travels around Britain spoke of the Lake District as the

(Left) Creech Grange Arch, set high on a ridge of the Purbeck Hills, was built to provide a focal point for the view from the big house *(Anthony Burton)*

(Below) Not part of a ruined abbey, but a successful fake: the Rousham eye-catcher at Steeple Aston *(Anthony Burton)*

Knutsford, Cheshire
Tatton Park has a garden full of oddities: the mysterious sheep-stealer's tower, a classical rotunda and a Japanese temple (NT).
Margate, Kent Lord Holland was responsible for a number of follies here, including Kingsgate Castle (now a hotel) and a round tower in the grounds of his home which is now a convent.
Middleton, Essex A pleasing little brick and flint arch stands near the church.
Newton Solney, Derbyshire Hoskin's Folly is a sham castle built to such a monumental scale that its builder was shamed into living in it, in some discomfort.
Renishaw, Derbyshire A splendidly Gothic building, the Renishaw arch stands in the grounds of the old Hall.
Rothley, Northumberland (4 miles (6.5km) north-east of Kirkwhelpington) Rothley Castle, a sham castle with two prominent towers.
St Columb Major, (Cornwall) Castle-an-Dinas, a sham castle on Castle Down and Roger's Tower, a small belvedere.
Scarrington, Nottinghamshire An obelisk built up from 35,000 horshoes,
Staindrop, Durham A splendid Gothic folly on a hill behind Raby Castle, 1 mile (1.6km) north of town.

'wildest, most barren and frightful' in all England, and he turned with relief to the 'very pleasant, populous and manufacturing' towns of Lancashire. By the end of the century, Lancashire was scorned and tourists flocked to the lakes and mountains. A new word entered the language: 'picturesque' which meant literally a view that would look attractive if it was painted. Wild scenery was fine, but what was really needed was a romantic ruin as the focal point. The great landowners turned away from rigidly formal gardens to the more natural seeming landscaped park. And, like the painter looking for the perfect scene, the owners of great houses wanted a focal point to the view from their window. A lucky few had a romantic ruin, others built their own. They had constructions erected which served no useful purpose other than to catch the eye. In time they became known as 'eye-catchers'.

Eye-catchers only make sense in the right context. It is disconcerting to be striding along the high ridge of the Purbeck Hills, between Corfe Castle and Lulworth, and then suddenly to be confronted by a stone wall, embellished with pinnacles and battlements with a high rounded arch in the centre. But look down through the arch, along a broad avenue through the trees and you will see Creech Grange at the foot of the hill. The arch was built in 1746 by the Bond family, who gave their name to London's Bond Street, and it made the perfect climax to the view from their home at Creech Grange. Creech Arch is one of Britain's earliest eye-catchers and is still one of the most attractive. The element of surprise comes because the eye-catchers are intended to be seen from a distance, so that the casual passer-by is simply bewildered. The Rousham eye-catcher stands alone in the middle of a field near Steeple Aston, Oxfordshire, a solitary wall with three arched openings. It could be mistaken for part of an ancient monastery if there was any sign of other remains – but, of course, there are none. Close up, the Rousham eye-catcher is unconvincing, but it looks splendid enough when seen from Rousham Park 2 miles (3.2km) away.

One of the great builders of sham ruins was Sanderson Miller, who inherited Radway Grange at Edgehill, Warwickshire, at the age of twenty. In 1747 Miller built a mock castle, Radway Tower, which was set at a suitably martial site, said to be the exact spot at which Charles I rallied his forces for the Battle of Edgehill in 1642. When it was built, the tower was even more grandly romantic than it is today, for it originally boasted a drawbridge as well as battlements. Many notable guests came to admire the view, among them the poet Richard Jaye, who left this verse:

> the broken arch
> Or mould'ring wall, well taught to counterfeit
> The waste of Time, to solemn thought excite
> And crown with graceful pomp the shaggy hill.

The shaggy hill certainly helps to bring the ruin into prominence, and some of the best of such mock antiquities are those which stand on hill-tops where they can be seen by everyone.

Mow Cop is certainly one of the best of the hill-top follies. It is ideally seen at a distance – usually, in the author's case, from a boat on the Macclesfield Canal. It then appears as a dramatic outline – a tall tower, with a high Gothic arch alongside and a jumble of ruined walls. It appears to be the perfect example of a medieval ruin, and it certainly satisfies the first rule for producing a convincing mock ruin as specified by Thomas Whateley in his influential work *Observations on Modern Gardening* (1770): 'The mind must not be allowed to hesitate; it must be hurried away from examining into the reality, by the exactness and force of the resemblance.' Its arrangement, too, with the high tower balanced by crumbling walls, conforms with Whateley's ideals:

> There should be one large mass to raise the idea of greatness, to attract the others about it, and to be a common centre of union to all: the smaller pieces then mark the original of one extensive structure; and no longer appear to be the remains of several little buildings.

Mow Cop was built in 1750 by Randle Wilbraham, twenty years before Whateley's book appeared, and it must surely have influenced his thoughts.

Seen close to, the sham is at once revealed for what it is, but this is

Stroud, Gloucestershire
Rodborough Fort is a massive sham castle rebuilt as a house. The nearby house 'The Gateways' was built as an eye-catcher by Sir George Onesipherous Paul.

Sudbury, Derbyshire
Sudbury Hall has an eye-catcher with a purpose: it also served as a deerfold (NT).

Twizel Castle, Northumberland A sham ruin on a massive scale, but planned to be even greater. After fifty years' work it was abandoned, unfinished.

Ulverston, Cumbria A lighthouse, the Hoad Hill monument, overlooks this inland town.

Werrington, Cornwall (2 miles (3.2km) north of Launceston) Three stone sugar loaves decorate the hillside in Werrington Park.

Whiteparish, Wiltshire 2½ miles (4km) west of the village is Pepperbox Hill, topped by the seventeenth-century folly which gave it its name (NT).

unimportant since its purpose was to provide a distant prospect. Mow Cop was, incidentally, to find fame in the nineteenth century as the home of Primitive Methodism, when a Stoke-on-Trent wheelwright, Hugh Bourne, organised a camp meeting on the hill-top to discuss the proposition that Methodism should return to simpler forms of worship. Bourne's arguments found little favour among other Methodists, so he left to form his own primitive religion. What a curious mixture this provides in this one spot: one man attempting to get back to a simple core of truth, in a place designed by another as a fraud, a monument to artificiality.

Everyone can choose their own favourite eye-catcher, but for the author it is Ralph Allen's sham castle at Bath. Designed to be seen from Allen's house in the city, it is most convincing when viewed from a distance, especially at night when it is floodlit. When seen close to, it resembles a film set: although its front looks realistic the sham it really is is revealed from the back. Even the splendid battlemented round towers are only empty semicircles. Others might prefer the delicate arches of Shobdon, set high on a hill at the end of a grassy avenue. Unlike Ralph Allen's castle, it is three-dimensional, and instead of relying on the long-distance effect is covered in finely carved detail. This displays its origins, for it was built from the stones of the Norman church at Shobdon, which was demolished in the eighteenth century to make way for Lord Bateman's new church.

Not all sham castles were intended to be empty shells, nor were all shams castles. At Carn Brea, a castle perches on an extravagant rock formation on the hill-top, in a style reminiscent of one of the less accessible Greek monasteries. Built as a hunting lodge in a Gothic style with castellations and pointed arched windows, it is the situation that makes the castle so extraordinary. It appears to be propped up against the rocks while the owner has gone away to find a more suitable site. Very different is Medmenham Abbey by the Thames. At the dissolution of the monasteries by Henry VIII, all Medmenham could boast was a cell for two monks, and the entire place was valued at £2 1s 8d. This did not match the aspirations of the house builders who followed, so they repaired the omissions of the Cistercians by building a sham ruined abbey. The Hell-Fire Club held their 'secret' meetings here, which, it seems, everyone for miles around knew about. The walls of the old abbey were covered in sexy paintings, although whether the infamy ever extended beyond turning a respectable house into a passable imitation of a modern Soho bookshop is uncertain. The abbey certainly attracted a good deal of attention, and Dashwood and his compatriots, growing tired of the inquisitive gaze of the hoi-polloi, retired to an even more romantic setting at West Wycombe. Here they constructed a new home for their revels in the Hell-Fire Caves, where they could take their whores and drink themselves senseless without the fear of interference. They now seem rather sad creatures, desperately looking for titillation to reawaken their long-sated appetites, but one has to confess that they strode off along the road to perdition with a certain style, and they displayed that style in West Wycombe Park. It could

be said, however, that the principal way in which they showed that style
was in having the good sense to hand over the entire design to one of the
leading landscape gardeners of the day, Humphrey Repton. Whether the
work is in fact, Repton's own or of one of his disciples is a question open to
discussion.

A number of pagan temples in the grounds of West Wycombe Park,
dedicated to gods who are not necessarily associated with the virtues –
Bacchus, for example, was exceptionally well housed – have been taken as
further evidence of wickedness and debauchery. These were, however, no
different from other classical fragments set down in English parklands.
Here, though, is one truly original concept. West Wycombe church is a
pleasant building in which irregular flint walls contrast with smooth brick
dressings, but which boasts one striking feature which makes the church a
landmark for miles around. On top of the bell tower is balanced a large
golden ball. From a distance it looks no more than a very odd form of
decoration, but when seen close at hand it appears to be remarkably large.
Even closer inspection reveals it to be hollow. The globe is in fact, large
enough to hold ten people, and it was here that Dashwood and his friends
would meet to make their plans and gaze at the world around them through
squints in the globe. They could, at least, be certain that they would not be
overheard, and they could look down on the tiny figures scuttling around
beneath them. As G. K. Chesterton pointed out in one of the Father Brown
stories, *The Hammer of God,* even the righteous can get strange thoughts if

they spend too long looking down on the rest of humanity. One can so easily end up looking down in a figurative, as well as a literal, sense. 'Humility is the mother of giants. One sees great things from the valley; only small things from the peak.' It is doubtful whether there was much humility present among the inhabitants of the golden ball above West Wycombe church.

It is pleasant to turn to a truly grand mock ruin, built for rather better reasons than the follies of Dashwood and his friends. High on a hill above Oban is what looks remarkably like the Colosseum at Rome, except that where the ancients had a round building with round arches, the Scottish one is oval with pointed arches and battlements. The builder, John Stewart McCaig, was a local banker with one abiding passion in life: the art of ancient Greece and Rome. He lectured on the subject to the young men of Oban and was always lavish in his praise of the Colosseum in particular. Then, in the 1890s, circumstances arose that gave him the opportunity to express his great love in lasting form. Unemployment was high in the town, so he decided to build a monument to his family, in the form of a museum for the town. It was a worthwhile project in many ways, not least in providing much needed work. He had no doubts about what form the museum should take: it would be in the shape of his beloved Colosseum. It would stand on top of the hill and become a prominent landmark. At that point he must have felt a twinge of dissatisfaction. If only a tower could be incorporated into the building, then it would provide magnificent views of the surrounding countryside and of the islands across the Firth. So he adapted his design and then realised that to have just the one anomaly would lead to charges of absurdity; he went on to make other changes. McCaig's museum was not, after all, to be a slavish copy of the original Greek temple, but an adaptation of an admired design in order to fit it to a new location and a new purpose. Various refinements were planned, including statues of illustrious Obanites (especially illustrious McCaigs) in the arches. £5,000 were spent, then McCaig died. No one else shared his enthusiasm for the project and it was left unfinished, much as we see it today.

The taste that led landowners to provide distant eye-catchers also led them to produce a variety of strange objects, temples and grottoes, towers and pavilions to enliven the grounds of their great houses. At their best they achieved sublimity, a perfect match between the arts of the landscape gardener and the architect. There can be no argument about which is the finest: the palm must go to Stourhead in Wiltshire. The garden was created in 1740, when the Stour was dammed to create the lake, but the work of folly construction had begun a little earlier. First to arrive was a grotto, then over the years classical temples to the gods – to Flora, Hercules and Apollo. Objects to grace the garden were brought over from their former homes in the streets of Bristol: a handsome conduit was set over a grotto and the medieval High Cross was erected to climax the view of the lake. But lording over all, in the literal sense, is a 160ft (49m) high triangular tower which was completed in 1772 (see p50). A plaque at the base announces

'Alfred the Great AD 870 On this summit erected his standard against Danish invaders'. After its warlike origins, Alfred's tower nearly had a warlike ending. In World War II a plane flew into the tower and one can still see where the brickwork was patched.

If Stourhead has the most elegant follies, the follies that are most perfectly in harmony with their setting, then Stowe in Buckinghamshire can boast the largest number. The house is now a school, but the grounds are often open to the public and one of the temples is let to holiday-makers by the Landmark Trust (see p211). Just quoting numbers is impressive: two arches, three pavilions, three bridges, four obelisks, eight temples, three monuments and ten oddly assorted structures ranging from a grotto to a menagerie, which now, perhaps appropriately, is the school shop. The buildings are of the highest quality, with architects as famous as James Gibbs, William Kent and Sir John Vanbrugh responsible for their design.

In Scotland, another famous architect, Robert Adam, was responsible for a magnificent house, Culzean Castle, in an equally splendid setting, overlooking the sea. To this great structure he added a home farm, almost as elegant as the house itself, and one charming little folly. In the grounds, surrounded by shrubs and trees is a little Gothic summer-house (see p38), looking at first glance like a mock ruin, with its unglazed windows, beneath an array of castellations and pinnacles.

It is certainly true that no one seeing the beauty of the buildings in any of the gardens mentioned above could ever seriously suggest that these follies are in any way foolish. They represent no more than an ordering and embellishment of natural surroundings. Anything can be used in the process and older buildings can easily be adapted to fit the scheme. The process continues. Perhaps the most bizarre example can be found in a setting as remote from the ordered English garden as one can imagine. On the distant island of South Uist, Mrs Johnson of Buailedubh somehow acquired a bus in her garden. Rusting buses are not very attractive, so she began to encrust it with seashells until now it would not disgrace an exhibition of the best of surrealistic art. For what could be more fanciful than a submarine bus?

Almost equally surreal are abandoned gardens where once delicate fountains and pavilions now peer out of the undergrowth. Raasay House on the Island of Raasay, off Skye, was praised by Dr Johnson for its elegance, but its new role as an outdoor sports centre has little need for formal gardens. It is a rather sad place, but also just a little enchanting. The fountains that once echoed the shapes of the natural world are now being engulfed in that same world. Incidentally, Raasay Forest is also a place of dark enchantment and there, in its green depths, is a broch, a ruined fortress that could well be an ogre's castle in a story by the Grimms.

Garden follies take almost any style or any culture as their models – for example, a Chinese pagoda at Cliveden or a Gothic temple at Stowe – but occasionally one finds a building with a more serious purpose. The best example can be found at Rushton in Northamptonshire. Sir Thomas

The Bristol High Cross re-erected as a garden folly at Stourhead *(National Trust/ Fay Godwin)*

SOUTH WEST ELEVATION

NORTH ELEVATION

The triangular lodge at Rushton: the drawings show with great clarity how everything relates to the number 3, for The Trinity *(Royal Commission on the Historical Monuments of England)*

Tresham was brought up as the son of a Catholic family during the Reformation. Open practice of their religion was very dangerous, so the boy was given the outward show of Protestantism, while being secretly educated in the Catholic faith. The life of secrecy and intrigue seems to have left its mark. He became obsessed with the more obtuse branches of theology, and with such arcane subjects as numbers and the power of numbers. It was a dangerous world, where witchcraft and orthodox Christianity were close neighbours. It was a world which expressed itself in ciphers. Tresham gave such ideas solid reality in his triangular lodge.

Everything about the lodge relates to the number three, and that in turn relates to the idea of the Trinity. The building is three-sided and three-storeyed. The rooms are either triangular or hexagonal. The building is decorated with trefoils and triangles, which themselves come in groups of three. Even the date on which it was begun is significant: it is recorded on the façade by the numbers 93, which is short for 1593, but which also serves as a plain hint to the building's numerical significance. There are Latin inscriptions, with thirty-three letters to each phrase, three gables to the roof, and so on. Wherever you look, the same number dominates everything. It is a building of astonishing complexity, for when you conclude that you have explored every conceivable variation of the number three, you find that there are still more to be discovered. If ever there was a monument to a single, or triple, obsession, then Tresham's lodge is one.

The Tresham family was much given to symbolism. Sir Thomas began to build a house nearby, Lyveden New Bield, its four wings giving it a cruciform shape. But the family was implicated in the Gunpowder Plot of 1605, and the house was never completed. It is now in the care of the National Trust and it seems as odd now in its own way as the triangular lodge.

Follies can also appear scattered in an apparently arbitrary way around the countryside. They are monuments to the great and famous which can take strange forms. The Kymin is a hill above Monmouth, up which a little road winds to bring visitors to the Naval Temple and the Round House. Once there were pleasure gardens here as well, but now all that remains is the tiny castellated tower house and the grand arch dedicated to sundry 'noble admirals'. The scene is completed by a pair of cannon. The views are stunning, but how many people would ever come here to enjoy them were it not for that famous admiral, Lord Nelson?

Others who have not had memorials erected in their honour – nor were ever likely to have them – repaired the omission by building their own. John Knill was mayor of St Ives in Cornwall – a respectable and honourable post – but he wished to be distinguished from all other mayors of St Ives. In his will he made provision for a monument to be erected to the south of the town. It is still there, a stone pyramid with the punning motto on his name 'Nil Desperandum' and the date 1782. He also left funds for a ceremony to be performed every five years at the monument, and, extraordinarily, it is still performed today. On the appointed day ten young girls, two

George Messiter was a great creator of follies: this is Jack the Treacle Eater. Who Jack was and why he ate treacle is unknown *(Reece Winstone)*

respectable matrons, the vicar, the mayor, the local customs official and a fiddler solemnly troop up to the pyramid and sing the hundredth psalm. The adults rest while the girls dance around the monument, then everyone sings 'Shun the Barter of the Bay', which is as inexplicable as the ceremony, after which they all troop down again and the parson, mayor and the customs official then give a dinner for two friends, by courtesy of Mr Knill. It would be pleasant to think that the widows are the *invitées*, for they have to make do with a paltry ten shillings each.

The best follies, however, must be those which celebrate nothing, provide no obvious focal point for any recognisable view but exist simply because their creator considered them to be good fun. If folly building is thought of as an expression of exuberance, a zest for the unusual for its own sake, then the king of folly builders must be Mad Jack Fuller of Brightling Park, Dallington, in East Sussex. Fuller was literally and metaphorically a larger-than-life character, who weighed over 20 stone (127kg). All his follies have a perverse logic about them. The Sugar Loaf, for example, a cone built of stone and concrete which stands on top of a

neighbouring hill, appears to have no function at all, to be the result of no more than a mad whim; yet, if old stories are to be believed, there is an entertaining explanation for its presence.

Mad Jack was dining with friends, during which he boasted of the fine view he had of Dallington church spire from his dining-room window. The statement was challenged by fellow diners, convinced that no view, fine or otherwise, was to be had from that vantage point. Bets were laid. Mad Jack hurried home, where he saw to his horror that the hill did indeed block the view. He was not a man to accept defeat easily, however, and called his workmen together and sent them off at top speed to re-create the top of the spire on the hill. Seen from a distance it was a convincing spire – more convincing, perhaps, than this old tale. The story has it that Fuller's friend, who had enough local knowledge to dispute the spire's visibility, did not have enough common sense to spot the Sugar Loaf. Fuller won his bet.

The Sugar Loaf is only one of Mad Jack's follies. On top of the hill to the west of the church there is an obelisk, and for once there is no story to explain its presence. It might be significant to note that in 1820, when

A Gothicised summer-
house at Culzean Castle
(Anthony Burton)

The Kymin stands high on a
hill above Monmouth
(Anthony Burton)

Fuller's folly-making was in full spate, Cleopatra's Needle was presented to Britain to mark the coronation of George IV – although it was to remain in the desert for another half century before it reached its present home on the Thames embankment. It seems reasonable that the Brightling Needle, as it is known, was built to show that anything the Egyptians could do, could be done as well by a Sussex squire.

Mad Jack Fuller saved his finest folly for the last. As local squire, Fuller owned much of the property in the village, including the village inn, the Fuller's Arms. This particular inn stood along the way from the village to the parish church, and the vicar complained that too many parishioners were stopping for a drink on their way to the service – and some never arrived at the church at all. Fuller was asked to change the site of the inn. He agreed to do so on condition that he should be allowed to design his own tomb to stand in the churchyard. The vicar agreed to this request, although if he knew Fuller at all he must surely have had some doubts. Fuller kept his word. The old pub was closed down and an empty cottage was converted into a new inn at a suitably safe distance from the church.

Fuller then insisted on his side of the bargain. The tomb was duly built – and the vicar's doubts were shown to be well founded. He built a huge stone pyramid, which dominated the churchyard. It was kept open to await Jack Fuller's demise, and when he eventually died in 1834 at the age of seventy-seven, he was duly interred in the enormous tomb of his own design. Local legend could not allow that such a colourful character was buried in any conventional manner. He was, it is said, buried sitting in his favourite chair with a table laid before him. What more fitting end could there be for the greatest of the folly builders?

George Messiter of Barwick Park is the one possible competitor to Mad

Hawkstone Park is full of strange edifices, including a hermit's cell, which once came complete with resident hermit *(Shropshire Libraries)*

Jack Fuller. He built four follies in the park in about 1820, including an obelisk with a distinct bend at the top. But the one monument which raises him into the ranks of the great folly builders is an almost perfect folly. Architecturally it is both incongruous and inexplicable. It consists of a rough stone arch, topped by a round tower, on top of which stands a winged figure of Mercury. What it is or why it is there are questions that remain unanswered, and its splendid name only adds confusion rather than clarification – Jack the Treacle Eater.

There are literally hundreds of follies of various sorts and descriptions in Britain. Some are on the grandest of scales, such as Hawkstone Park in Shropshire, where labyrinthine paths have been cut through and around the cliffs to create grottoes and caves, dizzying walkways and surprise vistas. There is everything here from the remains of a genuine medieval keep to the Victorian Gingerbread Hall where tourists could buy gingerbread and ginger beer from a little thatched hut in the rocks. Others are simply modest conceits, such as the Swiss Cottage brought to Osborne House on the Isle of Wight as a playroom for the royal children, who must have found it a relief from the somewhat claustrophobic stuffiness of Queen Victoria's favourite home.

The age of folly building is not yet dead, moreover. At Hartley Wintney in Hampshire there are a number of garden buildings, which date back no further than 1974 and which are the work of Lord McAlpine and the architect Quinlan Terry. The *Oxford English Dictionary* defines folly as 'any costly structure considered to have shown folly in the builder'. Lord McAlpine gives his answer in the inscription on a tall column. Translated from the Latin, it informs the reader that if it did nothing else, the money spent on the column was at least kept out of the hands of the taxman.

All the follies described here have been specially made, with the possible exception of Mrs Johnson's bus, but that is so transformed as to qualify as a specially manufactured object. But sometimes very little effort is required to turn a purely natural object into something bizarre and strange. A classic example can be found on Bute, looking out over the narrow channel that divides the island from the mainland. The Maids of Bute are two seemingly unremarkable rocks, but someone at some time had the idea that they looked like young ladies. So at regular intervals the rocks are painted and grey rock disappears beneath blushing cheeks and crevices become lipsticked smiles. Truth to tell, they are scarcely more convincing painted than they are unadorned, but that is not important. What matters is that the tradition continues. People plod out through a boggy wasteland to a remote corner of an island to daub paint on two otherwise undistinguished rocks which will be seen only by boaters as they pass through the Kyles of Bute. Inevitably, there are stories of love-lorn maidens waiting for sailors who will never return from the sea; the rocks even appear in fiction in the wonderful Para Handy tales, but their appeal surely lies in the glorious illogicality and inconsequentiality of it all. That explains the true nature of the folly.

A twentieth-century extravaganza: a shark nosedives through a roof in suburban Oxford. Folly or art? *(Anthony Burton)*

Pleasing Prospects

Alnwick, Northumberland
Brislaw Tower, also a column erected by the tenants for the Duke of Northumberland who thanked them by increasing their rent.
Bath, Avon Beckford's Tower, Lansdown Hill, stands 130ft (40km) high and offered its builder a view of his old home at Fonthill Abbey.
Bathford, Avon (3 miles (5km) north-east of Bath) Brown's Folly, a tower built to provide work for the poor in 1842.
Bridgnorth, Shropshire The tower of the old castle leans at an angle three times greater than the famous tower at Pisa.
Buxton, Derbyshire A folly tower known as Solomon's Temple stands on Grinlow Barrow.
Curry Rivel, Somerset (2 miles (3.2km) south-west of Langport) The Burton Pynsent column or steeple was once climbable by a spiral staircase. It was closed after a cow walked up and fell from the top.

PROSPECT towers are the opposite of eye-catching follies: whereas the latter are there to be looked at, the former are there to be looked from – but both owe their popularity to the picturesque movement. Phrases such as 'there is a wonderful view from the window' are now so commonplace that they are never questioned. Yet it is a modern notion that scenery can be enjoyed for its own sake. In an earlier age, a tower might have given a proud landlord a view of his estate or a warlord warning of attack, but it was seldom considered worth the effort of climbing many stairs just to see the unimproved works of nature. Change came with the comparative peace of the countryside during Tudor times. The fortress became a home, the courtyard a garden and there was time to stand and stare. There was also money to spare, money to erect buildings that did not need to fulfil any strictly practical function. As the taste for viewing the world slowly developed, those landowners who lacked a suitably superior hill from which to look down began to build towers. There were belvederes – turret rooms built into houses or pavilions in the grounds; gazebos – pavilions usually built into the garden wall so that the occupants could view the world outside the estate without actually having to encounter it; and, grandest of all, prospect towers – free-standing structures, with no role other than to support a viewing platform at the top. Most tower builders, however, decided that if they were going to have a huge tower on their estates, it should be amusing to look at as well. This is the chief appeal of prospect towers: they are attractive in themselves and can be enjoyed without the effort of making one's way to the top.

There is some dispute over which is the oldest prospect tower in the country. The honour is usually claimed for Freston Tower, which stands to the south of the River Orwell in Suffolk. It is definitely old, having been built by the Latimer family in 1549, but is it a prospect tower? It certainly offers a prospect that improves as you climb up through its six storeys, and the view is further improved by the fact that the windows get larger as you

Freston Tower, built in the sixteenth century to provide six storeys of schoolrooms – one for each day of the school week *(Suffolk Record Office, Suffolk Photographic Survey 14499)*

Eridge, East Sussex (3 miles (4km) south-west of Tunbridge Wells) Saxonbury Hill has a splendid, if somewhat decayed, prospect tower.
Faringdon, Oxfordshire Lord Berner's Folly is one of the rare twentieth-century follies, a prospect tower of 1935.
Harrogate, North Yorkshire Harlow Hill has a prospect tower which is now a public observation tower, while throughout the town are wells where visitors can taste the foul waters.
Hawkesbury, Avon (4 miles (6.5km) north-east of Chipping Sodbury) Tower of 1845 to commemorate the Duke of Somerset.
Hopton, Derbyshire Hopton Hall has a tower attached to a crinkle-crankle wall – the builder forgot to order any windows.
Horton, Dorset Sturt's Folly, a huge triangular tower used originally for watching deer on Cranborne Chase.
Kinglassie, Fife (2 miles (3.2km) south-west of Leslie) Blythe's Folly, prospect tower on the hill overlooking the town.
Lampeter, Dyfed A tall brooding monument

ascend, a reversal of normal building techniques.

Explanations of why the handsome tower was built include the somewhat unlikely suggestion that it was once part of a larger house, of which all trace has vanished. Another, much more interesting, explanation, is that the tower was built as a vertical study. According to this story the tower was built by Lord Freston for his beautiful daughter, Ellen de Freston, and he was determined that wisdom should be added to beauty. He devised a course of study, with one floor and one day for each subject. Ellen began on Monday by studying charity on the ground floor and then, ascending one floor each day, she learnt about embroidery, music, painting and literature, until on Saturday her lesson was in astronomy, very appropriately, on the top floor. There are two versions of what Ellen studied on Sunday. In the first, she left the tower for devotions

known as Derry Ormond tower, 2 miles (3.2km) north of the town.
Layer Marney Tower, Essex An eight-storey tower, built in 1520, originally intended as a gatehouse.
Little Berkhamsted, Hertfordshire Admiral Stratten's observatory, a charming Georgian prospect tower, now a private house.
Long Melford, Suffolk Melford Hall has an octagonal gazebo with gables and pinnacles (NT).
Matlock, Derbyshire A prospect tower on the Heights of Abraham.
Moel Famma, Clwyd At the top of the mountain is the stump of the jubilee tower.
Offwell, Devon Bishop's Coplestone's Folly, an 80ft (24m) prospect tower on Honiton Hill.
Pentlow, Essex (3 miles (4km) west of Long Melford) Bull's Tower, a 70ft (21m) prospect tower in a rectory garden.
Portquin, Cornwall Doyden Tower, a Gothic folly overlooks the bay (NT).
Powderham, Devon Powderham Castle belvedere looks down over the River Exe.
Sway, Hampshire Peterson's Tower, a tall folly tower with thirteen storeys built of concrete.
Wenlock Edge, Shropshire Flounder's Folly is a massive prospect tower on the top of Callow Hill, east of Winstanton.

and church; in the second, she went out on the roof to the arms of the tower's builder and enjoyed extra-curricular activity.

The best prospect towers combine a fine setting, a good story and interesting, preferably mildly absurd, architecture. Cotehele Tower manages to fulfil two of the conditions, and the house that it serves supplies the third. Cotehele House stands on the bank of the River Tamar in Cornwall in one of the most beautiful regions in England. The house is one of those splendid places that seem to have grown organically, one part evolving naturally from its neighbour throughout its long building period from 1485 to 1627. It was home to the Edgcumbe family, who seem to have been touched by a spirit of whimsy, for in their other house, Edgcumbe Park overlooking Plymouth Sound, they built an excellent sham ruin from which the whole city can be viewed, from the gleaming granite walls of the Citadel in the east right around past the dockyard to Brunel's great rail bridge in the west. But to return to Cotehele: here is a house imbued with a suitably murky medieval atmosphere and full of delights, which include a fifteenth-century clock that was built before the pendulum clock was invented. In the lovely terraced gardens, there is an odd stone building that looks like an overgrown beehive, which in fact is a perfect little dovecote, and the walk through the woods brings visitors out to a tiny chapel above the river. And here the romantic story begins. Sir Richard Edgcumbe was pursued down this path by Sir Henry Trenowth who intended to exact revenge for the Edgcumbes' rebellion against Richard III. Sir Richard hid in a tree on the cliff and threw his hat into the river far below to convince his pursuer that he had drowned. The ruse worked and the chapel was built as a thanksgiving.

For a prospect tower not be overwhelmed by architecture, scenery and history in such a situation it needs to be a good one, and Cotehele Tower is just that. It was probably built to commemorate a visit by George III and is a remarkable structure. At first sight it appears to be a church tower, although it soon becomes clear that no church is attached. It is only when you have reached the building itself that the full measure of the architect's ingenuity becomes plain. It is not even a four-sided tower at all, but a three-sided one – a perfect optical illusion, in fact.

A triangular church tower might seem an oddity, and is certainly a rarity, but triangular Gothic prospect towers are comparatively common – if such a grand object could ever be considered as common at all. The first appears to be Shrubs Hill Tower, built for the Duke of Cumberland in 1750 at Virginia Water. The lake itself was created for the duke as part of an elaborate landscape scheme, which involved building grottoes and sham ruins as well as the great tower. It began as a splendid Gothic tower and was later castellated, adapted as a house and renamed Fort Belvedere.

The name 'belvedere' is itself an alternative version of 'prospect tower', derived from the Italian *bello vedere* – beautiful sight. One of the finest examples of the towers to take the name is Powderham Belvedere in Devon, another triangulated, castellated and thoroughly Gothicised tower which entirely justifies its name, for it has no function whatsoever other than to provide a 'beautiful sight' in both senses of the word, for it is both attractive in itself and commands a fine view. Usefulness, however, always seems to detract slightly from a tower: it is the sense of absurdity of an immense structure built for frivolous ends that is the important element in the appeal.

Broadway Tower is a fine example of the unchanged prospect tower. It occupies a superb site on the edge of the Cotswold escarpment. It qualifies as a folly in every respect, for the building itself is a pastiche of a medieval fortress but a wonderfully unconvincing one, with pretty little round-headed windows, roundels and balconies in between the stern battlemented towers. A good tale is also attached to its building. It was built around 1800 for the Earl of Coventry of Croome Court, but the Countess had first to satisfy herself that their proposed scheme would work. The home of the Coventrys was, after all, 15 miles (24km) away from the hill on which the tower was to be erected, so she ordered a beacon to be lit on the site, and when she saw the flames from her house, she made sure that all her neighbours knew about it so that everyone in the county would be equally impressed.

What name would you apply to a prospect tower which no longer has a prospect? One such curiosity began its life as part of the old home of the Dukes of Sutherland at Trentham in the Potteries. This was a fine belvedere in the form of a tower, the top of which was a viewing platform surrounded by stone arches and topped with a balustrade. The house was pulled down in 1905, but Lord Harrowby was attracted to the belvedere and bought it for a modest £100. It was carefully dismantled, each stone being numbered, and then the tower was re-erected at Sandon Hall, just north of Stafford. It now presents an odd aspect, for it no longer stands on top of a hill but

Powderham Castle Belvedere is a perfect example of its type: Gothic in style, triangular in plan, its only true function is to provide a view over the River Exe *(Devon Record Office)*

sits forlornly on a low brick base in the grounds – a belvedere with no view.

Haldon Belvedere at Doddiscombsleigh between the Haldon Hills and Dartmoor in Devon is not so much a belvedere attached to a house as a prospect tower expanded to become a house. It was built in 1788 by Sir Robert Palk, in memory of his friend Major General Stringer Lawrence. It has two distinct personae, for the inside is in a different style from the exterior. Outside it is very much the fashionable Gothic. The plan is triangular with battlemented turrets at the corners and windows with pointed arches and intersected tracery. It seems a fitting building for a moorland setting. Inside, however, one is at once transported from the English Middle Ages to a land far away in the East. There are two stairways, built out of beautiful Indian marble, presented by the Nizam of Hyderabad, while the ballroom has a magnificent floor of mahogany from the East Indies. The delicate plasterwork decoration of the rooms could scarcely be more different from the rough, stern exterior.

The great attraction of prospect towers lies in their variety and there is something especially attractive to the collector of curiosities about these towers whose only true function is to act as ornate step-ladders. Some can be quite small and charming. Kimmeridge Tower, overlooking Kimmeridge Bay in Dorset, fits that description, although now, sadly, it is ruinous. It consists of a simple round tower with a quatrefoil parapet at the top and a Doric colonnade at the bottom. To purists, the mixture of classical and Gothic styles may be offensive, but it is so well proportioned and has such a marvellous situation on the cliff top, that one can only envy those who came here to laze away a sunny summer afternoon.

What could be in greater contrast to Kimmeridge than the outskirts of Birmingham? Birmingham has, of course, no shortage of tall buildings, but these are modern and plainly businesslike, the plainness being the dominant theme. But why, one wonders, should anyone build a prospect tower in Edgbaston – unless they were hoping for a free seat to view the cricket? But the tower was built as early as 1758 by John Perrott of Rotton Park, in the days when Rotton Park was still a country estate and before cricket came to Edgbaston. Then came the Industrial Revolution and Birmingham began to grow, and gradually the terraces crept up to the foot of Perrott's Folly until it was surrounded. Yet the encroachment has not detracted from the gracefulness of the tower: if anything, it has added to it, by acting as a foil. The tower, in turn, has added this touch of grace and individuality to a city sadly in need of both commodities. It stands seven storeys high, is decorated with Gothic windows and a castellated parapet, and, as with many such towers, comes complete with a variety of stories, each of which claims to be the true explanation of its existence.

One explanation is that Perrott's Folly was built by John Perrott in his old age to enable him to follow his favourite sport of hare coursing. In this splendidly unlikely version, an old gentleman who is so infirm that he cannot walk to the carriage that would take him to the coursing, is supposedly able to climb seven flights of stairs. In the second story, John

Broadway Tower, standing at the edge of the Cotswold escarpment, looks out over the Vale of Evesham
(Derek Pratt)

Perrott is a widower who built the tower so that he could see his wife's grave 10 miles (16km) away. In the third account, Perrott is an amateur astronomer who viewed the stars and planets through a telescope mounted at the top of the tower. There is an element of truth in the third version for the tower was used for a time as an observatory – but for viewing the weather not the stars. No one, it seems, has put forward a fourth explanation – that John Perrott built his tower simply because he thought it might be fun to have a tower on his estate.

Prospect towers might seem to non-aficionados to be boringly similar to each other, but closer acquaintance reveals a great richness of architectural styles and an even greater richness of stories attached to them. Some of these stories seem to put the towers well within the folly category, because of their exceedingly foolish conceptions. This applies particularly to those towers which were built to provide the owner with a specific view – which they then singularly failed to provide. Take, for example, Admiral Stratten's observatory at Little Berkhamsted in

The massive Horton Tower in Dorset did at one time fulfil a function: it was said to have been built for deer-watching, making it a contender for the title of world's grandest hide *(Royal Commission on the Historical Monuments of England)*

Hertfordshire. Outwardly, it is a pleasant, if not very dramatic, tower. The virtues of the building are those one associates with its period, the late eighteenth century: its proportions are exemplary, its aspect dignified; it is a classic piece of Georgian design. Look at the windows in the main, circular tower, which are held within the unifying enclosure of a tall arch. At the bottom is a square window, at the top a round one, while in between is an oblong window topped by a semicircular arch: it is a clever exercise in symmetry. Yet this eminently rational piece of design topples over, if only metaphorically, into absurdity if the popular story of its construction is true. It is said that the Admiral sorely missed his life at sea and he built his tower so that he could sit at the top with his telescope and watch ships on the Thames. But even with the best telescope, there was never any chance to see even a topmast from this tower, so all his efforts were wasted.

Kimmeridge tower in its heyday, a charming little tower on the Dorset coast *(Dorset Natural History and Archaeological Society, Dorset County Museum, Dorchester)*

Hull's Tower at Leith Hill in Surrey was built with not only the sensible purpose of providing superb views – which it does – but, as a plaque records, with the altruistic aim of making the view available to anyone prepared to climb the stairs. But it was not built simply to furnish the owner with a better view than nature provided unaided. The hill stands at a height of 965ft (294m) above sea level, and Hull was irritated by the fact that his local hill did not quite reach the 1,000ft (305m) mark. A hill under a thousand feet is a mere pimple on the land, whereas one that overtops the magic figure can properly qualify for the title of hill. So Hull built a tower, artificially extending the summit to reach that altitude. By the end of the century, however, the tower was being used as a hiding place by local criminals, who became such a menace that eventually it was decided to fill up the tower with rubble, thus closing it to everyone for all time. Later, a Victorian owner had a change of heart and built an exterior staircase, so that he could again enjoy the view from the top of his tower.

As with many such towers, stories were spread locally that Hull himself was buried in the tower – and, moreover, that he was buried standing on his head. The reason for this bizarre burial was the belief that the world was due to be turned upside down on the Day of Judgement, so Mr Hull would have remained uniquely on his feet. Such stories can normally be dismissed, but when the National Trust came to restore the property there they found the tomb – but not, alas, a hand-standing skeleton.

If there is a certain sameness about eighteenth-century towers, that criticism could never be levelled against their nineteenth-century successors, especially the Victorians. If, however, one begins with the early years of the century, there is no sudden break with the past, but rather a straightforward continuation of styles. Paxton's Tower near Llanarthney in Dyfed is on the old triangular plan with a battlemented tower rising from the centre. Yet it is one of the grandest of all such structures, as it needs to be for it has to compete with the genuine medieval fortress nearby. Dryslwyn Castle is famous as the seat of the turncoat Lord of Dryslwyn, Rhys ap Maredudd, who in 1282 supported Edward I against the Welsh and five years later revolted against the English king. He suffered the penalty of the unsuccessful rebel and was executed in 1291. Sir William Paxton, the builder of the tower, had a somewhat less dramatic history than the Lord of Dryslwyn and met a happier end. Nevertheless, there is one story that features in his life which typifies an aspect of life in Georgian Britain, just as the story of Dryslwyn typifies one of the more violent aspects of life in the Middle Ages. That story concerns the building of the tower.

Sir William Paxton was a Whig politician who was determined to beat the local Tory at the county elections of 1802. No expense was spared in an effort to woo the electorate. He treated them to 11,070 breakfasts, 684 suppers and 36,000 dinners, during which they consumed 8,879 bottles of porter, not to mention similar quantities of other gastronomic delights. The grand total for this exercise in mass bribery came to £15,690 4s 2d – but despite all Paxton's largesse, the ungrateful voters elected the opposition.

One hundred and seven of them drank his porter, ate his food and then voted Tory! But what has all this to do with the tower? Well, rumour spread throughout the district that all this extravagance had bankrupted Paxton, so he determined to give his critics visible and irrefutable proof that he still had money to spend. He built the tower, completed in 1805, to demonstrate to the entire neighbourhood that Sir William Paxton might have lost the election but he had not lost his wealth. Although another story exists that the tower was erected to honour Lord Nelson, the election story is undeniably true: the money was spent, the rumours did circulate, and there seems no reason why the two stories should not be combined. Perhaps Paxton built his tower both to honour Britain's most famous admiral and to prove his own wealth.

At almost the same time as Paxton was building his architecturally conventional tower in Wales, in Kent an eccentric gentleman named John Powell was constructing his own astonishing edifice. Quex Park lies near the village of Birchington in Kent. The tower itself is unremarkable – yet another Gothic structure – but towards the top of the building, a second, quite different structure looms over the battlements. This open-work spire of cast iron rises up on four legs like a Kentish Eiffel Tower. The spire and the tower that supports it make an incongruous pair, but there is a logic at work here. Powell was an enthusiastic campanologist and the tower contains a peal of twelve bells. Peals of bells are traditionally associated with churches and churches are associated with spires. Powell himself was buried in a mausoleum within the tower, where he can rest contented, for the bells are still in use.

Whatever one might say about the tower known as May's Folly at Hadlow in Kent, one could never criticise it for being plain. It is a Gothic extravaganza, a cross between a castle and a cathedral, a total denial of architectural logic and stylistic unity, a deplorable example of Victorian excess and lack of refinement. It is also wholly delightful. It was built as an addition to Squire Walter Barton May's house – actually a sham castle. The additions, in fact, literally overshadow the house, for the tower rises to a height of 170ft (52m). Arches and tracery, pinnacles and towers are built one on top of the other in this splendidly mad caprice of a building. Why was such an amazing structure ever built in the first place? There are a number of explanations, including the almost standard one that May wanted to see the sea, so he built a tower and only then noticed the Downs which stood in the way. Two other versions have rather more originality. In the first story, May's wife ran away with a local farmer, and the squire built the tower so that wherever she travelled in the neighbourhood she would be reminded of her abandoned husband. The second story is as bizarre as the tower itself. There was, it is said, a mysterious prophecy that foretold that when Walter May was buried beneath the earth, his family would lose the estates. To prevent such a travesty, rather than perch his coffin in a mausoleum a mere few inches from the ground, May determined that his body should be raised as far above the earth as possible. The tower

Alfred's Tower at Stourhead
(Derek Pratt)

was to be his mausoleum, and his body was to rest on the very top of it.

Not all towers that appear to be prospect towers are quite what they seem. Layer Marney Tower in Essex would be an altogether magnificent prospect tower, rising in splendour through eight storeys to a height of 80ft (24m). Built in brick and terracotta in 1510, it is, however, much too early for a folly and is, in fact, the gatehouse to what should have been a great Tudor mansion. It was the work of Sir Henry Marney, privy councillor to both Henry VII and Henry VIII. Work had scarcely started on the main house when Sir Henry died in 1523, to be followed two years later by his only son who left no heir. The project was simply abandoned, so that the tower was left alone in all its glory.

The same process appears in reverse, as it were, in several places where a great house has been destroyed, but the gatehouse remains. Kirtling Towers in Cambridgeshire is a particularly fine example. It dates from 1530 when the peace of Tudor times meant that the castellations of gatehouses such as this were purely ornamental. Kirtling Towers is now a fine home, which makes one speculate on how grand the house itself must have been. It was certainly grand enough to offer entertainment to Elizabeth I on one of her many tours of England, although it was not grand enough to accommodate all her vast entourage. So a small annexe was built nearby, which is now the Queen's Head pub. This boasts its own little small-scale curiosity: the logs for the fire that blazes comfortably through the winter are kept in an old brass kettle drum, minus its skin.

Clearly not a prospect tower, but what else could a lighthouse be in London E19? This is not a lighthouse for lost mariners, but for lost souls, a Methodist church of 1892 which manages a surprisingly good imitation of a cliff-top beacon, even though it looks out over a sea of television aerials rather than crashing waves.

Two personal favourites became prospect towers almost by accident. The Osmaston Garden Centre near Ashbourne in Derbyshire occupies what was once the kitchen garden of Osmaston House. The original house, built in 1849, was designed with a special central heating system of hot-air ducts that led to a single chimney. In order to get the necessary draught, however, it had to be 150ft (46m) high. The owner, the industrialist Francis Wright, sensibly decided that if he was going to have such a tall chimney it might as well enhance the scene, and if it was going to be embellished it might just as well be used. So the chimney became an Italianate tower which could be climbed by means of a spiral staircase. As it happens, the tower has outlived the house it was built to serve.

A similar story, but a more elaborate one as befits a more elaborate structure, can be told about the most prominent landmark in Halifax, Yorkshire. Wainhouse's Tower, 270ft (82m) high which is topped by a colonnade, a balcony and a cupola, is instantly recognisable as a typical nineteenth-century prospect tower. Nineteenth century it certainly is, built in the 1870s. Prospect tower it briefly was – but that is not why it was built. John E. Wainhouse was owner of a local dyeworks, and, being more

public-spirited than many of his neighbours, he was determined that he, at least, was not going to add to the level of pollution in the district. He decided to build the tallest factory chimney for miles around to keep the smoke clear of the town, so the chimney was duly built and named Wainhouse's Tower. He was not content to leave it at that – keeping smoke off the Monday washing. After all, a 270ft (82m) factory chimney was going to be a dominant feature in the landscape and might even be less popular than a lower, smokier version, condemned as an eyesore on the fair face of Halifax. So Wainhouse combined the notion of the chimney with that of a prospect tower. The chimney proper was to be built of plain brick, and then the tower was to be built of stone around it. As with so many of the best folly stories, everything went wrong. The chimney was supposed to be connected to the works by an underground flue, but before this was begun the works themselves were sold and the new owner declared that he had no qualms whatsoever about pouring soot over his neighbours' smalls. He declined to include Wainhouse's Tower in the purchase. Wainhouse was left with little option but to continue with the prospect tower plan, and this was duly completed. At least he was now able to trudge up the steps to view the world at large. Alas, Wainhouse was no giant, and when he reached the top he discovered that the architect had over-estimated his employer's stature – the unhappy mill owner was too short to see over the parapet. He now owned a chimney that would never smoke and a prospect tower with no prospect. At least he was able to do something about the latter, for he simply refused to pay the building costs until he was provided with a parapet that he could look over. The tower still stands, arguably the most ornate and certainly the least-used factory chimney in the land.

There are other versions of the Wainhouse story, but the tower itself is indisputably a folly on a grand scale. It does contrive to look as if it is both tower and chimney. Other industrialists and builders produced structures where the outward appearances bore little or no connection with their real purpose. Such follies are exercises in architectural disguise: they are not what they seem.

Not What it Seems

For many years, whenever I have travelled to London by train, my journey has taken me through Southall en route for Paddington. At first the scene was enlivened by a vast gas works, but this has long since been laid bare, leaving only the big gas-holders. They are in their way delightful objects, the hugely swelling holders seeming as if they are trying to escape from the delicately ornate frames. Alongside was an odd little building, a hexagonal fortress in brick which could have been almost anything, but most closely resembled a Gothic belvedere or gazebo. It was, in fact, a heavily disguised water tower. Over the years it became more and more dilapidated but suddenly it began to brighten up for it had been bought and converted into flats.

One might think that the notion of a water tower as a home is bizarre, but Southall is far from being unique. Appleton water tower, near the Sandringham estate in Norfolk, looks from a distance like a prospect tower: there is a double surprise, for this not only looks like a prospect tower but it *is* a prospect tower. It was built in 1877 and was given a royal start when the foundation stone was laid by the Princess of Wales. Its ornate appearance, no doubt, derives from its situation. Visitors could climb up an outside stair to a viewing room at the top of the tower, underneath which was the tower keeper's home. Each floor had a fireplace, and the flues were led up through the centre of the water tank, which very neatly kept the water from freezing in winter. Happily, this splendid building has been restored to its former glory by the Landmark Trust. But the prize for the most bizarre water tower of all must go to the one at Thorpeness.

In 1910, work began on an extraordinary holiday village on a rather bleak and desolate section of the Suffolk coast. Cottages were built around the focal centre of a clubhouse, and the notion was to make a holiday resort that would appeal to the comparatively wealthy. It was described in early brochures as 'the Home of Peter Pan' and the islands in the local lake were

given the names of Barry characters. The aim was to combine a certain amount of whimsy with modern, practical comfort which, of course, included an adequate supply of running water. A decent head of water to supply the taps was easily provided by the construction of two large water tanks, raised to a suitable height, but here was a problem. How do large iron tanks, raised high on metal frames, fit into the 'Home of Peter Pan'? The answer was found – they were to be disguised. One water tank was hidden away from view by enclosing it within a stone tower which resembles a cross between a church tower and a Norman keep. The second received far more imaginative treatment. The supporting iron frame of the tank was covered by weather-boarding, which was then pierced by windows and doors to make a five-storeyed tower. The tank on top overhung this main structure; it was also covered by weather-boarding into which windows were let and the whole was covered by a pitched roof. The result was that the tower looked like a giant fungus and it was given the name 'House in the Clouds'. And house it was, at least in part, for the lower part was and is habitable; the upper part that surrounds the tank is a sham, complete with false windows at which can be seen false curtains. It is a genuine curiosity, but then the whole of Thorpeness, as the 'Home of Peter Pan' is more prosaically known, is a happy hunting ground for the curiosity seeker. The boating lake was provided with a sham fort complete with sham guns, as well as sham concrete crocodiles lurking in the shallows. There is a pleasant conceit at the golf clubhouse, where the four towers are topped by giant tees.

The apparently mundane matter of water supply seems to bring out the best in imaginative designers. Goldney House near the Avon Gorge in Bristol has a charming round tower with little Gothic windows and pinnacled battlements at the top. It was built in 1764 and has a very special claim to fame, because the water tank at the top of the tower was filled by means of a Newcomen engine, the earliest form of steam engine. It seems very likely that this is the oldest surviving engine-house in the world, and there is a pleasing irony about the fact that this elderly survivor should not have been involved with the busy world of industry but with working cascades and fountains for an ornamental garden. Nevertheless, the very serious business of public water supply was not without its frivolities. Perth is a fair city as well as home to fair maids, and when a new waterworks was built, the job of designing it to fit its surroundings went to architect and engineer Adam Anderson. He chose a classical style and his water tank is a wonderfully convincing rotunda with a domed roof, which appears to be built of stone. The rotunda is, in fact, built of stone but the dome – the actual tank – is made of cast iron. The adjoining engine-house has gone, but the Round House is, at the time of writing, an information centre, although there are plans for a new use in 1990.

Such modesty did not carry over into the Victorian era. Water supply was a great public good and had to be seen as such. Huge steam engines were set to work and they were given suitably impressive homes. To the true

Burrington, Avon What looks like an ornate gazebo over a stream is a Water Board gauging station, measuring the flow.

Busveal, Cornwall (1 mile (1.6km) east of Redruth) Gwennap Pit appears a fine auditorium – Wesley preached here. It is, in fact, simply subsidence above an old mine.

Colchester, Essex The water tower with pyramid roof and lantern is known as 'Jumbo' after the famous circus elephant.

Driver's End, Hertfordshire The Node Dairy of 1927 is a circular building with a silo disguised as a medieval tower, but thatched.

Idlicote, Warwickshire A little octagonal, castellated building served as both dovecote and water tower.

Leicester Abbey Mills pumping station, a fine example of Victorian industrial extravagance is now a museum.

Linley, Shropshire Linley Hall grounds contain an ice-house disguised as a classical temple.

This is not a prospect tower, crept across from the last chapter, but the engine-house of the steam engine that pumped the water for the grotto at Goldney House, Bristol *(Rob Scott)*

House in the Clouds: a heavily disguised water tower (Derek Pratt)

aficionado of steam, the mighty engines need no embellishment. At Kew pumping station in London, one can see the mightiest of them all and they are miracles of ponderous yet graceful power. The biggest of the Kew engines is Harvey's Hundred Inch: that is the measure of the diameter of the cylinder. The piston moves not in fractions of an inch, but 11ft (3.3m) at every stroke, and as it moves it rocks the 24-ton overhead beam. Yet the whole process is almost silent, just a wheeze and a hiss like a gently snoring dinosaur. The setting for this great engine is austere, fluted columns rising up to frame the giant. Elsewhere, however, flamboyance is much more the order of the day.

Ryhope, near Sunderland, has what can best be described as a Jacobean engine-house, extravagantly gabled with a central turret and a triple-gabled engine-house alongside. Grander still is Stoke Newington Pumping Station in London which appears as an astonishing baronial castle. It looks remarkable and exotic to anyone who has not visited Papplewick pumping station in Nottinghamshire. The exterior is impressive, with what could well pass for 'Castle Dracula' standing beside an ornamental lake. But only when one pushes open the massive doors is the truly astonishing spectacle revealed. Archaeologists coming upon the site in the year 3000 might well decide that nineteenth-century man worshipped the machine, and they could be right. Certainly Papplewick is surrounded by an aura of devotion, a temple dedicated to the gods of steam. The great supporting pillars which both help to hold up the building and provide a frame for the engines are the first details to catch the visitor's attention. Magnificent gilded ibises and a relief of water-lilies decorate the capitals. The columns, too, are richly decorated with figures depicting suitably watery themes: lacquered brass plants entwine their way upwards, while an assortment of fish swim between them. Waterfalls, rushes and reeds appear and the same motif is continued in the windows. These have stained-glass insets, each one different and showing some water plant or creature. Until recently, when it was opened to the public, this lovely engine-house had few visitors. All this splendour, so lovingly cared for, was seen by no more than a handful of water-board employees. It represents a splendid example of Victorian self-confidence. The builders were certain that they were building for posterity, so they produced their best work. Perhaps the final irony is that the mighty engines in their elaborate setting have been replaced by an electric pump in a small, brick shed.

The majestic steam engines had themselves replaced an earlier form of power, represented in the familiar windmills and watermills of Britain. These are pleasing and welcome features in the landscape, but seldom come in any strange guise. There are exceptions, however. The Euston Hall estate at Euston, Suffolk boasts its fair share of ornamentation, including a temple and an eye-catching arch, but the watermill is the greatest curiosity. As far as work is concerned it is a perfectly conventional mill in which the waterwheel turns the stones that grind the grain. But the building itself has been disguised as a church, complete with a church tower, although the effect is made somewhat less convincing by the use of red brick. Windmills are themselves intrinsically so attractive that one might think that nothing was needed in the way of elaboration. The whole idea of a post mill is itself somehow vaguely unlikely. In these, the oldest type of mill, all the machinery is housed in a wooden 'shed' called the buck, and is powered by the sails on the outside. However, as the wind does not blow from just one direction, the medieval millers mounted the buck on a central post, and the whole structure – machinery and sails – would pivot. Later it was realised that only the sails needed to face the wind, so the machinery could be given a solid, unmoving home and the sails were attached to a rotating

Liverpool Albert Dock: the former dock office has a huge portico constructed from cast iron.

Carting Lane, London WC2 Old gas lamp was originally powered by sewer gas.

Nottingham The Lace Hall, High Pavement: a grand Unitarian chapel with windows by Burne Jones now houses the rattling machinery of the lace industry.

Rous Lench, Hereford and Worcester Village post boxes enclosed in little half-timbered building by nineteenth-century parson, Dr Chaffy, who also built a prospect tower in his grounds.

Shipley, West Yorkshire. Incorporates the mill village of Saltaire, built in the Italianate style by Sir Titus Salt.

Thetford, Norfolk Warrener's Lodge looks like a small castle, but was actually home to the gamekeeper responsible for rabbits.

Walsall, West Midlands The crenellated observatory tower in Highgate Road was originally a windmill.

Waltham Cross, Hertfordshire The impressive arch in Theobald's Park is not a sham triumphant entrance, but a real one transposed. This was London's Temple Bar.

Wexcombe, Wiltshire The village has a tiny pumping station with a pineapple roof.

This extraordinary building was originally Perth waterworks. The rotunda is actually a cast iron water tank *(Perthshire Advertiser)*

cap at the top. The cap itself is often decorative and is given attractive shapes, of which an ogee and a boat-shape are the most popular. But embellishments of the base are rare. The mill at Chesterton Green in Warwickshire is an exception. Where other towers sit solidly on the ground, this one is raised on a series of arches. It stands in its hill-top field, sparkling white on sunny days and visible for miles around, which explains why it was built to such an ornate design, for it acted both as a working mill and as an eye-catcher. It was built as early as 1632, and the design has been attributed to no less a figure than Inigo Jones. Modern experts tend to ridicule the notion that so grand an architect would stoop so low as to design a mere windmill, but one would like to think that Jones did so because the notion amused him.

The name 'mill' came to be applied to the textile factories of the

Industrial Revolution, which, in the early days were, like the grain mills, powered by water. The earliest looked like country houses, as unmistakably Georgian as an elegant town house. But the taste for the exotic that showed itself in other branches of architecture spread to the world of industry. One of the very finest examples is to be seen to the west of Chipping Norton in Oxfordshire. Bliss tweed mill was established in the middle of the eighteenth century, but the present distinctive building dates from the time when water power was replaced by steam power. The main mill building is no more than a standard, squared-off block with embellishments. It has four storeys with towers at either end, and the main decoration is a balustrade and cornice at the top of the walls. It looks as if it might be a second-rate country mansion, and if that was all there was to it, then it would scarcely rank as very extraordinary. The mill, however, is more than a building to hold machines, for it also holds a steam engine. Steam engines require boilers and boilers require tall chimneys to provide a draught to the furnace and to carry away the smoke. Mill chimneys are commonplace, and they were often built at the end of a main building. One can see what the builder had in mind. The mill resembles a country house and country houses often have domes, so if you put the chimney in the

Chesterton Green windmill, popularly believed to have been designed by Inigo Jones *(Royal Commission on the Historical Monuments of England)*

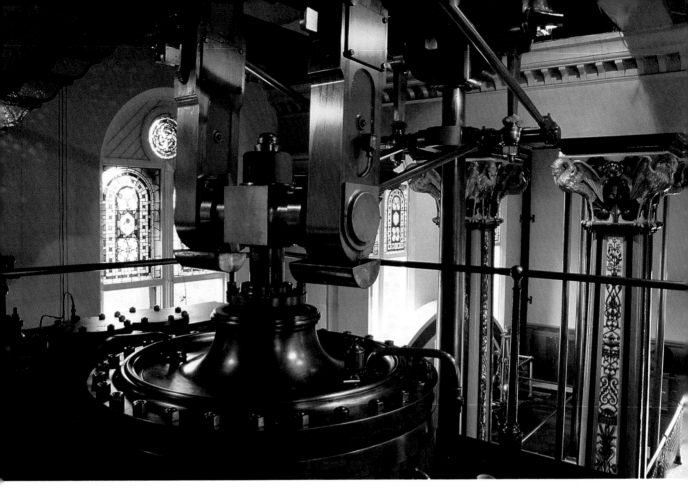

The giant steam engine in an exotic setting: Papplewick pumping station *(Anthony Burton)*

dome it does not look as tall and the structure will possibly still resemble a country house. The builders were trying a game of pretence with passers-by pretending that it was not a mill at all. The result does not look especially like a mill, but it looks even less like a country house. If it does have any associations, then it is reminiscent of a giant pepper pot. As a piece of disguise, however, it is a dismal failure, since its curious design – far from aiding it to find a comfortably anonymous place in the countryside – has produced an object for which the old cliché about sticking out like a sore thumb is all too apposite.

A far more successful piece of disguise can be seen at Coventry, although disguise was not intended. The introduction of the power loom and the removal of weaving from the cottage to the factory, aroused violent opposition during the nineteenth century. The hand-loom weavers rioted and their outbursts of machine-breaking recurred throughout the first half of the nineteenth century. One industrialist, Joseph Cash, felt that he understood the problem thoroughly. It was not, he felt, that the workers disliked the factories as such, nor was it the change from being able to work to times of their own choice to working hours dictated by the factory owners that upset them. The problem, Mr Cash decided, lay in their dislike of having to walk from house to factory in the morning, and then back again from factory to house at night. You can see his solution to that problem in Cash's Top Shops, built in 1875. At first, one sees what appears to be a perfectly conventional terrace of Victorian houses, except that they are

three storeys high and noticeably top heavy. The windows on the top floor are several sizes larger than the rest. In fact, the first two floors do represent a perfectly conventional terrace of houses, but the third floor is Mr Cash's factory. The houses surround a courtyard in which one can still see the ornate mill chimney, but the main work was carried out at the top of the houses. It was not necessary for the weavers to be unhappy about their walk to work, for, when the whistle blew, they simply opened the trapdoors in the ceiling and ascended to the factory – without even getting their boots dirty. What life must have been like in those houses with the machinery thundering overhead one can only guess, but in one sense at least the scheme was a success – Cash's are still at work. The factory above the houses is now only storage space, but down in the courtyard they turn out the Cash's name tapes which identify a million items of school clothing every year.

There is another way of disguising a factory. Instead of turning it into a facsimile of a country house or a medieval castle, it could be treated in such an exotic manner that no one could have any idea what it might be – for example, a factory could be turned into an ancient Egyptian temple. Early in the nineteenth century, John Marshall established a flax mill in Leeds in which flax was broken up into fibres for manufacturing linen – a mundane process. Marshall, however, was a man of vision, and his vision was of the glories of the Nile. So the mill was built in the style seen in temples such as that at Tanis, with a façade of massive palm columns. In its working days it must have been an even more extraordinary sight. The building has a flat roof which was covered with soil for insulation to ensure a constant temperature for the flax processing. Having taken the soil up to the roof, it seemed to Marshall to be wasteful simply to leave it, so he sowed it with grass. Having got the grass there, it seemed equally wasteful simply to let it grow, so a flock of sheep were put up there to graze. The sheep, alas, are gone, as is the flax business, but the Egyptian temple remains in the heart of Leeds. The architect responsible for Marshall's flax mill was Joseph Bonomi.

There must have been something particularly appealing about ancient Egypt for this family, as Bonomi's brother Ignatius was responsible for the country's grandest pyramid. Blickling Hall, in the heart of Norfolk, is a noble Jacobean house, which makes it all the more surprising to find a 49ft (15m) high stone pyramid in the grounds, the last resting place of the second Earl of Buckingham and his two wives. But if an Egyptian pyramid is an unlikely discovery in an English country garden, what is one to make of a carpet factory in Glasgow that does a passable imitation of the Doge's Palace in Venice?

Templeton carpet factory on Glasgow Green has now been converted to offices. To describe the building as highly decorated would be an understatement. Anything that can be decorated is decorated – in colour. It is such an amalgam of bits and pieces that you would need a short book just to give a description of the façade. The staircase tower in one corner, for

example, has simply been turned into a minaret, and one would not be surprised to hear that the workforce was summoned in the morning not by bells and whistles but by incantations. There is colour everywhere, and not just the multi-coloured bricks popular with the Victorian designers. Tiles are inlaid to simulate mosaics, in brilliant reds and blues. There is an equally colourful mixture of styles – a medieval oriel window stands above an Arabic-style arch. The circular tower at one corner is balanced – if that is the right word – by an octagonal tower at the next with a bartizan, a form of turret, in between.

It was not only mills and factories that were given the exotic treatment, for the warehouses where the end products were stored were often equally elaborate. At Ironbridge in Shropshire, for example, the warehouse by the Severn was built in the 1840s as a miniature castle, with sufficient battlements and arrow slits to withstand a major invasion – though it is doubtful whether the brick walls would provide a very stout defence. It is an incongruous building, but so in its way is the iron bridge that gave the town its name. The bridge is famous as the first of its kind in the world, which necessarily means that there was no previous experience to draw on. So the iron sections were treated as though they were pieces of timber. You can see how it works by going down to the towpath and looking at the details. Sections slot through each other, fit together in mortice-and-tenon and dovetail joints and are kept firm by iron wedges. It is unique.

Returning to warehouses and textiles, the only building that can match Templeton in style is found in Leeds. Park Square is one of the city's gems, a quietly charming Georgian square, but a brash newcomer appeared on the south side in 1878, a wool warehouse built in the style of a Moorish palace. It has fine detailing, including minarets at the corners, but if you look very closely at the detailing you will see that some of the stone has been replaced by fibreglass. Somehow it adds to the piquancy to have a wool warehouse that has been designed on the lines of a Moor's palace, decorated by fibreglass disguised as stone. The replacement comes from a recent highly successful refurbishment which converted the warehouse into offices.

The grandest warehouses, however, must be those of Manchester. A wander around the area of the Rochdale Canal is a memorable experience, especially for those who raise their eyes to the upper storeys. Here stony ships can be seen sailing out of the walls, and roofs are topped by elaborate weather vanes, but the greatest warehouse ever built was S. and J. Watts' cotton warehouse of 1851. It is a giant of a building in every sense, big and flamboyant. The style is Renaissance, with each floor of the building designed in a different variation of the main period style. It is a mark of its urbanity that its conversion into the Britannia Hotel, far from seeming incongruous, is altogether fitting. The architecture certainly seems to blend with the blue and the gold and the sweeping staircase of the lobby. Imaginative effort is not required to see the warehouse as a hotel, but to conceive how this hotel could ever have been a warehouse.

This Moorish palace in Leeds was built as a wool warehouse *(Anthony Burton)*

This colourful imitation of the Doge's Palace was built on Glasgow Green as Templeton's carpet factory *(Glasgow Tourist Board)*

(Opposite) It looks like a summer-house, but it is in fact used for measuring earthquakes and sits above a fault line at Comrie in Scotland *(Anthony Burton)*

Conversions can lead to some very strange results. One would be surprised not to find a bank in a city centre, but it is less usual to enter The Bank. It is not hubris, however, nor an attempt to denigrate every other bank. This restrained classical building in Plymouth was indeed once just one bank among many, but now it houses a very successful pub, where the emphasis is on the quality of the draught rather than on the overdraft.

Redundant churches are not uncommon and often make suitable conversions to shops, offices and even, in Bradford, an Indian restaurant. It is nevertheless still surprising to discover a church used as a pub, but that is exactly what has happened in Dundee. The pub is called 'Angels', although the jukebox plays a good deal less angelic music than the organ which would once have sounded for the Sunday hymns. In Leeds it is not a church but a synagogue that has undergone a transformation into the Northern School of Contemporary Dance. To some it can seem sacrilegious to convert any building of this sort, but an old former worshipper who came back to see what had happened to the synagogue summed up his feelings to the change. The synagogue was built, he said, to give thanks for the beauty of life, and the beauty of life is still here.

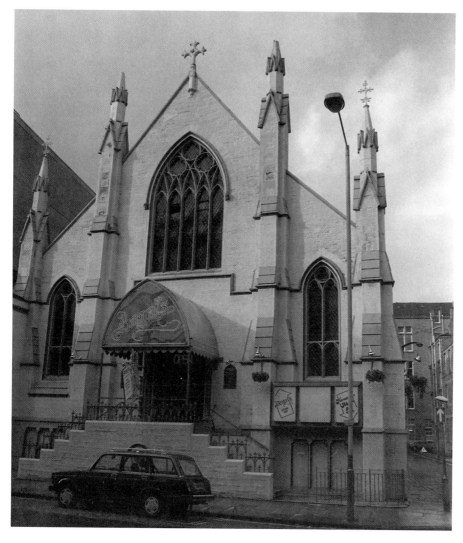

What a dour Scots minister would think of this conversion it is difficult to imagine, but this Dundee church is now Angels pub *(Anthony Burton)*

Conversions are not, perhaps, true 'not-whats', for they lack the element of conscious disguise. The very best of the true imitations are not only convincing shams but display a touch of humour as well, and none can match the Tattingstone Wonder in Suffolk – a folly of renown. The local squire looked across from his house to a pair of cottages and thought the view a little dull. He added a third cottage and then gave each a new façade with Gothic windows and a square tower at one end of the row and a rose window at the other. He looked out now on a convincing church, but from the rear the cottages were still cottages with a patently false front. Whether this can be classed as an example of disguise, as an eye-catcher or simply, as local legend has it, a wonder for the inhabitants of Silly Suffolk to gawp at is uncertain, but a wonder it certainly is. It dates from the end of the eighteenth century, a time when there was a great vogue for one particular group of buildings – a vogue that became so widespread that it deserves a chapter all to itself.

(Opposite) The Bank is not a bank, though it was once. It is now a pub in Plymouth *(Anthony Burton)*

Birds of the Air and Beasts of the Field

ONE expects to know where one is with domestic animals: hens live in hen houses and cows in the field or byre – or they did at least until the factory farm was invented. Dogs sleep in kennels, horses rest in stables. But animal homes were not always designed just as shelters for creatures but as embellishments of the scene. One such building is now so exclusively thought of as ornamental that we sometimes lose sight of the fact that it was originally useful: the dovecote. The utilitarian aspect does become clear when you step inside the very best of the preserved dovecotes.

Erddig in Clwyd is a seventeenth-century country house, situated on an estate that is as important as the dwelling. The dovecote looks attractive in its setting, but it is the interior that is most impressive. All around the walls are literally hundreds of nesting holes, and in the centre of the building is a potence, a central pole supporting a ladder that protrudes from a bracket. The ladder itself rotates, so that the estate worker could climb up and push himself around, collecting eggs and young birds. The dovecote was not built to house ornamental birds, but as an important source of food. A large dovecote could hold up to two thousand birds, and in Scotland a fifteenth-century law required every laird to maintain a 'doocot', as they were known north of the Border. One of the best known of these is the Phantassie Doocot at East Linton, which is generally believed to be of fifteenth-century origin. It is a massive stone structure, like an oversized beehive of which

the top has been sliced away at an angle. It is now in the care of the National Trust for Scotland. Later doocots were altogether more ornate. At Balerno in Lothian, the doves had a little stone house with a pitched roof – an attractive home-from-home for about 1,800 birds. The gardens of Balerno are also well known, if only for the great yew trees that were planted in 1603 – one for each of the twelve apostles. As they grew, so the house became steadily gloomier, until in the 1960s drastic action was taken. Now the garden has only four 'apostles'. The garden of Haddington House, also in Lothian, was restored in 1771 for Lady Catherine Charteris, and it is still known as Lady Kitty's garden. The dovecote reflects the Gothic taste of the period: a little round crenellated tower above a square pavilion. In the nineteenth century when doves were no longer kept at Haddington, the dovecote became home to an elderly couple. Some English dovecotes seem equally desirable residences for humans, if a trifle cramped. The one at Wichenford Court in Hereford and Worcester could easily pass muster as a timber-framed Tudor cottage, apart from its total lack of windows. In later years, the dovecote found a new and unlikely importance. The bird droppings were collected and used to provide saltpetre for the manufacture of gunpowder. The bird of peace thus unwittingly fuelled the engines of war.

Most of us can conceive of a dovecote as being used as a bijou

The dovecote in the gardens of Cotehele House, Cornwall
(Anthony Burton)

Bodmin, Cornwall The town car park contains a memorial to Prince Chula of Siam's dog.

Brecon Beacons, Powys Memorial to Harry Llewellyn's horse Foxhunter.

Branxton, Cornhill-on-Tweed, Northumberland 'The Fountain' is home to the Cement Menagerie, a garden full of beasts and gnomes created by John Fairnington, who died at the age of 99.

Bruton, Somerset ½ mile (800m) south of Bruton is an unusual gabled sixteenth-century dovecote (NT).

Carisbrooke, Isle of Wight Carisbrooke Castle has a donkey wheel used for raising water from a deep well.

Castor, Cambridgeshire Milton Park has kennels disguised as a medieval gatehouse.

Chastleton, Oxfordshire (2 miles (3.2km) west of Chipping Norton) Opposite Chastleton House, a gabled dovecote built on massive pillars.

Cotehele, Cornwall A well-preserved stone dovecote can be seen in the beautiful gardens (NT).

Ford, Northumberland Village smithy with a horseshoe-shaped entrance.

residence, but would we take equally kindly to the notion of living in a hen house? Leighton, near Welshpool, is a model (ie exemplary) farm. Everything is on an impressive scale, including the housing for the livestock. The Fowl House resembles a cross between a Swiss chalet and a stockbroker's mock-Tudor home. It was built to house ornamental as well as purely useful birds, and each species had its own apartment. It is notably grander both in size and style than the house provided for the mere human, the poultry keeper. Given a choice, the Fowl House looks the better option for a potential house purchaser.

The Fowl House seems unremarkable, however, when set against the home provided for the birds of Tong in Shropshire (p79). The local landowner, George Durant, who came here in the late eighteenth century, had a strong taste for the fantastic, and he passed it on to his successors. What George Durant senior had begun, George junior was to continue with gusto, and nothing on the estate is more fantastic than the Egyptian aviary of 1842. It can still be seen standing in front of the farmhouse, an unlikely brick pyramid, with egg-shaped holes to let the birds hop in and out. Having built a pyramid for hens, Durant turned his hand to designing a porcine pyramid. This very cramped little pyramid pig-sty can be seen in a garden at Bishop's Wood in Staffordshire. An inscription reads 'To Please The Pigs', but even piglets might have cause to complain. There seems to be something about pigs which causes people to produce odd buildings – even farmers unaffected by whimsy. The Welsh, for example, often favour circular pig-sties, and there is a lovely example preserved at the Welsh Folk Museum at St Fagans, near Cardiff. But the prize for incongruity must surely belong to a sty at Robin Hood's Bay in Yorkshire. Here the animals are housed in a classical temple that looks for all the world like some splendid garden pavilion. The Robin Hood's Bay pig-sty is being refurbished by

A circular pig-sty in Cardiff *(Anthony Burton)*

the Landmark Trust as a holiday home. In the not-too-distant future when people say that they have holidayed in a pig-sty, they will not necessarily be alluding to an unfinished hotel – they might in fact be telling the truth.

This classical temple at Robin Hood's Bay must be the world grandest pig-sty *(Landmark Trust)*

Some animals might be thought to have a somewhat higher status, at least as far as human judgement is concerned, than the pig. Horses did, and still do, inspire affection in their owners, which was occasionally reflected in grand homes. One of the most grandiose of all is the stable block at Silverton Park at Broadclyst in Devon. No one coming upon the building by accident could ever guess what it was. At first sight it is a country house, but obviously a somewhat unconventional one. A Palladian mansion might be one guess, with porticos on all four sides, but the porticoes rise higher than the single-storey building behind them. In the event, it looks just what it is – an extraordinary building, whether intended for man or beast.

On the great hunting estates, the stables were always given due prominence. In 1697, the first Duke of Richmond bought Goodwood House, in West Sussex, to enable him to ride with the Charlton Hunt which had just introduced the novel activity of pursuing foxes instead of deer. It was the duke's grandson who built the stable block which must be the only stables in Britain that outdo the house which they serve. The kennels were built on an equally gargantuan scale, but they have long since found a new use as Goodwood Golf Club.

Often it seems that very grand stables are simply another example of

Fulking, West Sussex
The path up to the
Downs has a stile for
humans and a separate
one with sliding door for
dogs.
**Garway, Hereford and
Worcester** Close to the
church is a fourteenth-
century dovecote built by
the Knights Templar.
**Great Milton,
Oxfordshire** Circular
stone dovecote in the
churchyard.
**Hawford, Hereford and
Worcester** Sixteenth-
century half-timbered
dovecote (NT).
**Horsenden,
Buckinghamshire** (1
mile (1.6km) west of
Princes Risborough) A
timber dovecote of 1550
built over archway.
Hurley, Berkshire A
circular dovecote stands
beside the tithe barn.
**Kinwarton,
Warwickshire** (1½
miles (2.5km) north-east
of Alcester) A circular
fourteenth-century
dovecote (NT).
**Little Comberton,
Hereford and
Worcester** Medieval
dovecote at Nash's Farm
and seventeenth-century
dovecote at Manor
House.
**Long Crendon,
Buckinghamshire** A
medieval square
dovecote at Notley
Abbey.

Not a half-timbered
cottage, but the dovecote
at Wichenford Court
(National Trust)

owners' love of ostentation. The stables and kennels of Berkeley Castle appear in a startling black-and-white stone building, an elaborate structure with a castellated arch in the centre. However, the stables and kennels here pale into insignificance compared with another stable block on the edge of Bristol known variously as Arno's Castle, the Black Castle and the Devil's Cathedral. In the eighteenth century, Bristol was the centre for a thriving brass industry. William Reeve married into the Andrews family who were smelting copper in the area. When he came to add the stable block to his house he found the ideal building material – ideal because it came absolutely free – shiny, black slag from the furnaces. He built in the fashionable Gothic style, producing an extraordinary black-and-white castle that now looks more than a little out of place in the surrounding suburbs.

Sir Christopher Sykes of Sledmere on Humberside went one stage further by turning an entire farmyard into a castle – although it was not intended originally for that purpose. When 'Capability' Brown landscaped the park in 1776 an eye-catcher was deemed necessary, and a medieval castle seemed appropriate. Sir Christopher, however, felt that it should be useful as well as decorative and declared that it would make an ideal dower house. The dowager was less amused at being classified with old ruins, even false ones, so the 'castle' with its turrets and grand entrance arch now leads into the farmyard. Sir Christopher might well have been feeling a little piqued by his mother's scorn of his folly. She had always loved gardens and flowers, and when she died he had all the flower beds in the village destroyed and he ordered the tenants to plant no more. Sir Christopher Sykes cannot be placed among the more amiable folly builders.

Amiability is certainly present at Attingham Park in Shropshire, where instead of a conventional hive, the bees have been given a delicate little house of their own. It looks at first glance like a summer-house, although one would be unlikely to sit in it for long. It was designed to be both practical and ornamental, and perhaps even instructive, for the bee's industry was considered by our forebears to be a model of virtuous behaviour. Perhaps so, but one suspects that those who delighted in the house were happy to listen to Tennyson's 'sweet sound' of the 'murmuring of innumerable bees'. It is, however, entirely possible that many visitors took the view of Edward Lear's old man:

> There was an Old Man in a tree,
> Who was horribly bored by a bee;
> When they said, 'Does it buzz?'
> He replied, 'Yes, it does!
> It's a regular brute of a bee!'

The goats of Blithfield in Staffordshire have no exotic home – in fact, they have no home at all. The goats roam wild in Bagot's Park, their ancestors having been presented to Sir William Bagot of Blithfield by Richard II. To

This is not the ruins of a manor but the stables at Silverton Park, Devon *(Landmark Trust)*

The stables at Arno's Castle in Bristol were built from blocks of furnace slag *(Rob Scott)*

commemorate the event, if somewhat belatedly, a Goat Lodge was added to Blithfield Hall in 1839. It is a splendidly grotesque building, from which stony goats' heads pop out in the most unlikely places. Stone animals often appear in unexpected places. A positive menagerie of beasts peers over the wall outside Cardiff Castle: lions wait to pounce on unsuspecting shoppers, while more bashful creatures look as if they would dearly love to escape the fumes and noise of the busy road outside. It is the element of surprise that makes the Cardiff animals memorable. The same is true of other similarly memorable animals.

The Crystal Palace, which was built for the Great Exhibition of 1851, must have been a great marvel, but although the building has gone, the park in which it was rebuilt in South London, after the Hyde Park show was over, remains. And there, lurking in the undergrowth are dinosaurs – splendidly realised, full-scale models cast in bronze and then painted. They were made for serious educational purposes, but for generations of children they have been good, slightly scary, fun. Our own age has produced an equally memorable sculptured group. In the post-war years, new towns have been added to the countryside, and one new city. Milton

Mavesyn Ridware, Staffordshire The old hall has gone but the gatehouse, dovecote and rare nesting-boxes survive.

Monk's Risborough, Buckinghamshire (adjoining Princes Risborough) Dovecote in field behind church square.

Northchurch, Hertfordshire Norcott Court, a brick and timber Tudor dovecote.

Rotherfield Greys, Oxfordshire Grey's Court, 3 miles (5km) west of Henley-on-Thames on the road to Rotherfield Greys; the well house has a huge wheel which was turned by a donkey to raise water from the well (NT).

Sevenoaks, Kent Knole Park in the grounds of which stands a tiny Gothic folly house built as a home for birds.

South Harting, West Sussex Uppark has two pavilions: one a highly decorated stables, the other a pretty dairy.

Westdean, East Sussex (6 miles (10km) east of Eastbourne) Medieval dovecote in the grounds of Charleston Manor.

Willington, Bedfordshire (4 miles (6.5km) east of Bedford, just north of the A603) Sixteenth-century dovecote is all that remains of a large estate (NT).

A pyramid for hens at Tong
(Anthony Burton)

Keynes has spread itself in a regular grid over acres of old farmland, giving rise in the process to a bewildering signposting system using letters and numerals rather than names, so that the visitor half expects to find the instruction P to KB2 among all the MK1s. As a memorial to the bucolic past, the citizens have been provided with a herd of concrete cows and their calves.

Sculpture with a purpose appears in another unlikely setting, decorating the lineside on the railway between Birmingham and Wolverhampton. A succession of sheet metal horses appear in fields along the way. One of the more dramatic figures is of a horse caught at the moment of leaping a fence. When last observed, the iron horse was evoking no sign of interest from the flesh and blood horses which were sharing the field.

In most cases, one comes across a statue and it is easy to say just where it is, what it is and in most cases why it is. But to end this short catalogue of notable creatures, here is one which remains a delightful mystery. Drivers travelling north on the M5 between Exeter and Bristol can see by the roadside an animal peering over a hedge. Although there is nothing surprising in that, this animal is not real but manufactured, and it is not a common English beast but a camel. As it is beside the motorway one cannot stop for a closer look, and one never seems to have time to turn off to make enquiries. But the camel provides a welcome diversion from the tedium of motorway driving – so from this driver at least, a big thank you is offered to the anonymous sculptor.

As well as the ordinary statues of animals the country boasts a surprisingly large number of monuments dedicated to animals. Sometimes the reasons are plain to see. At Stratfield Saye, in Hampshire, the Duke of Wellington's country house, there are memories of his favourite horse, Copenhagen, which carried him through the day at Waterloo. A lock from the horse's mane is kept in a case in the library and a headstone marks its grave. Lord Byron was not content to commemorate his favourite dog Boatswain with a mere headstone. The monument at Newstead Abbey has an urn on an engraved plinth, and Byron wrote a memorial verse which includes the lines:

> But the poor dog, in life the firmest friend,
> The first to welcome, foremost to defend.

The monument stands not far from the lake, where two mock forts inspired the poet to hold his own private naval battles on the water.

Byron's lines were used on a memorial at Woburn dedicated to a former Duchess of Bedford's pet Pekinese, Che Foo. The dog itself, modelled in bronze, is curled up on a plinth, looking out at the world with a singularly distrustful air as though it is not greatly enjoying its uncomfortable new home in a draughty temple, consisting of a cast-iron dome supported on stone pillars. Che Foo might have been somewhat unhappy with the inscribed verses (not by Byron):

The famous naturalist Gilbert White of Selborne so disliked the sight of meat in the village butcher's shop that he planted these trees to shield him from the view *(Royal Commission on the Historical Monuments of England)*

When the body that lived at your single will,
When the whimper of welcome is stilled (how still!)
When the spirit that answered your every mood
Is gone – wherever it goes – for good,
You will discover how much you care,
And will give your heart to a dog to tear.

Such lines are enough to make any self-respecting Pekinese sneer.

One of the most famous monuments is the statue to the Edinburgh dog which never forgot its master, Greyfriars Bobby. Tell's Tower in West Kirby in Merseyside stands 25ft (8m) high, a large monument for a large dog, for Tell was a Saint Bernard. Hounds also figure largely, although generally in the metaphorical rather than, as in Tell's case, the literal sense. Set in a wall at Euston Park is a commemorative tablet that records the death in 1788 of Trouncer. It carries the message: 'Foxes Rejoice: Here Buried Lies Your Foe'. More foxes slept easily in the vicinity of Rousham, the fine Oxfordshire house, when the best hunting hounds' days came to an end, and these hounds were given a grand memorial in the grounds.

Cats, are, for some reason, less well represented – perhaps because it might seem an impertinence to attempt to do anything for such

Sheep farming on the South Downs is remembered in the gateway to Pyecombe Church, which incorporates a shepherd's crook, made at the local forge *(Anthony Burton)*

independent creatures. An exception can be seen in a splendid cat monument, with the animal crouching on a high pillar, in the grounds of Shugborough Hall in Staffordshire. More modest memorials mark the graves of a pair of church cats. A simple gravestone at St Mary Redcliffe in Bristol simply states 'The Church Cat 1912–1927'. Tiddles of Fairford, Gloucestershire, was given her own portrait stone in the graveyard, commissioned by the verger. Tiddles lived in the church from 1963 to 1980 and earned her place in the graveyard, having spent far more time in the church than most of her human neighbours.

One of the grandest of all memorials can be seen on Farley Mount in Hampshire. It is a pyramid with four porches at the base, through one of which one may enter to discover the following inscription:

> Underneath lies buried a horse, the property of Paulet St John Esq, that in the month of September 1733 leaped into a chalk pit twenty-five feet deep a-foxhunting with his master on his back, and in October 1734 he won the Hunters' plate on Worthy Downs and was rode by his owner and entered in the name of 'Beware Chalk Pit'.

Memorials to horses, dogs and cats seem easy to accept, but some creatures seem less worthy of, or certainly less likely to receive such post-humous tributes. To prove this point, here are two memorials to less likely recipients, and a small group which seem to defy explanation. In the grounds of Mount Edgcumbe overlooking Plymouth Sound, is a fine obelisk erected in memory of the countess's pet pig, Cupid, while the following tablet can be found near a stream at Fish Cottage, Blockley, in Gloucestershire:

The delicate beehive at Attingham Park *(Mike Williams/National Trust)*

In
Memory
of the
Old Fish
Under the soil
The Old Fish do lie
20 years he lived
And then did die
He was so tame
You understand
He would come and
Eat out of our hand.

And what of the inexplicable? There is a group of four carvings in the churchyard at Dacre in Cumbria, depicting a bear and a cat. In the first

carving the bear is asleep, then it is woken by the cat, grabs it and in the fourth eats it. There is no inscription and no explanation. On that mysterious note, this section ends.

It would, however, be a pity to end the chapter on a mournful note, and there is one other popular association between animals and man which occurs constantly – the pub sign. All kinds of beasts appear in pub names, but some deserve a special mention. The Beehive, for example, is a popular name, and sometimes, as in an Abingdon hostelry, comes complete with a rhyme:

> Within this hive we are all alive
> Good liquor makes us funny
> If you be dry step in and try
> The value of our honey.

But a similarly named establishment in Grantham goes one better, for it uses an actual beehive, populated by genuine bees, for its sign, to which are added these lines:

> Stop traveller, this wondrous sign explore
> And say, when thou hast viewed it o'er and o'er;
> Grantham, now two rareties are thine
> A lofty steeple and a living sign.

It is not just the pubs that have animal connections, for many breweries boast of their dray horses. Young's of Wandsworth have some of the finest animals, which are still used regularly for deliveries in the surrounding streets. Young's emblem, however, is a ram, and by tradition a ram has always been kept on the premises. He has his own handsome little house and frequently wanders out to watch the ducks and geese on the pond in the stable yard – and all this within yards of some of London's busiest streets.

No Place Like Home

Banwell, Avon (5 miles (8km) east of Weston-super-Mare) Banwell Castle, a typical Victorian castellated house privately owned and notable for a belvedere in the form of a round tower.

Brixham, Devon The Old Coffin House, so known simply because it is coffin-shaped.

Bunbury, Cheshire The Image House is an otherwise ordinary home, but covered in carved figures.

Chysauster, Cornwall (north of Madron) A surprisingly well-preserved Iron Age village.

Eagle, Lincolnshire Eagle Moor, 1 mile (1.6km) north-east, boasts an amazingly convoluted farmhouse known as The Jungle, privately owned.

East Cowes, Isle of Wight A suburban semi-detached house almost entirely covered in seashells.

Greystoke, Cumbria (5 miles (8km) west of

ODDNESS lies in the eye of the beholder, and perceptions change all the time. At the height of the Gothic revival, for example, buildings were put up which were then merely fashionable but now seem extraordinary. The little market town of Brewood in Shropshire seems at first glance to be a place of unspoiled charm, where the tone is set by restrained Georgian houses. Then you meet Speedwell Castle: the style is Gothic on the rampage, with a riot of tortured ogee arches on the main façade and one delightful note of incongruity. There, perched on top of the arch that frames the main door is a cheery, red-cheeked garden gnome. The name is said to derive from a racehorse which did indeed speed well enough for one fortunate punter to build this amazing house out of his winnings. Other buildings, however, intrigue and fascinate, although in themselves they are ordinary enough, at least in terms of the period in which they were built.

Looking far back in time to a house of the Neolithic or New Stone Age, what would you expect a dwelling of four thousand years ago to look like? Two possible stereotypes come to mind: the cave of the caveman or the stone house of the cartoon Flintstone family, with stone walls, stone beds, chairs and tables. The surprise is that the cartoon version is nearer to reality. Some time in the third millennium BC, a great sandstorm completely buried the village of Skara Brae on the coast of Orkney. It remained covered until the middle of the nineteenth century when another great storm ripped the sand away again to reveal the houses and their contents. These were very practical, if a touch aromatic, homes, for they were built into a giant midden. The decaying rubbish protected the inhabitants from the cold winds and generated heat as it rotted. The real shock is the furniture, for it is genuine stone furniture: stone beds that would be filled with bracken, stone cupboards and what can only be described as stone Welsh dressers (p87). Moving closer to our own time you will find an example of houses which are in their own way just as intriguing.

Penrith) An extraordinary collection of farms commemorating American battles: Bunker's Hill, Fort Putnam and Jefferson Farm. There is also a farm with a spire.

Grimspound, Dartmoor, Devon A group of circular stone huts enclosed by a circular wall.

Henfield, West Sussex A platoon of cats clutching canaries marches round the eaves of a sixteenth-century cottage in the lane leading to the church.

Lincoln The Glory Hole or High Bridge: houses that span the Witham. Aaron the Jew's House is claimed to be the oldest house in the country.

Midford, Avon (3 miles (5km) south of Bath) Roebuck's Folly, a castle-like building shaped in a plan like the ace of clubs – the card that made its owner's fortune, or so the story goes. Folly 'Priory' in grounds.

Newquay, Cornwall The Huer's house on the cliff is a small castellated tower from which the huer kept a look-out for pilchard shoals.

St Michael Caerhays, (Veryan Bay) Cornwall Caerhays Castle, a Gothic masterpiece by John Nash. Privately owned.

Speedwell Castle in Brewood: a Gothic fantasy, but why the gnome? *(Anthony Burton)*

Twickenham, London
Strawberry Hill: Walpole's
Gothic fantasy which is
now the home of a
Catholic training college.
**Weston-in-Gordano,
Avon** Walton Castle, a
particularly convincing
sham ruin built in a
mixture of styles. Now a
private house.

On the western edge of Basildon in Essex is what was once the Dunton Plotlands. The story starts with the agricultural-depression years at the start of the nineteenth century, when a good deal of farming land was sold off to land speculators. It was then marked out into small plots and sold again to individual buyers. The main years of development came between the two world wars when London families began building their holiday bungalows here, avenues of trim little houses. This was very much a do-it-yourself project with no help from the authorities. Houses were laid out in rows and named First Avenue, Second Avenue, and so on, but no one paved the new roads, no one brought in mains services and no one helped with the building either. Families would come down for weekends, sleeping out in tents and getting on with the job. Then, during World War II, Londoners began to move out of the bombed city and the holiday homes became permanent homes, but still without amenities. The end of the Plotlands came with the establishment of Basildon New Town. The authorities began buying up the cottages as people moved out, and today most of the plots have gone back to nature. The avenues are grassy tracks and the carefully tended gardens have run riot. But you can still wander through the area and find the foundations of the little bungalows and the few survivors, and the local authority has provided a Dunton Plotland Trail to help the visitor. One bungalow, The Haven, has been kept as a Plotland Museum. Built by Frederick Mills in the thirties, he lived here for over forty years. It is tiny but trim, the perfect suburban villa in miniature; but a suburban villa without a suburb. Instead there is a little wilderness, where domestic flower-beds riot among the more familiar buttercups and dandelions.

There are a number of houses which have always been considered strange and bizarre. My own childhood was spent in Yorkshire and each

Self-built holiday home for
a Londoner: one of the
survivors at Dunton
Plotlands, now a museum
*(Basildon Development
Corporation)*

A Stone Age Welsh dresser in a Stone Age house at Skara Brae on Orkney (Anthony Burton)

day I travelled 3 miles (5km) to school in Knaresborough. The school devised an annual torture for its male pupils in the form of a compulsory cross-country run which involved running, stepping, staggering or walking – depending on personal fitness and inclination – up the steps that led from the path by the River Nidd to the top of the cliffs that dominate the northern bank. The less energetic among us had a chance to ponder the work of Thomas Hill, who some two centuries before had expended even more energy on those same cliffs than had we, the unwilling schoolboy athletes. Thomas Hill decided to make himself a house not on the cliff, but inside it. In 1770 he began the long task of carving his dwelling out of the

Home from home for Bronze Age man: looking out of the doorway of a stone hut at Grimspound, Dartmoor *(Anthony Burton)*

rock face. This was no troglodyte cave, but a proper home, multi-storeyed and many-roomed. It took Hill sixteen years to complete his house, during which time he continued to earn his living as a weaver. His extraordinary house soon attracted a good deal of attention and a great many visitors, including the Duchess of Buccleuch, in whose honour he renamed the house Fort Montagu. The local inhabitants tended, as is the nature of Yorkshire folk, to mock such pretensions and began referring to the owner as Sir Thomas Hill. But Hill himself was not to be that easily put down, and went one better by adopting the title 'Governor of Fort Montagu'. He even issued his own currency in the form of a tuppence ha'penny note,

suspiciously similar in design to a conventional £5. In the fullness of time, Hill died. His banknotes vanished, but the house he had hacked from the rock has survived to fascinate generations of visitors to the quiet market town on the Nidd.

Another example of a house that has been built in a cliff can be seen in the Rock Cottage at Wolverley in Worcestershire, which also claims to be one of the smallest houses in the country. The claim of being the smallest might be disputed for there is a strong contender in the restricted shape of 10 Lower Street, Conwy. The house has a total frontage of a mere 6ft (1.8m), is 8ft 4in (2.5m) high and just over 10ft (3m) deep. It has two rooms, one

above the other, and was lived in until 1900, although there is something of a mystery as to how its last inhabitant survived his tenure, for he was 6ft 3in (1.9m) tall. Another contender for both titles of smallest and most unusual rock dwelling can be seen carved out of the cliffs at Porthcurno in Cornwall.

Still in Cornwall one finds not just another odd building, but a whole collection of them: the Round Houses of Veryan. The village of Veryan would attract attention without the round houses, for it is one of those pleasing little places, full of narrow undulating streets that are such a feature of the South West. The houses are, however, unique. They are not all strictly round: some are hexagonal, although the corners are rounded to give an impression of circularity, an impression heightened by the conical roofs. Taken individually, they are curious buildings, with oddly shaped windows and doors, the shape often picked out in pebbles and shells; in each case the conical roof is topped with a cross. They become even odder when seen as a group, each one slightly different from its neighbour, yet all fitting into the same general pattern. They are spread out around the edges of the village, and no one knows exactly why or when they were built. There is, however, agreement on one point: they were intended to thwart the Devil in his evil designs on the good citizens of Veryan.

There are two main theories as to how these odd little houses would thwart diabolical schemings. The first rests on the well-established view that the Devil, ever on the look-out for souls to drag to the nether regions, spends a good deal of his time lurking in dark corners. It follows then that a house with no corners of any description, dark or light, would provide no suitable lodging place. Surround the village with such houses, and Old Nick would soon become discouraged and slope off to look elsewhere for more congenial surroundings. In version two, the Devil comes to the village and is confronted with a house topped by a cross, which keeps him away. He then moves off to be faced by more of the same houses, all identical, which greatly confuses the Satanic mind. Discouraged by this, he gives up and goes in search of a less well-protected village. The citizens of Veryan could sleep easy in their beds, untroubled either by the Devil or the thought of what evils he might be perpetrating nearby.

There is always a particular appeal about buildings which are odd by design, and an even greater appeal when there is a good story to be told about them as well. The Pack o' Cards Inn at Combe Martin in North Devon looks very much what you would expect from its name. But why would anyone build a house to resemble stacked-up playing cards? And why would they carry the card motif even further, by building the house with four floors to correspond to the four suits, and then emphasise the point by installing fifty-two windows? The builder, George Ley, made his fortune at the gaming tables in the late seventeenth century and this seemed an obvious way for him to commemorate his good fortune. But why did someone build a cottage in Lyme Regis to look like an umbrella? Did they make a fortune on a wet day? The answer is, sadly, dull: no one built it to

The Veryan round houses were designed so that they had no corners for the devil to lurk *(Derek Pratt)*

The Pack o' Cards Inn, Combe Martin has fifty-two windows and celebrates a gamester's good fortune (S. Griffin, Pack o' Cards, Combe Martin)

look like an umbrella at all, for the cottage was built long before the first British umbrella was unfurled. It is a cottage which has been changed and added to over the years, the additions including the hemispherical thatched roof that overhangs the walls by over 2ft (60cm). The shape of the roof is entirely appropriate for a house built on a hexagonal plan, and the shape of the building itself is equally appropriate for the cottage's original function as a toll house, so all the oddity derives from the shape and the shape was the answer to a practical problem.

The shape of the house known as 'À La Ronde' in Exmouth, Devon, serves no practical end, and, to add to the confusion, it is not round at all. It is in fact octagonal, built to the same plan as the famous Church of San Vitale at Ravenna. It has, at its centre, an octagonal hall, and all the rooms radiate out from this. The idea for the house came from two sisters, Mary and Jane Parminter, who visited Ravenna in the 1790s. The house would, by its design, qualify for any list of strange buildings, but the passing years have greatly added to its character. Inside it has become like a grotto with, it seems, every inch of surface decorated with shells. This reaches its culmination in the shell gallery, where abstract design and pictorial representation mix happily together.

The octagonal hall with its encrustations of shells in À La Ronde (The British Tourist Authority)

Elaborate decoration joins with an interesting history to make Plas Newydd, near Llangollen in Wales, an outstandingly interesting house. It was the home of the 'Ladies of Llangollen', Lady Eleanor Butler and Sarah Ponsonby who eloped from Ireland and set up house here in 1780. They

became famous local characters, dressed in dark riding habits, wearing tall hats and having close cropped hair. They came to a plain Welsh cottage and then set to work on it until it was completely Gothicised. They added oriel windows, stained glass and carved oak in profusion. Their many visitors, who included such famous people as the Duke of Wellington and Wordsworth, would bring oak carvings as gifts for their hostesses. The carvings festoon the walls, both inside and out: lions look across at cherubs and Hindu gods consort with the ancient Greeks. The effect is sombrely extravagant, for the odd pieces of wall that appear between the dark carvings in the rooms are covered in embossed leather. Attitudes to the house are as varied as were the attitudes to the ladies themselves, who were described by one contemporary as looking like 'respectable superannuated clergymen' and by another as 'hazy or crazy old sailors'. But neither the ladies nor their house could ever be described as dully conventional.

Plas Newydd became extraordinary by the steady accretion of details added during the half century that the ladies lived there. It is, of course, much easier to make an effect by starting with something bizarre. A very strange building can be found by the Norfolk Broads at Potter Heigham. It is round, ribbed and has a conical top. It once lived on the pier at Yarmouth as the top of the helter-skelter. When its fairground days were over it was brought to Potter Heigham and adapted as a holiday cottage.

Living in a helter-skelter must be fun, rather more so, one might think, than occupying a gents. A round, stone building at Gayhurst in Buckinghamshire is topped by an extraordinary conical roof with arched dormer windows, the whole structure culminating in a pinnacle on which perch two hounds, back to back. It was built as an outdoor lavatory for Lord Carrington's man-servants by one of the most flamboyantly playful of Victorian architects, William Burges, whom we shall be meeting again shortly. Locally it is known as the 'Dog House', giving a new slant to the popular expression 'in the dog house', and is now a pleasingly eccentric family home.

The 'Dog House' is a good example of a local landowner indulging his taste, but some went ever further. Not content with the occasional building being produced in a style they deemed appropriate, they made themselves responsible for the appearance of whole villages. Often this produced no more than dull, regimented rows of cottages, standing guard on either side of the main road. Occasionally, however, the landowner had decidedly quirky notions about how such a new village should appear. The villagers had, at best, only a slight say in the matter, and had to make do with what they were given, no matter how bizarre.

Marford in Clwyd was a typical village of little cottages, scattered around the main road from Chester to Wrexham. Then, in 1805, George Boscawen set about modelling the whole village to suit his taste, and eleven years later the work was complete. Gone were the low-walled, thatched cottages scattered higgledy-piggledy; in their place came the new, on a neat and

The sundial stands surrounded by John Nash's picturesque cottages ornées at Blaise Hamlet
(Rob Scott)

formal plan. Neatness and formality, however, begin and end with the overall plan, for the houses themselves are disorderly in the extreme. No two cottages are alike, and each is more than a little strange. They conform to no known style, although they could be classified as rural picturesque with Gothic overtones. Roofs are tile instead of thatch, but have been 'aged' by the architects who designed them with curving ridges to imitate the sagging roofs of older buildings. Walls also curve, in regular undulation. Windows come in all shapes and sizes – rounds, ovals, extravagant ogees, lancet – everything, it seems, except the common rectangle. In addition, Gothic detailing is stuck on almost randomly. And so the Marford cottage was created, which seems to be not merely the brainchild of Boscawen the

landowner, but the work of Boscawen, amateur architect extraordinary.

Some village planners showed their idiosyncratic designs in the odd building rather than in an entire village. A fine example can be seen in the village of Ripley in North Yorkshire, alongside Ripley Castle, the seat of the Ingilby family. William Ingilby was Lord of the Manor during the early years of the nineteenth century and in the 1820s he set about rebuilding Ripley as a model village. Houses were arranged in neat terraces and built of the dark, local stone which gives such a distinctive character to this part of the country. They possess almost a compulsory hint of Gothic, but are otherwise pleasantly unremarkable. The family home had been plain Ripley Castle since the middle of the fourteenth century, but to this member of the family it was 'The Schloss'. Ingilby dreamed of bringing European style and grandeur to little Ripley, and decided that what the village most needed was a hall – not a village hall nor a town hall, but an Hôtel de Ville in the French manner. What the villagers would do with an Hôtel de Ville was clearly of little interest and of less importance. An Hôtel de Ville they would have, and in the grand manner at that. And there it stands in mock medieval splendour, with turrets and battlements, mullioned windows and all the trimmings, lording it over the terraces of stone cottages.

The most famous of all planned villages is Blaise Hamlet, the village near Blaise Castle just outside Bristol. We have already seen how stately home owners in their enthusiasm for all things picturesque had set about transforming their parks and gardens with imitation ruins designed to suit the style. One aspect of this construction movement was the cottage orné, an idealised country cottage, irregularly shaped, preferably thatched and representing a romanticised pastoral ideal. Such cottages had about as much to do with the genuine cottages of farm labourers as pastoral poetry did with the actuality of working life in the country. The cottages were, however, undeniably attractive additions to the large estates. John Scandrett Harford, a local banker, took the concept one stage further. Where others had been content with one cottage orné, he was determined to build a village full of them. Unlike other landlords, such as the builder of the over-ordinary village of Nuneham Courtenay near Oxford, he did not have to destroy existing cottages and transfer existing tenants, willing and unwilling alike, to their new homes. Blaise Hamlet was an entirely new construction. Harford called in one of the most distinguished architects of the day, John Nash, who, with his associate George Repton, set out to construct an idealised English village. The cottages were individually designed and grouped around a green. There are only nine cottages, but between them they cover every conceivable pastoral style. There are thatched roofs and tiled roofs, although no cottage is allowed a single, unadorned roof: each has a multiplicity of levels. There are verandas and porches; leaded windows and plain. There are Tudor chimney pots, and one cottage has little holes cut in the boarded façade in imitation of a dovecote, although heaven help the elderly residents for whom the

cottages were intended if pigeons ever decided to use them. Blaise Hamlet is an artifice, a conceit, an exercise in nostalgia, and the forerunner of thousands of countrified houses that make up twentieth-century suburbia.

The wealthy who indulged their taste in designing other people's houses showed themselves just as eager to indulge in fancies when building or rebuilding their own. Of all the styles that flourished, if only briefly, none seems more unlikely than that which came to be known as Indian or Hindu Gothic. The name is an apt description, for the characteristic onion domes and open turrets clearly derive from the Moghul architecture of the great buildings of India, such as Fatehpur Sikri or the Red Fort in Delhi, while much of the elaborate detail shows a stronger local influence. The best known example of the genre is the Royal Pavilion at Brighton, but the style first appeared in the unlikely setting of the Cotswold countryside of Moreton-in-the-Marsh. Sezincote was built in the early nineteenth century for Sir Charles Cockrell, who had spent many years of his life in India. It is really an English country house with oriental motifs, although the dome is a little startling. The astonishing thing is that it manages to look exotic without looking silly, which is no mean feat. The great landscape gardener, Humphrey Repton, also pursued an oriental theme in his design, with Hindu shrines and an oriental bridge.

No style, however, has ever had such sway among those who yearned for

'Hindu Gothic' at its most extravagant at Sezincote *(Royal Commission on the Historical Monuments of England)*

The magnificent hall at Cardiff Castle with its elaborate fireplace *(City of Cardiff)*

a romantic home as the medieval. And no one set about re-creating it with more vigour than John Patrick Crichton-Stuart, 3rd Marquess of Bute, with the more than enthusiastic help of the architect, William Burges, who brought to his work a child-like delight in fantasy, a point made in a limerick by Dante Gabriel Rossetti:

> There is a babyish party named Burges
> Who from infancy hardly emerges,
> If you had not been told
> He's disgracefully old
> You would offer a bull's-eye to Burges.

The Butes were a powerful family of industrialists who brought prosperity to Cardiff and in the process acquired the Lordship of Cardiff Castle. When the young Lord Bute took over, the work of transformation began, and even now nothing on the outside prepares you for the strange glories of the

interior. It was Burges who added the clock tower and other towers, furnishing them with suites of rooms decorated with a richness that it is almost impossible to describe. Knights ride out above castle-like fireplaces, from the battlements of which ladies wave farewell while heralds sound the departure on their trumpets; even a bathroom boasts sixty different types of marble and a mermaid wash-basin. Artists, sculptors, tile-makers and glass-makers were all brought together to give reality to Burges's vision. The framework might be a medieval castle, and rooms such as the Chaucer room gave the theme out in full measure, but that did not prevent other styles from creeping in. There is an exquisite Arab Room and, perhaps most surprising of all, a roof garden complete with tessellated floor, wall paintings and a fountain. It is a sort of cross between a Roman bath and the courtyard of one of the great Moorish temples of Spain. And the two men did not stop there. They also turned their attentions to a ruined castle just outside Cardiff, Castell Coch. The ruin was transformed not into what it would have been, but into what it should have been in an idealised medieval world of chivalrous knights, demure ladies and colourful pageant. It is no accident that it has been seized on by Hollywood for more than one swashbuckling adventure. The inside is alive with colourful ornamentation, with no surface left undecorated.

A detail of the Cardiff Castle fireplace *(City of Cardiff)*

Lord Penrhyn, a Welsh industrialist, made his fortune from the slate mines of North Wales. Unable to acquire a real castle, in 1827 he commissioned the architect Thomas Hopper to build him one on a superb site between the Menai Straits and the mountains of Snowdonia. The result, Penrhyn Castle, is a Norman fake on a gargantuan scale. There is no gleeful cross-over from period to period, style to style here: every effort has been made to create a facsimile of a great Norman castle, even down to specially designed 'Norman' furniture and decoration in the rooms. It is a bold attempt, but ultimately it looks less reminiscent of a medieval fortress than of the equally ambitious house that Orson Welles dreamed up for his film *Citizen Kane*. Penrhyn Castle is Wales's Xanadu.

Occasionally, the clash between styles in one building leads to absurdity. Burges got away with it by sheer panache, but Castle Goring near Worthing in West Sussex is simply hilarious. It was built in the 1790s for Sir Bysshe Shelley, the poet's grandfather. There were at the time two overwhelmingly popular styles, the classical and the Gothic, and either Shelley or his architect – the resoundingly named John Biagio Rebecca – seemed undecided which to adopt. So they chose both. At the front, the house is a fortress, with castellations and arrow slits, and at the rear it is pedimented classical. The building looks fine from the front and fine from the back, but where the two meet at the sides, with Gothic window next to Ionic pilaster, the effect is extraordinary. It is as if two houses had been cut in half and the disparate parts jammed together to make a new whole. And the change is not limited to the outside, for the same mismatch is repeated inside. Castle Goring, the house with a split personality, is the oddest of all our odd houses.

Holy Disorders

CHURCHES and their accompanying graveyards are generally thought of as more sombre than curious. In our own secular age we treat them solemnly but not seriously; earlier periods regarded them seriously but did not feel that they had to be unduly solemn. The church was a vital part of the community, involved in all aspects of life, and all aspects of life were often represented in church architecture and decoration. Nowhere is this more evident than in carvings. Pew ends and choir stalls are an especially rich source of illustrations showing different aspects of the everyday business of local life and death. One of the most macabre church carvings must be Death who stands on a pew at Little Barningham in Norfolk. He is shown as a shrouded skeleton, carrying a scythe and an hour-glass with the cheerful message: 'As you are now, even so was I. Remember death for ye must dye.' Hell-fire sermons at Little Barningham no doubt received more than the usual concerned attention.

In many churches, the seats for the choir tip up but have a shallow projection on the underside to give support to the standing choristers. These are misericords and are often beautifully decorated, and the richer the church, the richer the decoration. In medieval times, East Anglia prospered on a thriving wool trade, and perhaps the finest of all the wool churches is to be seen at Lavenham. The entrance is an ornately carved porch and everything inside the building proclaims the wealth of the church's benefactors. Yet among all this opulence, the misericords strike a pleasingly refreshing note: pomp and ceremony disappear in favour of the birds and beasts of the countryside. Even more down-to-earth are the carvings on the pew ends of another Suffolk church at Blythburgh. These show the Seven Deadly Sins: a personal favourite, for reasons that will not be elaborated, is the drunkard who is clearly going to wake to a richly deserved hangover. There are other carvings to admire in this splendid church. Wooden angels spread their wings over the nave, but also still

Ely, Cambridgeshire Memorial tablet in Ely Cathedral contains a long poem to two dead railwaymen.
Esher, Surrey Churchyard monument: 'This tombstone is a milestone. How so? Because beneath lies John Miles who's miles below.'
Fenny Stratford, Buckinghamshire On 11 November, six miniature cannon are fired in the churchyard.
Firbank, Cumbria The outdoor pulpit where George Fox preached.
Henham, Essex Anti-body-snatcher cage in churchyard.
Milber, Devon (near Newton Abbot) 'The Dream Church' is so called because its unusual design came to the vicar in a dream.
Morwenstow, Cornwall The rectory has five chimneys in the form of church towers and the churchyard has a figurehead memorial from the wreck of the *Caledonia*.
Oldhamstocks, Lothian Watch-house in the graveyard for guarding bodies.

show the holes left by Cromwellian musket balls. It is difficult now to imagine these carved figures giving offence, but once they were far gaudier creatures. One angel has been fully restored, painted and decorated with a variety of materials including, of all things, tinfoil; seeing it in its original glory makes it easier to understand how it might have seemed a painted idol to a zealous Puritan. Even that, however, is not the end of Blythburgh's delights, for it also has a Jack-o'-the-clock or Jack the Lad. This painted Tudor gentleman with a handsome feathered hat originally struck the hours on a bell. Now you have to pull a cord to make Jack work, although he does nod his head in thanks. Many churches feature interesting clocks, but none is grander nor more elaborate than the astronomical clock in the north transept of Wells Cathedral. Built in the fourteenth century, it is not only very ornate but provides a surprising amount of information. It is a 24-hour clock, and instead of the familiar hands, the hours and minutes are told by rotating stars. It also gives the days of the month and the phases of the moon, and, to add to the entertainment, little armoured knights ride round above the face every hour.

The alternative to the clock is the sundial, which is not perhaps the ideal instrument for Britain's cloudy land. Sundials are, however, still very popular. One of the most enthusiastic of dial builders was William Watson of Seaton Ross, Humberside, whose epitaph in the local churchyard reads:

> At this church I so often
> With pleasure did call
> That I made a sundial
> Upon the church wall.

A mermaid flanked by sea beasts: a misericord in Ludlow church *(Anthony Burton)*

An open air church in
Cornwall: Gwennap Pit was
formed in a hollow created
by mining subsidence, and
later used for religious
meetings *(Anthony Burton)*

He also built a sundial on the front of his own cottage nearby, with the dial
itself forming a semicircle some 12ft (3.6m) in diameter which starts under
the eaves and reaches to the top of the ground-floor windows. It might well
be the largest sundial in the country, although it is insignificant by
international standards. When the Rajah of Jaipur constructed his sundial
at Delhi in 1724, he built it with the gnomon (the part in the centre that casts
the shadow) in the form of a triangle with a base over 100ft (30m) long and
a 56ft (17m) perpendicular.

Most sundials are comparatively simple affairs, but not the one in the
churchyard at St Neot in Cornwall, which is beautifully made and is, one is
assured, remarkably accurate. Unfortunately, I was wholly defeated by its
intricacies and had, and still have, not the least notion of how to read it.
This makes it not just the most modern but also the most curious sundial to
be seen in the country. It is possible that when I visited St Neot I was
distracted by arriving at the church on the day of a strange annual
ceremony. On Oak Apple Day, a whole young oak tree is hauled up to the
top of the church tower, where it stays for a full year until it is replaced.

Clocks and dials tell the time for those who can see them, but in the days
before every household had its own timepiece, it was necessary for the
church to have a means of calling the parishioners to the services, hence
the church bells. In time, everyone became bored with the monotonous,
repetitive clanging of a bell, and unless the church has a towerful of bells –

St Benet's Abbey on the Norfolk Broads fell into ruins after the dissolution by Henry VIII, but the gateway found a new use as a windmill base in the nineteenth century. Today, the windmill too is ruined *(Norfolk Library and Information Service)*

eight will only give you an octave with no semitones – tunes must be of the simplest. It was the parish clerk of St Benet's in Cambridge who solved the problem by inventing change-ringing. It is an art more mathematical than artistic: the closest analogy might be with a Bach fugue. The secret lies in changing the order in which the bells are rung. The church tower announces the presence of the church visually, and the church bells have become a traditional feature, especially in villages. But before looking at bells and bell towers, there are two diversions here. The first takes us back to clocks, where another Cambridge church, Great St Mary, has a decidedly familiar chime. It is precisely the same as that of London's Big Ben, but do not accuse them of copying: Great St Mary was the first to chime. The other diversion is suggested by the name of St Benet. An abbey dedicated to the same saint was built in the heart of the Norfolk Broads. At the dissolution, it was annexed to the see of Norwich, but was never suppressed. Nevertheless, it gradually fell into ruins and suffered the fate of many such buildings, as the stone was carted away. The gatehouse, however, survived, largely because one local decided it was too much effort to carry the stone away, so he simply built a windmill into the old structure.

Returning to church bells, however, one expects to find them hung in a tower attached to the church. This does not always occur: sometimes they are hung in separate campaniles, but they can look very odd. The strangest must be the one at Brooklands in Kent which has the shape of a stylised Christmas tree. Built in the thirteenth century, it consists of three cones of diminishing size, stacked one on top of the other. It was always intended as a separate structure, but not so the bell tower at East Bergholt in Suffolk. Cardinal Wolsey had begun providing funds for a bell tower at East Bergholt's church to house the massive bells, but the Cardinal fell from favour and died in 1530 before a tower was built. The bells have remained in their 'temporary' home for over four centuries and will probably stay there for many years to come. The bell tower at Great Bourton in Oxfordshire serves a dual purpose, for it is also the lych-gate giving access to the churchyard.

It seems fitting for church bells to be found in a lych-gate; it is, however, far less common to find one that also houses the village lock-up as at Anstey in Hertfordshire. The fifteenth-century gate was bricked up in 1831 for its new role as a gaol. But St George's is an odd enough place in any case. The stones came from a demolished castle and still show signs of military graffiti; the misericords are thirteenth century and show gentlemen modelling the fashionable headgear of the day, while mermen disport around the Norman font.

Another remarkable connection between church and gaol is to be found at Stratton in Cornwall, where the door of the south porch is boldly emblazoned with the name 'Clink' spelled out in square-headed nails. How it came to be there is a mystery, but there are examples on record of churches which became, if only temporarily, the local prison. An outstanding example, in every sense, is the church at Westonzoyland in Somerset. It is a magnificent church in a comparatively humble setting. Parts at least date back to the early thirteenth century, but like so many churches, the interior is the most impressive. Angels, reminiscent of those at Blythburgh, fly out from the king posts above the nave and the delicate window tracery is a model of its kind. But the church door, if it does not actually announce itself as a 'clink' is heavily barred and bears a massive lock. In 1685, the Duke of Monmouth's rebellion was ended at the Battle of Sedgemoor, fought near the village. The church was, for a time, prison for some five hundred rebels, of whom five died from wounds and twenty-two were hanged.

Sometimes churches seem odd because of their contents, sometimes because of their history, but others appear simply to be curious in their

Ormskirk, Lancashire
The Sisters' Folly, a church built with both tower and spire. The sisters, who endowed the church, disagreed over which was more appropriate so decided to build both.
Reepham, Norfolk was formed by amalgamation of three villages and all three churches shared the same churchyard; two still stand.
Remenham, Berkshire
A solitary church spire in a meadow once graced St Bride's, London.
St Mawgan, Cornwall
Churchyard memorial, like a boat stern, to sailors who froze to death.
Sydenham, Oxfordshire
A small brass sundial now acts as a keyhole plate on the church door.

own right. The church of Burgh St Peter in Norfolk could be just another attractive parish church in a county famed for its churches: it has a simple, conventional nave and a pretty thatched roof – then one discovers the tower. If ever a contest was held for Britain's ugliest church tower, then this would surely be a contender. It looks exactly what it is: a tacked-on afterthought. Everything about it is wrong. The material is red brick, pierced with blank-faced arches, and the tower rises in a series of crude, stepped boxes in which the only note of grace is some flint and brick diaper work near the base.

Shape also plays a part in making other churches notable. Maldon church, in Essex, for example, has a most unusual triangular tower, topped by a hexagonal spire. It was built in the thirteenth century, and the emphasis on the number three may well have had significance, as at Rushton Lodge (see pp33/36).

Circular churches are equally uncommon, and one of the finest examples must be the building known simply as the 'Round Church' in Cambridge. This was a Norman foundation, built in the twelfth century, and inside a ring of stone heads stare down at the visitor. Some are fiercely moustachioed warriors and others even fiercer demons.

Situation rather than shape distinguishes the bridge chapel at St Ives in Cambridgeshire. It stands in the centre of the medieval bridge across the River Ouse, and it was here that travellers could give thanks for a journey successfully completed or pray for fortune to be kind to one about to begin.

Another bridge chapel can be found at Bradford-on-Avon in Wiltshire, but this one has had a rather more lurid history. The bridge itself dates back to the fourteenth century, but by the seventeenth century it seems to have been generally agreed that travellers could cross the bridge in safety, without divine intervention. Alternatively, the authorities might have decided that safety could be better assured by gaoling footpads, highwaymen and the like. The little chapel became the town lock-up.

Bridge chapels are undeniably striking, but it is very doubtful that anyone would spare a second glance for the parish church of St Michael on the outskirts of Liverpool. It looks to be an absolutely standard Victorian parish church, and in respect of its design it is. I would certainly never have become aware of it had I not been taken there by a local inhabitant. There is a hint of what makes the church special in the surrounding houses which are notable for their decorative ironwork. The whole village was, in fact, built for the workers of the Mersey Iron Foundry. They specialised in building cast-iron churches, which were designed in sections so that they could be crated up and sent off to missionaries in the far corners of the British Empire. Few people have the opportunity to view metallic Gothic in the jungle, but the iron church of St Michael can be seen in Liverpool. Sadly, the impact has been lost: the Liverpudlians might have been only too pleased to send out do-it-yourself churches to the rest of the world, but they were far less enthusiastic about receiving one on their own doorstep. So the church was given a cosmetic skin of brick, making it disappointingly

indistinguishable from dozens of other Victorian churches in Britain.

From a church that looks more ordinary than it is, we can move on to one which does not look like a church at all. The Reformation brought a period of Catholic persecution which was slow to die out. Even in the late eighteenth century, religious prejudices were still strong, so when in 1786 permission was finally granted for a new Catholic church to be built at Lulworth Castle, in Dorset, it was on condition that it did not look like a church. When Thomas Weld built a chapel beside the house, therefore, it was designed to look like a fashionable belvedere.

All kinds of circumstances conspire to produce strange results, and here are just a few examples. Swaffham Prior in Cambridgeshire was once divided between the Prior of Ely and a group of knights from Brittany – Ely had got there first and had already endowed a church, St Mary's, in Saxon times. The newcomers from France, however, decided that they should build a second church, SS Cyriac and Julietta, around 1250. After that matters become complicated. The original St Mary began to decay and was rebuilt. Then it was sensibly decided that one church was sufficient, so the nave of St Cyriac was demolished, leaving only the bell tower. A century later, St Mary's was hit by lightning and rather than repair it, a plain Georgian church was built on to the old St Cyriac tower. It was not a great success, so it was abandoned and St Mary's was restored yet again. And there they stand – for the moment at least – two churches in one churchyard. Even that is not quite the end of the story, for St Mary's was given some extraordinary windows after World War I. All around the

church are stained-glass bombers and roaring cannon, and there is even a window showing young ladies filling shells in a munitions factory. After that warlike note, perhaps a brief look at a cheerier theme will not be amiss. At Halstead in Essex, Fremlin's Brewery built a chapel for their workforce actually within the brewery grounds.

Other churches have been overtaken by events. Chesterfield is famous for its twisted spire. Legend has it that the devil sneezed and bent it or that it twisted itself following the progress of a particularly attractive local maiden. The truth is more mundane. The timber frame was not adequately seasoned and it warped. It is not, in fact, the only twisted spire in the country: there is a second at Ermington in Devon, but it is not so grotesquely corkscrewed.

The event that overtook Normanton church was deliberate rather than accidental. Built in 1826, it was described by landscape historian W. G. Hoskins in the *Shell Guide to Rutland* as 'the little white church that seems to float alone in a large, denuded park'. Since those words were written, Rutland has disappeared by Act of Parliament and the church has almost vanished with the creation of Rutland Water. Now it really does seem to float, like some strange stone ship on the waters, for only the upper part has survived, a memorial to all that was lost when the great reservoir was created.

Perhaps the most extraordinary church in the whole of Britain is to be

Liverpool's cast iron church *(Anthony Burton)*

This looks like a garden pavilion, but is actually a Catholic church, built in 1786 and the first to be built after the Reformation. It is at Lulworth Castle *(Dorset Natural History and Archaeological Society, Dorset County Museum, Dorchester)*

Where God and Mammon meet: the chapel at Fremlin's Brewery *(Brewery Chapel Museum, Halstead)*

found at the northern extremity of the country in Orkney. On the island of Lamb Holm you will find a Nissen hut, part of what was once a camp for Italian prisoners-of-war. But this hut is unique: Nissen hut it may be on the outside but inside it is a chapel that would not be out of place in Florence or Venice. Every inch of the interior has been decorated to simulate mosaic, tile and stone. It is, in its way, a masterpiece, but not for the quality of the painting so much as for the wonderful ingenuity of the transformation.

Churches exist to minister to the living and to provide last resting places for the dead, either in the building or in the churchyard. The rituals of death have been important for all civilisations at all times, and some of Britain's most impressive ancient monuments are tombs. One of the grandest and most interesting is in Orkney. Maes Howe is described in the guidebooks as a Neolithic chambered cairn with runic inscriptions, but that does nothing to prepare you for the site itself. At first it seems unimpressive, a

Normanton church, just before most of it vanished under Rutland Water
(Brian and Elizabeth Nicholls Photography)

Lamb Holm church, Orkney, created out of a Nissen hut by Italian prisoners-of-war *(Highlands and Islands Development Board)*

large grassy mound surrounded by a ditch. But then you make your way down a low narrow passage formed from massive stone slabs; this leads to a great, beautifully constructed chamber of stone, which originally rose to a height of over 16½ft (5m). Once there were burials in the small side chambers and the whole structure is carefully aligned so that at the winter solstice the setting sun shines straight down the entrance passage to light the tomb. Originally the dead were surrounded by the riches they would need in the next world, but the Vikings looted the tomb. The runes cut on the wall tell us that Earl Harold sheltered from a storm in the church and left with a great treasure. The other runic graffiti are not very different from the scrawlings of a modern world – Viking versions of 'Kilroy Was Here' and 'Norse Boot Boys Rule OK'.

Different ages have different notions of how to dignify their dead, and for funerary monuments on a grand scale no one can beat the great Victorian cemeteries. The Necropolis in Glasgow, for example, is a wonderful spot to see how, just as at Maes Howe, those who were wealthy in life wanted to keep the symbols of wealth around them in death. Paths wind up the hill between ever more exotically carved memorials. Bradford's Undercliffe Cemetery has a similar effect; again, it is perched on a hill with wide views over the mills where the graveyard inhabitants made their brass. All the well-known Victorian emblems are here: pinnacles and towers, urns and angels, row upon row of them, soot-blackened by the mill chimneys. These are essentially very British places; not so Highgate Cemetery. It can seem very foreign and one is liable to meet troops of solemn-faced Chinese and Russians on their way to pay homage at the tomb of Karl Marx. If, however, one penetrates deeper into the cemetery one comes across a section of mausolea which look for all the world – or, should one say, all the other world – like imports from Transylvania. Behind an entrance in the Egyptian style lie the catacombs, vaults through whose crumbling weed-covered walls one catches unnerving glimpses of coffins. It is, without question, the most unnerving place in London. Forget the Chamber of Horrors, forget the London Dungeons. If you want to have your spine chilled, then visit Highgate Cemetery on a misty November evening.

Not surprisingly, a number of strange stories surround this eerie spot – and not merely tales of events long gone. In 1970, there was a great furore over evidence of black magic and satanic rites at the catacombs. There

A mortsafe at Henham, built to preserve the grave from body snatchers
(Anthony Burton)

were also stories of a mysterious apparition and at least one vampire was reported. All kinds of people from sensation seekers to amateur exorcists and television teams swarmed around the area of the catacombs, and eventually the authorities were forced to close off this area of the cemetery. The stories all seem incredible, just so much mumbo-jumbo, when read in the comfort of an armchair, but in the cemetery, when the mist is just beginning to smoke around the crumbling vaults . . .

A reminder of one of the grimmer episodes in history can be found in some churchyards in the measures that were taken to thwart the resurrectionists, those grave robbers who disinterred newly buried corpses to sell to the anatomists at the local medical schools. The most famous of these somewhat unsavoury gentlemen were Burke and Hare who, failing to find enough bodies to satisfy the Edinburgh doctor Knox, solved the shortage problem by creating corpses for themselves. There was a rhyme that became popular after their crimes were discovered:

> Down the Close and up the Stair
> But and ben wi' Burke and Hare.
> Burke's the butcher, Hare's the thief,
> Knox the man that buys the beef.

Most resurrectionists stopped short of murder, and it could be argued that they performed a public service by aiding medical research. Grieving relatives took a less altruistic view, and took steps to ensure that once they had buried their relatives, their kin should remain buried.

One solution to protect corpses from exhumation was to hire a watchman to guard fresh graves, and at Wanstead in London you can still see the stone sentry box where he kept vigil. Another solution was to make it as difficult as possible for the resurrectionists to get into the graves. At Aberfoyle, in Scotland, one grave is most securely guarded by a vast iron mortsafe, a contraption placed over the grave which is so heavy that it could only be lifted with the aid of a block and tackle. Even the most enthusiastic grave robber would have second thoughts about arriving in a churchyard at midnight with a small derrick.

Other, apparently equally impregnable, graves are not always quite what they seem. A monument in Pinner churchyard would appear to have a coffin set half-way up a great stone pyramid, but the coffin, too, is stone and empty. John Claudius Loudon, the landscape gardener and publisher of Humphrey Repton's work, was not noticeably whimsical in his working life, but when it came to executing his father's will he showed that he possessed a somewhat bizarre imagination. He had been presented with something of a problem, for his father had expressed the desire to be buried above ground – hence, the pyramid. The 'coffin' was buried within the pyramid, well above ground level. It was, however, no more than a gesture, for there is no body in that airy resting place.

The great pioneer of the iron industry, John Wilkinson, was less fortunate in his choice of memorials. When he died in 1801 he had to his

Two sisters of Ormskirk, Lancashire, wished to endow a church: one wanted a spire, the other a tower – so they gave it both! *(Anthony Burton)*

credit the invention of a machine for boring through iron, making it possible for steam-engine cylinders to be bored with accuracy; he had built the first iron boat, a barge which was launched on the Severn near the Wilkinson works, and he played a part in the construction of the famous iron bridge over the Severn at Ironbridge. Not surprisingly, he wanted an iron memorial. He was buried in the garden of his house and an iron obelisk was erected to mark the spot. The house was then let, and the new tenants were reluctant to include the late Mr Wilkinson in their inventory. The church was happy to accept his remains, but was less happy about taking the obelisk. So, iron master and monument were parted: the master was settled inside Lindale churchyard near Grange-over-Sands and the monument was left outside hallowed ground.

Staying with the world of industry, the Railway Age was responsible for many deaths in the early years. It began in the construction period, and the work of tunnelling was especially dangerous. Bramhope tunnel on the Leeds and Thirsk Railway is notable for its impressive portals, with castellated arches flanked by towers. It appears again, in miniature, in Otley churchyard, complete with its four towers and an arch to represent the tunnel itself. It was erected by the contractor, in memory of the navvies who died building the tunnel between 1845 and 1849. The completion of the railway did not mean the end of accidents: early locomotives were not the safest of machines, nor were practices such as screwing down safety valves to get higher pressure particularly conducive to safe running. In 1840 the driver and fireman of a locomotive on the Birmingham and Gloucester Railway died in a boiler explosion. They were buried side by side in Bromsgrove churchyard, each headstone carrying a representation of the locomotive. An anonymous friend added these lines on the memorial to one of the engineers, Thomas Scaife:

> My *engine* now is cold and still.
> No water does my *boiler* fill:
> My *coke* affords its flame no more,
> My days of usefulness are o'er.
> My *wheels* deny their noted speed,
> No more my guiding hand they heed.
> My *whistle* too has lost its tone,
> Its shrill and thrilling sounds have gone.
> My *valves* are now thrown open wide,
> My *flanges* all refuse to guide.
> My *clacks* also, though once so strong
> Refuse to aid the busy throng.
> No more I feel each urging breath,
> My *steam* is now condens'd in death.
> Life's *railway*'s o'er, each *station*'s past
> In death I'm stopp'd and rest at last.
> Farewell dear friends and cease to weep.
> In Christ I'm safe, in Him I sleep.

A railway locomotive turns up again, in very different circumstances, in the graveyard at Stoke Poges. A ten-year-old child died, and the enthusiasms of his short life are preserved in his memorial. A capstan and an anchor record his love of sailing, and beside them lie his toy yacht and railway engine. It is a sad place but surprisingly, there is humour to be found in death.

Epitaphs can be jolly as well as grim. At Woodditton in Cambridgeshire is the grave of William Symons that bears this epitaph:

> Here lies my corpse, who was the man,
> That laved a sop in the dripping pan.
> But now believe me I am dead,
> See here the pan stands at my head.
> Still for sops till the last I cried
> But could not eat and so I died,
> My neighbours they perhaps will laugh,
> When they do read my epitaph.

Joseph Wright, auctioneer of Corby Glen, Lincolnshire, was killed when he fell from his trap and was dragged along behind the horse, until:

> grim Death, with visage queer,
> Assumed Joe's trade of Auctioneer,
> Made him the Lot to Practice on,
> With 'going, going' and anon,
> He knocked him down to 'Poor Joe's gone'.

A farmer and his wife rest side by side at Ashby, Norfolk *(Royal Commission on the Historical Monuments of England)*

The quirkiest epitaph must surely be that at Bampton in Devon, dedicated simply to the memory of 'The Clerk's Son'. It reads:

> Bless my i.i.i.i.i.i.
> Here he lies
> In a sad pickle
> Kill'd by an Icicle.
> In the year, 1776.

But the prize for the best pun goes to Charles Knight of Walsoken, whose epitaph simply reads: 'Good Knight'.

There seems to be no end of strange memorials in Britain. Sarah Hare of Stow Bardolph in Norfolk can be seen as an eighteenth-century waxwork effigy, wearing her own favourite clothes. Others received very grand memorials. When the famous explorer Sir Richard Burton died in 1890, his wife designed his mausoleum: a stone tent with a frieze of crescents and stars. It can be seen in the Catholic cemetery at Mortlake in London. An even grander wifely tribute is to be seen at Compton in Surrey. Mary Watts designed a mortuary chapel in memory of her husband, the artist G. F. Watts. It is somewhat dourly monumental on the outside, but the interior is art nouveau at its most ornate, with no surface left undecorated. But the grandest memorial of them all reversed the pattern: it was built by a husband for his wife.

Any visitor to the city of Lancaster cannot fail to notice the Ashton memorial, which stands on top of a hill surrounded by the formal gardens of Williamson Park. It dominates the city. Lord Ashton made his fortune from linoleum, and a considerable fortune it must have been to allow him to spend £87,000 in 1906 on this memorial. It is a tall building, colonnaded at the base and topped by a dome, and it fulfils no practical function whatever. Dedicated as it is to the wife of one of the great Victorian industrialists, it is perhaps not altogether surprising to find some odd little details among the strictly classical forms of the main structure. They certainly help to make the memorial unique, for how many other Victorian ladies could boast a monument across which a 4-4-4 locomotive steams in perpetual stone?

The ecclesiastical railway connection reached its finest moment in the little village of Cadeby in Leicestershire. Visitors wandering across the churchyard might once have been confronted with the somewhat Pickwickian figure of the vicar, the Rev Teddy Boston, steaming up the rectory drive at the controls of his traction engine *Fiery Elias*. But even more startling were the days on which the sound of a steam whistle was heard and puffs of smoke rose up above the headstones to announce that the Cadeby Light Railway was in full operation. This is no toy railway, not even a miniature railway, but a genuine narrow-gauge railway run by locomotives which once earned their living in the harsher world of industry. Sadly, Teddy Boston died in 1986 but Audrey Boston has kept the railway going: the unique churchyard railway steams on.

Transports of Delight

M AN has been working at improving the means of getting from place to place for thousands of years. The oldest known manufactured road was discovered preserved in the peaty bogs to the north of the Polden Hills in Somerset. Around 3000BC, the settlements on the islands above the marsh were joined by causeways of brushwood hurdles pegged to the ground or by paths made of split logs. A section of the hurdling can be seen in the Woodspring Museum, Weston-super-Mare. But when we think of old roads the first word that comes to mind is 'Roman'. Everyone knows about the Roman habit of charging across country in an unwavering straight line. Nevertheless, it still comes as a surprise to encounter a section of Roman road and to discover just how well it was constructed. The finest section can be seen on the North Yorkshire Moors, near Goathland. Known as Wade's Causeway it shows the main characteristics of Roman construction. It is raised on a little embankment, or aggar, which is pierced by beautifully constructed stone culverts for drainage. The surface of large stone slabs is well preserved and is generally believed to have been covered by gravel. But even Roman roads can present their mysteries. A cobbled way crosses the Pennines at Blackstone Edge with a shallow groove all the way down the middle. Various theories have been put forward to explain the existence of the road, but none of them has been entirely satisfactory, so if you stroll along this Roman moorland road you are free to invent your own theory. The Roman road system also boasts one oddity. Walkers on the South Downs Way, itself an ancient street, will cross the line of Stane Street, where a signpost helpfully points them in the direction of Noviomagus and Londinium.

Medieval roads were seldom, if ever, as well built as Roman ones, so few have survived in recognisable form. An exception is Maud Heath's causeway, which is marked by a memorial at East Tytherton in Wiltshire. Maud Heath died in 1474 and in her will she left a legacy to pay for a causeway to be built across the flood plain of the Avon to help her old

Museum runs vintage trams past the façade of the old Derby Assembly Rooms.

Chard, Somerset An attractive thatched Gothic toll house stands in the angle between the A30 and a minor road to Axminster, west of the town.

Conwy, Gwynedd Two castellated bridges, one for rail and one for road, stand beside the real castle.

Devizes, Wiltshire Shane's Castle is, in fact, a toll house at the junction of the Chippenham and Trowbridge roads.

Drayton Bassett, Staffordshire A funny little castellated footbridge crosses the Birmingham and Fazeley Canal.

Haworth, West Yorkshire Among the Brontéana is the grave of Lily Cove, balloonist.

Honiton, Devon Castellated toll house 1 mile (1.6km) west of the town on the A373.

Linslade, Bedfordshire The north end of the railway tunnel has a castellated entrance.

Llanuwchllyn, Gwynedd The Bala Lake Railway, a preserved steam line, boasts a unique halt where trains were stopped by flag signal from across the lake.

Stanton Drew, Avon (6 miles (9.6km) south of Bristol on the B3130) The toll house is unusually rural because of its thatched roof.

neighbours to reach the local markets. Maud's causeway still stands, as does the memorial that was erected in 1698. This consists of a sundial mounted on a column, the dial occupying three faces of a cube. The south-facing part has the familiar triangular gnomon, while the east and west faces have bell-shaped gnomons giving an appropriate ecclesiastical air to fit the monumental function. The dial is surrounded by suitably moral homilies, such as:

> Haste Traveller the sun is sinking now
> He shall return but never thou.

These lines were presumably not intended to cheer the lonely traveller. An equally cheerless message can be seen on the Mail Coach Pillar by the A40 between Llandovery and Pentre-bach, where the road skirts a wooded cliff above the River Gwydderig. It shows that drunken driving is no modern phenomenon, and records the fate of an intoxicated coach driver who, in 1835,

> drove the mail on the wrong side of the road and going at a full speed or gallop met a cart and permitted the leader to turn short round to the right hand & went down over the precipice 121 feet where at the bottom near the river came against an ash tree when the coach was dashed into several pieces.

Roads seldom provide much opportunity for their builders to indulge in flights of fancy. The coming of the turnpike roads, the early toll roads, did, however, bring some novelties to the land. The toll houses where travellers stopped to pay their dues are always of interest. They usually stand at or near junctions, so the collector had to peer down every avenue to ensure that nobody slipped past without paying their dues. To ease the toll-collector's task, the builders of toll houses produced a splendid variety of multi-angled buildings with windows facing in all directions. Toll houses are usually built on a somewhat unorthodox plan, often hexagonal, sometimes circular. They often have apparently illogical details, such as a blank window above the main door. It is actually not a window space, but the spot where the notice-board was placed, informing travellers of the different charges they should pay. The toll house at the end of the famous iron bridge from which the town in Shropshire gets its name, records the slightly bizarre information that if you travel in a horse-drawn carriage it will cost you the same money whether you are alive or dead: travel for a live body in a chaise being 2s, as is that for a dead body in a hearse. Livelier individuals able to cross on their own feet went a good deal cheaper. Such toll houses are common enough, but only a few have that extra ingredient of oddity that might turn the head of the passing motorist.

An excellent example can be seen on the outskirts of Devizes, at the junction of the Chippenham and Trowbridge roads. It may have been built merely for toll collection, but it seems ready to withstand siege from an

Trinity Bridge, Crowland. The triangular medieval bridge still stands, but the streams it once crossed have gone *(Derek Pratt)*

army of highwaymen and footpads. It is a massive stone structure with heavy battlements on top. It came to be known locally as Shane's Castle, although no one any longer remembers who Shane was.

Bridges have always been considered sufficiently important to warrant a little extra in the way of embellishment, and some might quite reasonably be thought of as a little odd. One of the oddest of all must be Trinity Bridge at Crowland in Lincolnshire, so called because it has three arches set in a triangle. This in itself is unusual, but what makes it odder still is the fact that today the arches span nothing whatever. Once, however, they crossed three streams that met in the village, but they have all moved away to other courses, leaving the bridge, quite literally, high and dry. The carved figure in the bridge is thought to have come from nearby Croyland Abbey. The most ingenious bridge, however, must surely be the Mathematical Bridge in Cambridge, which crosses the Cam at Queen's College. It looks a simple, elegantly curved arch, but a closer look shows it to be an ingenious assembly of straight timbers designed to notch together and to stand without the benefit of nails. Unfortunately, this puzzle of a bridge proved

Telford's iron bridge at Craigellachie, given the baronial treatment with battlemented towers
(Anthony Burton)

When the new railway at Conwy met the old city walls, something had to give: the walls received a new Gothic gateway *(Anthony Burton)*

too much for generations of drunken undergraduates who were quite able to dismantle it, but found the task of reassemblage far beyond their abilities. Reluctantly, authority was forced to step in and the parts are now securely bolted together.

The eighteenth century was a tumultuous time in Scotland, but marked the start of a new, improved road system for the Highlands. Military roads were planned after the first Jacobite rebellion by General Wade, and the finest monument is the bridge over the Tay at Aberfeldy. It is an unlikely marriage of military necessity and elegance, for the design was entrusted to William Adam. However, General Wade claimed some of the credit for himself and there are two plaques, inscribed with both Latin and English, proclaiming that Wade's roads and bridges were the finest to be seen in Britain since Roman times. The process of modernising Scottish transport was continued in the early nineteenth century by the engineer, Thomas Telford.

Telford favoured the Gothic and the application of medieval defences to

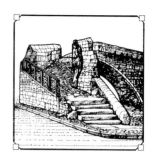

the most modern structures of the day. He was particularly fond of applying such styles in Scotland, where he felt they were especially appropriate. It certainly fits well with the stone bridges, such as the one across the Dee at Tongland, but when you get a thoroughly modern iron bridge, such as the one across the Spey at Craigellachie in Grampian, it does begin to look a little odd. The stone towers with arrow slits might convince us that they were put there to defend a stone bridge against attack. At Tongland one can just about accept the notion of armed knights galloping across the stone bridge in full armour – but over an iron bridge? There the effort becomes too much, and in any case the illusion is totally destroyed by a prominent cast-iron plaque set on one of the towers and carrying the message 'Cast at Plas Kynaston, Ruabon, Denbighshire, 1841'. One can scarcely get more prosaic than that. Telford's best-known castellated bridge is probably the Conwy suspension bridge in Wales. Here the presence of Conwy Castle at one end of the bridge encouraged him to supply the supporting towers with crenellations and arrow slits, and to build the accompanying toll house in an equally medieval style.

The Devil's Bridge near Aberystwyth became such a popular tourist attraction in the nineteenth century that a special narrow-gauge steam railway was built up to it. This remained as the last bastion of British Rail to be regularly run by steam locomotives until it was sold off to private enterprise in 1988. The bridge itself is not, in fact, one bridge but three, built one above the other. The oldest and lowest was built, it is believed, by monks, in the twelfth century; the second in the eighteenth century and the top layer, a simple iron bridge, was added early this century. The bridges cross a wooded ravine of spectacular waterfalls which visitors who are prepared to tackle the Jacob's Ladder of steps can see close up, while the more leisurely can enjoy the view from the hotel terrace.

The bridge across the Stock Beck in Ambleside is far from grand: the stream itself is a mere 10ft (3m) across, which makes it all the more remarkable that anyone should have chosen to build a house on it. But a house there is, although there is some doubt as to whether it was ever used as a dwelling. The National Trust, who own the property, suggest that it may have been a gazebo in the eighteenth century. One reason it is believed that the house was never inhabited is the external staircase; it would certainly have been very inconvenient, but there is no room in the house for it anyway.

Modern bridges are often elegant, but tend to be severe in their refusal to spoil the purity of line by unnecessary adornment. Occasionally, however, a purely practical solution to a purely practical problem results in something which appears to be quite outlandish. What, for example, do you do about building a bridge across a river which is a busy shipping lane? The obvious solution is to build a very high bridge. The next option is to build a bridge that can be moved out of the way. The best-known example of this is Tower Bridge in London, which, like Telford's Conwy bridge takes its inspiration from being close to a great castle. One of the

most elegant of swing-bridges is the one across the Tyne at Newcastle, lurking under the shadow of the high-level bridges. Surprisingly, it has what appears to be a gazebo perched on top, where the bridge-keeper observes the river and road traffic. But it is the third solution to the problem that is the most bizarre. There is no problem building a high bridge over a deep gorge, but it is very expensive to build a high bridge where river banks are low. The ingenious answer is the transporter bridge. What you have, in effect, is a short length of road suspended from a tall frame. Vehicles and passengers mount this moving road which can be trundled across the river to the opposite bank. There are two fine examples, one at Newport, Gwent, and the other at Middlesbrough, both of which look as if they have been built by an enthusiastic schoolboy who was given a gargantuan Meccano set to play with.

The real transport revolution of the eighteenth century began with the Canal Age in the 1760s and lasted until it was overwhelmed by the Railway Age of the 1830s. The canals, like the turnpike roads, had their toll houses to which they also added lock cottages. Most are plain, no-nonsense buildings, but there are exceptions. There is a pleasant little castellated cottage at Camden Town on the Regent's Canal in London. Somewhat odder are the circular cottages on the Thames and Severn Canal. No one seems to know why they are circular but here is a personal theory, for which it has to be said there is no hard evidence. The canal runs through what was once a thriving woollen industry based in and around the town of Stroud. A part of that industry involved drying the wool in special wool-stores, which were once commonplace, and were invariably circular towers. One of these towers, at Woodchester, has recently been converted into a home, and looks remarkably like one of the lock cottages.

The Thames and Severn Canal can also lay claim to one of the rare examples of 'architectural' engineering in the canal world. Sapperton tunnel has decorated portals, which are classical with pilasters and niches at one end and castellated at the other. Tunnels are dark, mysterious places and Sapperton, much of it carved out of the bare rock, is no exception. But it is not just the portals that appear on view. All long tunnels have air shafts, which usually appear as little round brick or stone towers above ground. Standedge Fell to the west of Huddersfield is pierced by adjoining rail and canal tunnels, but walkers can always tell which shaft is which when they are out on the moors, for whenever a train passes through, clouds of diesel fumes shoot up. In the working days of the canals, however, life in the canal tunnel could be grim, for smoke from passing steam locomotives would billow in. Air-shaft tops can appear anywhere, and the oddest one can be found in a suburban front garden in Dudley, covered by a metal grille, giving it the appearance of a giant pepper-pot. It marks the Gosty tunnel on the Dudley Canal: it is strange, but nowhere near as strange as the Dudley tunnel itself. Whereas most tunnels are no more than holes going in one side of a hill and coming out the other, Dudley is a labyrinth, for it connected a series of underground workings

A bridge on the move: the Middlesbrough transporter bridge
(Anthony Burton)

where limestone was quarried. The tiny main tunnel opens out into great basins and there are underground watery crossroads, of which the most spectacular has a vaulted roof, known very appropriately as Cathedral Arch. One wide section is not unlike a grotto, and it is said that if you follow one of the side arms and make your way to the surface you emerge in the lions' den at Dudley Zoo. This theory, it has to be said, has not been tested by the author, but the other delights of this subterranean world may be enjoyed by means of a special trip boat.

Canal structures are seldom excessively elaborate, although they can be made so if the canal passes through or close to some stately home. In such cases it was common for the landowner to insist on a little extra decoration to make the intruder more palatable. This can be seen, for example, at Grove Park, Watford, on the Grand Union Canal, where an otherwise ordinary canal bridge is transformed into an elegant structure by the addition of pilasters and a balustrade. But the Kennet and Avon can provide a whole series of special bridges for the passage through Sydney Gardens, Bath. The Sydney Gardens No 2 tunnel, to give it its correct, if prosaic title, is decorated with stone swags, niches and carved figures, and in the gardens themselves the waterway is crossed by delicate iron bridges.

Macclesfield Road bridge over the Regent's Canal in Regent's Park, London also has a touch of class, and an interesting history. If you go down to the tow-path, you will see that tow ropes have cut grooves into the iron supporting columns of the bridge, but they are on the wrong side. As it is not very likely that boats were dragged along the tow-path, something must have happened. It did, in 1874, when a boat loaded with gunpowder exploded under the bridge. Boat and bridge were shattered and the boat crew were killed. The remains of the bridge were collected up, but when the columns were returned to place, they were reversed – hence the illogically placed grooves of what is still known as 'Blow-up Bridge'.

The canals were not totally exempt from the fashion for adding Gothic decorations. Aqueducts are always popular, if only because there still seems to be something vaguely unnerving about one boat sailing high above another. The Engine Arm aqueduct on the Birmingham Canal is one case where the lily has been thoroughly gilded: the iron trough has been decorated by rows of pointed arches, giving the whole structure an oddly ecclesiastical air.

Like the transporter bridge, it is the notion that makes the Anderton boat lift so extraordinary. Boats float into large water-filled tanks which can be raised and lowered, the idea being to join the Trent and Mersey Canal at the top of the hill at Anderton with the River Weaver down below. To lift this huge tank of water, complete with boat, would be very hard work unless the load was counterbalanced as in an ordinary lift in a tall building. As the tank goes up, so a weight goes down and vice versa. But in this case, one weight was insufficient, so a series of heavy weights were hung around the frame of the lift, giving it a decidedly Heath Robinson appearance.

Modern developments that have changed the appearance of canals have usually not come from inside the canal world at all, yet some of these developments have had the effect of transforming what was a perfectly plain, conventional little canal into something altogether strange. Take, for example, the Gravelly Hill interchange on the M6 motorway, which is better known as Spaghetti Junction. In itself it is a remarkable piece of civil engineering and can be bewildering for motorists trying to thread their way through it. In a car, it is impossible to capture the complexity of the structure. This becomes immediately apparent when it is seen from the air, or from the canal, for the old canal runs right through the junction. The road's concrete pillars stand on either side and even in the middle of the canal, while the roadways themselves swoop in giant curves overhead. What one of the boatmen who first used the canal two centuries ago would think of this concrete maze if he could see it one cannot imagine.

An even more remarkable transformation has been effected in Manchester. Here the Rochdale Canal plunges through the heart of the city and was, in its day, one of the major transport routes to serve the growing industries of Lancashire. That role has long since ended, and now the canal is usually thought of as a nuisance to planners who must fit it into their new building schemes.

What do you do if you have a prime site for a new office block just off Piccadilly, but in the middle is a canal and an inconvenient lock? The answer is to build over it. Few people up in the busy streets around Piccadilly are aware of the canal's existence, but those who travel by water are very aware of the presence of the office block, for they are presented with the daunting sight of their canal disappearing underneath it. There, among the foundations, is the lock, and the boat crews must fumble around in the dark while office workers are busy overhead.

The first railways were built in the Canal Age, but before the arrival of the steam locomotive. Horses, not engines, pulled the trucks on those early lines and they were invariably built with industrial use, not passenger traffic, in mind. The strangest of these lines, the Haytor Granite Tramway, can be found on Dartmoor. Its name has a dual significance. It was used to transport stone from the quarries, but the rails themselves were also made from stone. As iron was expensive on Dartmoor and stone was being quarried every day it was obvious to use it wherever possible. So the stony rails run over the moor, past stony sidings and even over stony points, although the actual switching was done by a metal plate spiked into place. Many other more conventionally iron-railed routes were built, and one at least was destined to have a special place in railway history.

A narrow-gauge railway was built to take slate from Blaenau Ffestiniog to a new port, Porthmadog. It was completed in 1811, with the rather surprising support of the poet Shelley. Experiments were later made with steam trains, although a contemporary reported that any speed over 8mph (13kmph) ran the risk of 'breaking the springs or loosening the driver's teeth'. The problem of running a locomotive on a narrow track with tight curves was solved by building 'double-ended Fairlies'. These look like two

Gothic arches on
Birmingham's Engine Arm
aqueduct *(Anthony Burton)*

locomotives that have backed into each other and become inextricably stuck. The cab is in the middle and sprouts boilers fore and aft. It was, in fact, an ingenious way of getting two boilers on the one engine for power, but making it possible to cope with the curves by having each mounted on a separate bogie. And these weird push-me-pull-you engines worked – and still work, for the Ffestiniog Railway is a thriving line carrying passengers on a beautiful scenic route through the hills.

By the time steam had reached the Ffestiniog, the whole country was in the grip of railway mania. When it came to building a new station for city, town or village every architectural style known to man was investigated, and most were tried. There are stations like castles and stations that are doing their best to pass themselves off as stately homes; some stations are like cottages and others are like cathedrals. Among mock-medieval structures, few are more convincing than the little station at Battle, in East Sussex. Outside, there are the predictable trappings, such as thin lancet windows, but the interior holds the greatest surprise, with a waiting-room like a baronial hall boasting a beamed roof and hooded fireplace. A train of knights might as easily appear beside the platform as the 3.15 from Tunbridge Wells. The station at Stoke-on-Trent, on the other hand, preferred its hurrying passengers to believe that they were going to a Jacobean house party – although today's travellers, once they are behind the ornate façade, will find the station itself transformed into just another set of British Rail tea-rooms and echoing platforms. Façades such as those of Stoke-on-Trent's station are all too commonly fronts disguising a duller reality, duller nowadays than the original builders intended. The hand of

The stone rails of the
Haytor granite tramway
(*Anthony Burton*)

A typical West London terrace – until you look behind. Nos 23 and 24 Leinster Gardens are façades bridging the Metropolitan Railway *(Derek Pratt)*

conformity has fallen heavily on the glorious individualism that characterised the earlier buildings.

The station hotel across the square, however, still shows the same exuberant Jacobean style, inside and out, although sadly the station and hotel are no longer linked by tunnel.

Old station buildings had a message to convey to travellers – an 'image' in modern jargon. They might be homely cottages, such as that at Fenny Stratford in Buckinghamshire with its elaborate half-timbering, where the message for the would-be traveller was 'don't be frightened by these new-fangled engines – look here where you start off in a nice, comfy little house, just like your own home'. Alternatively, a station such as Monkwearmouth, Tyne and Wear, in the Greek revival style with porticoed entrance, wants travellers to know that they are in the presence of something gentlemanly and imposing. Different styles, different messages, but both Fenny Stratford and Monkwearmouth are buildings of character. It is sad to see the indignities that even the finest of such structures have suffered in recent times. Look, for example, at the splendid mock-medieval style of Temple Meads Station in Bristol. Its old train shed has a wonderful roof that might have graced a grand hall or an Oxbridge college library; today the hammerbeams preside over ranks of parked cars. It is now, however,

slowly being restored to more dignified uses.

As with station architecture, the Gothic style has often found its way into railway structures. One of the best known, and most attractive, examples has graced a thousand calendars – the viaduct across the Nidd at Knaresborough in Yorkshire. It is actually the second Nidd viaduct, the first having fallen down.

The same love for the grandiose was to be seen in tunnel entrances. One notable example of a castellated entrance is at the north end of Clayton tunnel on the London to Brighton line, and there is another at the northern end of Bramhope tunnel outside Leeds. At one side of the latter is a three-storeyed circular tower. This was no mere embellishment for it was the tunnel-keeper's house. Here, in this lonely spot, he guarded the entrance, controlling traffic through the tunnel in the days before efficient signalling systems made his job superfluous. His was not only a lonely life, but it must also have been hopelessly inconvenient in the narrow, circular house, which was built not with the occupant's convenience in mind, but with a view to making an imposing effect on the landscape. Not every grandiose plan, however, reached fruition. The citizens of Tadcaster in north Yorkshire, for example, built themselves a most impressive viaduct across the River Wharfe. It is still there, and still waiting for the railway that never came. A grandiose scheme that did work, however, can be seen in a parkful of follies at Shugborough in Staffordshire. The London to Stafford main line runs in a tunnel topped by a replica of Hadrian's Arch in Athens, and trains emerge triumphantly into the light through a wonderfully convincing medieval fortress.

When it came to building their railways, the planners were generally fairly ruthless about whatever was in the way. Sometimes, however, they had to make special arrangements. When the railway came to Leeds, the scheme called for an embankment that not only passed close to the parish church, but actually went right through the graveyard. The bodies were disinterred and reburied, but the headstones were laid out in rows on the steep slopes of the embankment like carved paving stones, and they remain there still. The builders of the line through Conwy faced a different problem. Conwy is an ancient fortified town with castle and encircling walls. In his approach bridge, Robert Stephenson was influenced by an earlier engineer and designed a bridge with castellated portals, but the city wall had still to be pierced. Pierced it was, however, and the gap was covered by a tall Gothic arch, which far from being in keeping with its surroundings, looks totally unconvincing (see p124).

The most bizarre solution to a structural problem came when the Metropolitan Railway wanted to drive their line through the middle of a typical West London terrace, Leinster Gardens. The essential feature of such a terrace is its unity, yet the new line would create a gap between numbers 22 and 25. A solution was found that allowed the railway through, yet preserved the essential unity of the buildings. The railway came, yet 23 and 24 Leinster Gardens are still there – or at least they appear to be. In

reality they are just a façade: like the street fronts on a Hollywood set, they are no more than walls propped up by heavy timbers.

To conclude this tour of transport oddities, here are three favourites and one failure. One does not expect much from underground railway systems in the way of amusing buildings, but when Glasgow's underground was built in the nineteenth century, St Enoch's Station appeared as a little building, looking like a cross between a Jacobean home and a Scottish castle. Although it is now used as an information centre, it still looks distinctly odd. Berney Arms Halt in Norfolk has nothing in its appearance to suggest oddness, but it comes complete with an excellent tale. Mr Berney was a local landowner who only agreed to allow the railway across his lands on condition that a halt was built and kept there in perpetuity. The railway agreed, but Mr Berney's delight was short lived. There was nothing in the agreement, according to the railway company, that actually required trains to stop for Mr Berney – so they didn't. It took years of legal argument before Mr Berney won the case and trains stopped at the halt. It is still there, a lonely little spot, but the rail route is the only way, other than a boat journey, of visiting the fine windmill nearby. Finally, I made an unexpected discovery in a city centre while I was walking through an underpass. I noticed a metal plate at the entrance cut with deep grooves, similar to the columns of Blow-up-Bridge. Furthermore, there was a raised walkway

This exercise in Scottish baronial architecture was the entrance to Glasgow's St Enoch underground station *(Anthony Burton)*

Beer on the move. This bottle van is preserved at the Bass Museum *(Anthony Burton)*

down one side of the underpass. Could I really be looking at a canal tunnel passing under one of Cardiff's busiest streets? Indeed I could: the raised walk was the old tow-path, the dried-out tunnel was the pedestrian path, and a long-disused section of the Glamorgan Canal had found a new use.

Finally, then, to an odd transport failure, and one of the few associated with Isambard Kingdom Brunel: the Atmospheric Railway he built in Devon. The principle was not unlike that used in old-fashioned department stores, where air pressure drew canisters of cash in pipes around the building. On the Atmospheric Railway pumps sucked air from one end of a tube and the atmospheric pressure at the other end sent a piston shooting along. All that was needed was a projection on the piston passing through a groove in the tube. When a train of trucks or carriages were fastened on to this projection they were transported silently and speedily. The system was not a success, however, as air leaked out and the plan was abandoned. All that remains is the 1844 pumping station at Starcross, near Exeter, where demonstrations of how this glorious failure *should* have worked are regularly given.

Collectors' Corner

THIS is not primarily a chapter about great collections, or at least not in terms of size, but rather about the collections that reflect the personal enthusiasms of the collector. It is one of the marks of the true collector that he or she regards as perfectly normal an activity which the rest of the world would think mildly eccentric. Sometimes the enthusiasm for collecting is so overwhelming that it becomes obsessive. Sir John Vanhatten would seem to have been just such a collector – in his case, of fossils. Not content merely to collect, he was determined to have an appropriate home for his beloved objects. So, in 1769, he built a mock castle, Dinton Castle, which actually incorporated all kinds of fossils into the fabric of the building. The castle can still be seen, standing a forlorn ruin, beside the main road from Thame to Buckingham. There is no definite record of what happened at Dinton Castle. Did Sir John ever finish his exotic museum, or was his intention simply to preserve the ammonites and the rest of his fossil collection by turning them into a picturesque folly?

Few collectors go to the extremes of Sir John Vanhatten. Many begin, however, with a few items, the number of which gradually grows and grows, until a point is reached where it seems unfair to keep them for oneself and the general public are allowed to see the treasures. For many of us, such collections are a delight. One can admire modern display techniques and the new sense of excitement that they can bring, but nothing can match the privilege of sharing a true enthusiast's passion. A great personal favourite is the collection of railway memorabilia at Shackerstone Station on what is now the Market Bosworth Railway. The place itself is a delight to the railway enthusiast, with its beautifully restored steam locomotives running outside, and it has achieved one gloriously comic moment in its history. Edward VII was expected at nearby Gopsall Hall to spend a weekend shooting birds. The railway company decided to make the most of the royal occasion. To save His Majesty the unnecessary bother of clambering down from carriage to platform, a

Holt) The shell museum is a collection of shells from around the world.
Glasgow, Strathclyde The Burrell Collection, Pollock Country Park, is now a superb gallery of the arts. It began as the personal collection of Sir William and Lady Burrell.
Lamberhurst, Kent Mr Heaver's Model Museum on the A262 has model scenes covering everything from Ancient Rome to nursery rhymes.
St Thomas Street, London SE1 Old St Thomas' Hospital operating theatre is preserved. Not a collection perhaps, but a macabre museum.
Woolwich, London SE18 The Museum of Artillery, Repository Road. It is not the collection but the setting that is remarkable: a Nash rotunda built to celebrate, of all things, the Year of Peace.
Winchcombe, Gloucestershire The Railway Museum is a collection of railwayana including a bewildering array of working signals.

section of the platform was raised and covered in red carpet. All went well at first, and the driver performed his part to perfection, but someone had boobed: the raised platform was too high. Irritated royal attendants were seen trying to open the carriage door, but to no avail. There was nothing for it but to move the train while the red carpet remained untrodden. The king was not amused. But to return to the station museum.

John Jacques was a British Rail signalman who, thirty years ago, noticed that when the old-style semaphore signals worked by levers were being replaced by modern electrical systems, the old ones were simply thrown away. Jacques therefore acquired them and then began acquiring anything else concerned with the railway that no one else wanted – tickets and timetables, posters and pictures – anything, in fact, from station signs to uniforms. They are all on show in the old station buildings and if there is an order it is not easy to see. Every inch of wall is covered, objects fill so much of the floor space, there is scarcely room for visitors. It is the sort of museum where you make your own way and make your own discoveries. It is a collection put together by an amateur in the very best sense of that word – 'one who loves'.

Museums have been described as one of Britain's biggest growth industries, but they began with amateur collections, just as the little railway museum at Shackerstone did. There is one city – Oxford – where you can see virtually the whole development of the museum story. It began when Elias Ashmole put his collection of objects gathered on his journeys, especially the Grand Tour of Europe, on public display. Ashmole's Cabinet of Curiosities was given a home of its own in the seventeenth century when it became the Ashmolean Museum, the first public museum in the world. The old building still exists in Broad Street, but it has been transformed into the Science Museum, a marvellous collection of intricate, beautifully worked old scientific instruments. The Ashmolean had outgrown its old home and moved from what was, in effect, an attractive town house to a more imposing classical building in nearby Beaumont Street. By the nineteenth century, however, the emphasis had changed. Museums were not there for fun – they were serious, part of the educational process. A Natural History Museum was clearly required, and another new museum was built, this time in a style that was a true reflection of the age. The engineering of the building was the latest idea – glass on an iron frame, like the great railway stations or the Crystal Palace – but the style looked back in time. The University Museum is one of the most Gothic of Gothic buildings. Yet, in part at least, it also has something of the spirit of the Shackerstone Railway Museum. It incorporates the Pitt-Rivers Collection of Ethnography. No doubt it all makes great sense to the serious student, but to the casual visitor it is a glorious jumble of anything from shrunken heads to shadow puppets.

Not every natural history museum has impeccable scientific origins. Some collections saw animals merely as items placed on earth for man's amusement. Lionel Walter, second Baron Rothschild, rode around the

grounds of his house at Tring in Hertfordshire in a carriage pulled by zebra, while other exotic animals, such as giant tortoises, roamed the grounds like mobile garden ornaments. Today, the house is home to the Tring Zoological Museum in which animals, birds and insects are beautifully displayed – but dead! Taxidermy has a role to play in properly organised scientific museums such as Tring, even if the museum's origins were less organised and considerably less scientific. But what is one to make of Potter's Museum of Curiosity at the Jamaica Inn in Cornwall?

Walter Potter was a taxidermist who founded his museum in 1862. Where most Victorian taxidermists were content to mount birds on branches and to cover them with a glass dome, Potter had grander ideas. He produced a series of tableaux. 'The Rabbits' School' has a score of genuine stuffed rabbits sitting on benches reading books and doing arithmetic. Extraordinarily, all the animals look very natural – if a rabbit standing on its hind legs with a book in its paws can ever look completely natural! The kittens' tea and croquet party has thirty-seven furry friends gathered together for these delights. The kittens – ladies in jewels,

Kittens having tea and enjoying a game of croquet: just one of the many bizarre tableaux in Potter's Museum of Curiosity *(Potter's Museum of Curiosity, Jamaica Inn)*

The message seems clear: just a small part of the collection that makes up Moseley's museum of railwayana in Birmingham *(Moseley Railwayana Museum)*

gentlemen in cravats – sit at a table where they are served by the maids who pass around such culinary delights as baked mouse tart. Other tableaux represent traditional stories, such as the death of Cock Robin. There are conventional exhibits as well, but it is the tableaux that draw the visitors. This riot of anthropomorphism either attracts or repels utterly.

Another collection which many people find repulsive, yet which nevertheless was based on serious, and often brilliant, scientific work, can be seen in the Hunterian Museum at the Royal College of Surgeons in London. It contains the collection of John Hunter, one of those remarkable polymaths who flourished in the eighteenth century. He was one of a group of 'scientific and literary men' who met regularly to exchange ideas in the coffee houses of Soho, a group which included such eminent individuals as Sir Joseph Banks and Captain Cook. Hunter himself was a brilliant anatomist and researcher. His own work was too far ahead of its time to earn him much in the way of recognition during his lifetime – he moved a long way towards establishing a theory of evolution before Charles Darwin was even born. Hunter's pupil Jenner left the world the techniques of vaccination; Hunter himself left his strange and wonderful collection.

Many of the specimens, pickled and bottled, are just what you would expect to find in the collection of a man concerned with the complexities of nature. Over three thousand specimens are carefully arranged to show the interdependence among animals that is the basis of evolutionary theory. The pickled portions make the collection seem like a cross between an exotic delicatessen – woodpecker's tongue is, no doubt, a delicacy somewhere – and Frankenstein's laboratory. Then there are the freaks and aberrations. There is the 8ft tall Irishman who actually left a plea in his will that his body should be kept out of the hands of the anatomists. His efforts were in vain however. Five hundred pounds to the undertakers secured the giant's skeleton for Hunter's collection. There are other macabre remains, from the double skull of a child to examples of the ravages and deformities caused by venereal disease. The Hunterian Museum is not a place for those with weak stomachs which is, perhaps, why special permission is required to view it.

Other collections do have somewhat jollier themes. It is tempting not to

John Hunter and oversized friend at the Hunterian Museum, Royal College of Surgeons *(Hunterian Museum, Royal College of Surgeons)*

mention the Paul Corin collection to anyone, so that they, too, can have the delight of stumbling upon it by accident. St Keyne is a tiny village in southern Cornwall, and until I met Mr Corin my only knowledge of the place came from the fact that it once stood on the long-vanished Liskeard and Looe canal. Hunting for a crumbling lock chamber in the undergrowth, I was astonished to hear the unmistakable sounds of a fairground organ – and not just one but several, following each other in succession, to which were added the sounds of an electric piano. I had found Paul Corin's Magnificent Music Machines. The collection would be extraordinary anywhere, let alone in the depths of the Cornish countryside. There are street organs from Europe, a fairground organ and a pair of Belgian café organs, the latter being a cross between a live band and a juke-box. Rather more serious in intent, though equally fascinating, are the Welte reproducing pianos. Unlike the pianolas which simply banged out a tune in a very mechanical, featureless way, these pianos are electrically driven and can reproduce fine nuances of tone and expression. The pianist played the music, and a series of pens marked notes and expressions, which could then be transferred to a roll of paper which was then fed back into the machine. The resulting playback is a faithful reproduction of the original performance. With such an instrument you can hear Paderewski play again or Debussy interpreting his own work. And if the classics are not to your taste, you can always turn instead to the Welte Jazz Piano, which comes complete with mandolin, drums, cymbal and wood block. And for those who like music every hour on the hour, there is the Orphonian Disc Music Box. When the discs are inserted into the clock, it not only strikes the hour but plays a tune for the hour as well.

The Nickelodeon at Napton in Warwickshire also specialises in music, from one of the most ornate juke-boxes imaginable to the street hurdy-gurdy. The gem of the whole collection is the Compton Cinema Organ that once held a place of honour at the Hammersmith Regal. Then it would rise, flashing its colour changes while the organist bowed and flashed his pearly teeth at the audience. Those were the days of interval music when the audience were expected to join in a sing-song as the little white ball bounced along on top of the words on the screen. Its new home, the Heyday Kinema, may not be quite as grand as the Odeon, but it does re-create the atmosphere of a thirties cinema. Recitals are given regularly and vintage newsreels are shown, including such true museum items as Elizabeth Taylor's first wedding and London's last tram. Visitors to East Anglia can enjoy remarkably similar entertainment at the Cotton Mechanical Music Museum, near Stowmarket. A cinema with a slightly different theme can be found at Pocklington, Humberside. This is now the Penny Arcadia, home to an amazing collection of all kinds of coin-operated amusement machines. There are antique games and slightly naughty 'What-The-Butler-Saw' specials that once titillated visitors to seaside piers.

All kinds of museums exist with all kinds of collections: some display a collection of very large items, others very small ones. On the grand scale,

A colourful street organ
attracts a crowd of
admirers. This is one of
Paul Corin's Magnificent
Music Machines *(Paul
Corin)*

what could be more impressive than a collection of buildings? St Fagans
near Cardiff has already been mentioned (see p72), but the range of
structures is very impressive, and includes an entire row of cottages. And it
is not just the cottages that have been collected, for they come complete
with gardens, one of which has a typical do-it-yourself pigeon loft.

Few museums, however, can boast such a variety of buildings that have
been dismantled and then reassembled on one site as the Avoncroft
Museum of Buildings, Bromsgrove. Here one can inspect such diverse
structures as a three-seater loo, a surprisingly grand structure for
communal lavatorial use, and an ice-house, a subterranean chamber and
predecessor of the modern refrigerator. But the museum has a serious
purpose: to preserve buildings which would otherwise be demolished,
buildings which are not necessarily particularly grand, but represent

important examples of building techniques and uses. So there are old houses and barns set alongside forges for making chains and nails, a windmill and a cockpit and much, much more. It is a place which manages a very clever balance, for it satisfies the serious student of vernacular architecture and the casual visitor who asks for nothing more than to be shown things both interesting and amusing. If one had to choose one building at Avoncroft to sum up the slightly quirky yet basically serious nature of the museum, then it would have to be the prefab. How easy it would have been to allow this vital example of post-war rebuilding simply to vanish from the landscape without a trace – and how sad if it had. For here is a wonderfully ingenious example of problem solving, replacing houses lost in the devastation of war by homes that were cheap and quick to build, yet managed to arouse genuine affection.

One can understand the rationale behind Avoncroft, but who in his right senses would start a dog collar museum? The collection consists of canine wear rather than clerical dress, but that scarcely makes it any less remarkable. It is only when one sees it that one becomes at least partially convinced that the thing was worth doing at all. Here is an amazing variety of dog collars, ranging from collars for hunting dogs with protruding spikes

to prevent the hunted from damaging the hunter to baroque masterpieces in brass, wrought iron and even silver and gilt. There are even occasional forays into wit, even if on occasion the witty inscriptions are blatant plagiarisms. Alexander Pope had the following lines engraved on a collar which he presented to the Prince of Wales for his pet pooch:

> I am his Highness' dog at Kew;
> Pray, tell me sir, whose dog are you?

The down-market version in this collection reads: 'I am Mr Pratt's dog, King St, Nr Wokingham, Berks. Whose dog are you?' Somehow Pope's version has more of a swing to it. The collars are on display at Leeds Castle, Maidstone, Kent.

Avoncroft and Leeds Castle, then, represent two extremes, but happily there is no shortage of in-betweens, catering for a wide variety of tastes. It is always difficult to decide what to include in a list of eccentric collections and museums. What one person regards as strange, another will see as the most natural thing in the world. Take, for example, the Morpeth Chantry Bagpipe Museum in Northumberland. The population can be divided between those who regard bagpipes as divinely inspirational and those who marginally prefer the noise made by a cat whose tail has just been stepped on. But if it does nothing else, this museum does show that the bagpipes are not a peculiarly Scottish instrument, since, not surprisingly, the Northumbrian pipes hold a place of honour. This museum successfully combines the ancient and the modern: the ancient tradition of the pipes is displayed in a restored thirteenth-century building: the infra-red sound system ensures that visitors hear precisely what they want to hear.

The Geological and Folk Museum of North Wales is comprised of two collections which could scarcely be further apart, whatever yardstick is taken for measurements: one has hard exhibits, the other soft; one shows objects formed over thousands and even millions of years, the other has exhibits unknown before the present century; one involves walks in the open air, the other can be found in just one building in a town centre. The Museum is centred on an old quarry near Wrexham. The difficulty that many people have with geological museums, and indeed with many kinds of museum, is the inability to relate the objects seen inside with the world seen outside. There is, for example, a rock garden at Bwlchgwyn, but somehow in nature rocks refuse to arrange themselves into neat, docketed order. From the museum you can set out and explore the surrounding countryside armed with museum leaflets, and when you follow the recommended routes you find miraculously that museum world and natural world do actually meet. There are two walks, neither very arduous. One takes you on a tour of inspection of the Nant-y-Ffrith stream as it gurgles and plunges down the hillside; the other takes you around a disused quarry. The latter is, in some ways, the more interesting walk, for once you have grasped what you should be looking for, you find yourself discovering

fossils of shells and plants and a rich variety of rock formations. This is an open-air lecture, where the script is written in stone and earth in the changing patterns of the landscape itself. With just a minimum of help, you find that a simple walk has been turned into an engrossing lesson.

What could be less similar to a garden of rocks than a house full of teddy-bears? President Theodore Roosevelt can rest easy in the knowledge that however historians may assess his period as President of the United States, generations of children will continue to love and cuddle their teddies. The Teddy Bear Museum at Stratford-upon-Avon has teddy bears of all sorts, big and small, famous and anonymous. Here visitors can see such illustrious bears as Winnie-the-Pooh and Rupert not to mention William Shakesbear. There are hundreds of bears, and although the museum pretends to cater for children, it is really a museum for adults who wish to wallow in unashamed nostalgia.

The great difference between the old museums and collections and the new, is that now no one feels constrained any longer to keep to 'worthy and educational' subjects. Objects can be collected which are just tremendous fun – which is not to say that they are not important. Ephemera and amusements can say as much about a society as high art. One example is Lady Bangor's Fairground Collection. She began the collection in the 1960s, when the old wooden carved and painted fairground objects began to disappear in favour of easily maintained plastic and metal. Collecting such marvellous, rich objects needs no excuse, for they are wonderful in a very real sense, their sole purpose being to instil a sense of wonder in the fairs' visitors. They succeeded when they were first built as much as a century ago and they still succeed today. Lady Bangor had originally intended to display the collection herself, but in 1974 she sold it to Madame Tussaud's, who added it to another of their attractions, the Wookey Hole Caves in Somerset. So the bioscope and the fairground organ, the gallopers and the spinner have left the open air where they spent their working lives, and have a new home. And they have some odd companions. Madame Tussaud's is celebrated for its waxwork figures of the famous. But fame is transitory, and Wookey Hole is full of likenesses of the once-glamorous, forlornly waiting in the hope that one day their originals' reputations will revive and they will return to glory in the Marylebone Road showrooms.

There is a certain reassuring durability about fairgrounds, but packaging is essentially ephemeral. You take out the contents and throw away the container, but the packages are often fascinating objects in themselves. For a start, they are intended to be attractive, to shout out 'Look how pretty I am – buy me!' to the passing shoppers. But the art of selling is as changeable as any other art. Packets reflect changing notions on design, typography and art; they are social documents which everyone can appreciate and understand because everyone buys them. Robert Opie has a huge collection now on display at the museum of Packaging and Advertising at the Albert Warehouse, Gloucester. It is a curious fact that

A splendid example of fairground art: a merry-go-round lion from Lady Bangor's Fairground Collection (*Lady Bangor's Fairground Collection*)

packets and posters may look dated but they are nowhere near as dated as the old television advertisements that are screened at the museum. Many people visit the collection to enjoy a nostalgic look at the recent past; and the same motive might take them to the National Waterways Museum in another of the warehouses in the Gloucester Docks complex. This is a fine museum, but it does share one feature with the Opie collection in being housed in a superb industrial building. In fact, one could say that with the virtual death of trade in the old canal basin, the whole dock complex has acquired museum status – even the little sailors' church tucked away among the tall warehouse blocks.

A comparatively recent trend is that a museum is no longer necessarily a place in which a collection is housed in a building; it can be the building itself. To take one example, as different as it can be from the jollity of bright and cheerful packaging, consider one of William Blake's 'dark, Satanic mills' or, better still, an entire mill village. Quarry Bank Mill at Styal in

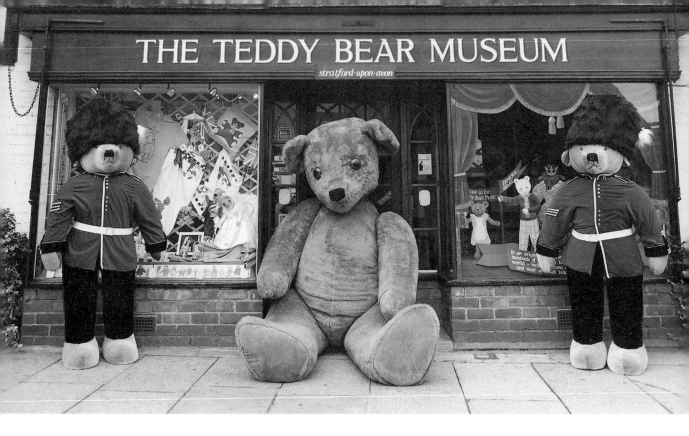

THE TEDDY BEAR MUSEUM
stratford-upon-avon

Guarding a 15ft teddy bear
at the Stratford museum
(The Teddy Bear Museum)

Cheshire was built to spin cotton in 1784 and later weaving was added so that the mill could produce anything from yarn to finished cloth. The mill's working days have ended, but it lives on as a museum: the shuttles fly again across the looms; the giant waterwheel rumbles slowly round and one can enjoy the sight of one of the most elegant of all machines, the spinning mule at work. But Styal is more than just a mill. Samuel Greg who founded it came to what we would now call a 'green field site'. Such sites create no problem to the modern commuter, but when workers had to walk to work, they needed to live near the factory. So Greg built a village across the fields, and a delightful spot it seems today, with attractive houses each with its own garden. We no longer see the chronic overcrowding, with two families sharing each house, but by the standards of the day, Styal must have seemed near-paradise. The same could never have been true of one house, separate from the rest. It looks now to be a grand family home, but two centuries ago it housed over a hundred young boys and girls, some no more than nine years old, who worked in the mill from six in the morning to seven at night. It was hard, dull, repetitive work, and it was dangerous, for the children worked with unguarded machines. Ask any parents with a nine-year-old child, standing watching the lovely machines from behind the safe guard-rails, if they could let them crawl into the moving machinery to repair broken cotton threads. Styal brings many aspects of the past into sharp focus: on the one hand the ingenuity of the early inventors, on the other the inhumanity that the inventions brought to the lives of the mill children.

But this chapter will not end on such a sombre note. Let us instead celebrate the squirrel-like collecting instincts of Charles P. Wade of Snowshill Manor in Gloucestershire. He was a scholar, an architect and an artist, but above all he was a collector. He bought the old house in 1919 when it was in a shocking state of disrepair, restored it to its former glory and set about filling it with whatever took his fancy. If he saw something he fancied, then he bought it and brought it back to the lovely old Cotswold manor. He ended up with what must be the least coherent collection in the country. Some of the items do look at home in a Tudor home – old musical instruments, for example, of which there is a room full. Spinning and weaving tools have relevance in an area that once had a thriving wool trade. Toys and clocks might just about fit in as well. But why bicycles? The Great Garret, also known as 100 Wheels, boasts a huge collection of two-wheelers, and why is there such a collection of things nautical in a house as near to the centre of the country as you can get? The answer is simple – Wade liked the sea and he gave several of the rooms nautical names: Admiral, Top Royal, Top Gallant, Mizzen. The collection starts to seem logical after all, until one comes across the Samurai warriors, a small army huddled together in martial conference, their weapons around them. It appears that Charles Wade was walking past an antique shop when he saw a suit of Samurai armour. He liked the look of it so he went inside. The shopkeeper, catching the powerful scent of a collector, casually remarked that this was just one suit but there were several more to be had. The hint was sufficient: Wade bought the lot, and began collecting Japanese weapons and armour on the spot. No doubt there are collectors even now gathering objects which most people would pass by without a second glance. In time, their collections, too, might go on display. Long may the squirrels thrive.

Just a few examples from thousands at Robert Opie's Museum of Packaging and Advertising *(Robert Opie Collection)*

Out of Sight

Bradwell, Derbyshire
The Caverns, Bradwell
Head Road, offer the
usual .cave visit plus
more adventurous
explorations.
Cheddar, Somerset
Gough's Cave is a
beautiful show cave and
visitors can also try
'adventure caving' and
visit a cave museum.
**Greenhow, North
Yorkshire** There is a
pleasing paradox in
finding a deep cavern at
the highest village in
England. It was originally
a lead mine.
Guernsey, Channel Isles
The German Underground
Hospital was carved out
of solid rock by slave
labour.
Hastings, East Sussex
St Clement's Caves, West
Hill are cut deep into the
hill and were said to be
the haunt of smugglers.
**Ingleton, North
Yorkshire** White Scar
Caves are 1 mile (1.6km)
outside the village on the
Hawes Road.
Newtongrange, Lothian
The Scottish Mining
Museum is based on the
old Lady Victoria Colliery.
St Neot, Cornwall The
Carnglaze Caverns are
vast caves formed by
slate mining.

THERE are things which are out of sight, because they are deliberately hidden away from view, and others which are hidden only in the sense that they are not normally visible. Secret hiding places come very much into the first category, and of these by far the most common are the priests' holes, into which Catholic priests crept to escape religious persecution. Harvington Hall in Hereford and Worcester is a late-medieval moated manor house which in 1630 was owned by the Throckmorton family who had been involved in the Gunpowder Plot. Although Thomas Throckmorton was the only conspirator who escaped suspicion, he decided that it was only prudent to ensure that Harvington Hall should be liberally supplied with hiding places. He must have employed a master of false doors and secret passages to turn the family home into a warren of hidden passages. An upright timber on a wall pivots to reveal a hiding place; a stair riser rises on a hinge to give access to a cosy room. There is a false chimney, a false drain under a lavatory and a secret chamber over a bread oven; all three hiding places would have been satisfactory only for as long as no one mistook the false for the real. Chingle Hall in Lancashire gives a hint of its religious significance in its cruciform plan. Built in the thirteenth century, it became a place of secret worship during the Civil War. It has four priests' hiding places, which are neither very large nor very comfortable. They certainly seem to have made the priests unhappy, for they are said to have haunted the house ever since.

Not all secret passages were necessarily intended to be secret. Nottingham, for example, turns out to be a positive Swiss cheese of a city – it is riddled with caves and tunnels. Special cave tours are organised by the council which claims that there are more man-made caves in Nottingham than anywhere else in the country. Looking through the list, it is impossible to disagree and these underground passages certainly afford a novel view of the city. Broadmarsh on the surface is shopping centre and bus station; underneath is a cave complex excavated in the eighteenth century for use by tanners – which must have been a boon for the citizens, as tanning was a notoriously aromatic activity. The Oxfam shop in Bridlesmith stands next to the entrance to another group of caves which includes an ice-house. In pre-refrigerator days, cool holes in the ground were the only places where ice could be stored. Yet another set of caves can be found at Brewhouse

Yard, where they form part of a museum complex. All the caves were carved out for some special purpose – as stores and workplaces – and over the centuries their use has changed many times. A cave that began as a medieval fish store might have become a Georgian wine cellar and in more recent times may have served as an air-raid shelter.

The caves, however, are only part of the story of underground Nottingham. Down below the castle, in the depths of the rock, is a secret passage, known as Mortimer's Hole. It gained its name from an event in 1330 when the Regent, Roger Mortimer, was holding his own parliament in what he believed to be the safety of Nottingham Castle. But someone knew of the secret entry and Mortimer was captured. Wollaton Hall, the rather grand Elizabethan house on the edge of Nottingham, home to an excellent museum, also has underground passages, and not only this – it also boasts its own subterranean reservoir, known as the Admiral's bath. You can have a guided tour *under* instead of *through* Nottingham, the details of which you can get from the local information centres.

Stoke-on-Trent, Staffordshire Chatterley Whitfield Mining Museum, near Tunstall, is based on a former working mine, but the underground section had to be specially cut.
Uley, Gloucestershire Hetty Pegler's Tump: a chambered long barrow which invites exploration of its underground chambers.

Exeter may not be able to boast of such an extensive underground labyrinth as that of Nottingham, but its underground passages are no less intriguing. Because water supply has been a problem for Exeter since Roman times, as the city sits on a hill with no instantly available water source, aqueducts and channels have been cut at various times from Roman times up to the medieval period. Not that visitors get a very medieval start to the underground visits, since access is down a flight of steps in the middle of Princesshay, a modern shopping precinct. Once underground, however, exploration becomes fascinating, with glimpses of the old city walls and even the grooves for the portcullis that closed off the city gates. Children have their own very narrow passage through which only the more nimble, and slim, adults can pass.

We tend to think of water mains running under a town as a recent phenomenon, yet Exeter has a complex of aqueducts dating back hundreds of years. This is not surprising, as wells are an ancient way of obtaining fresh water from deep below the surface. The need to ensure water supplies may lie behind one very strange and mysterious little passage. Carreg Cennen Castle in Dyfed is everything a castle should be, perched high on a precipice above the River Cennen. Although it seems impregnable, during the wars of the thirteenth century it changed hands several times and was captured by the Yorkists during the Wars of the Roses. They ordered its destruction but, fortunately for posterity, the demolition gang were less than conscientious. So we have a fortress that proved more vulnerable than appearances suggest and more vulnerable than its builders anticipated, for they expected to withstand lengthy sieges. A passage was therefore cut through the rock to reach a spring that would supply fresh water to the castle. That, at any rate, is the most popular theory explaining the passage. Whatever its purpose, the old tunnel now provides an entertaining addition to the castle's list of attractions – especially if, as our family did, you arrive not knowing of the tunnel's existence and not

armed with lights. We all stumbled around in the dark, while the children tried to terrify us, each other and anyone else who happened to be there at the time.

Coming closer to our own age, and rather more sinister burrowings, the island of Guernsey was honeycombed with tunnels and excavations during the German occupation of World War II. The work was performed by slave labourers brought across from Europe. The largest of these caverns, the Underground Hospital at St Andrew's, is open to the general public. Many of the other caves were used as shelters, bunkers and ammunition stores and have either been filled in or used for more peaceful purposes. The story told at the museum is an uncomfortable reminder to those who lived in mainland Britain at that time of how close the country came to invasion.

Narrow, dark passages beneath city streets and tunnels dug by slave labour may not be everyone's notion of fun, but almost everyone seems to

The mysterious underground passage at Carreg Cennen castle *(Cadw: Welsh Historic Monuments, Crown copyright)*

enjoy caves, provided that access is not too difficult. Some caves are simply natural phenomena which exist to be explored by anyone prepared to make the effort. Some require the special equipment and expertise of the trained caver, but others are very accessible. Caves such as Smoo Cave in the cliffs near Durness on the north-west tip of Scotland are particularly rewarding. After scrambling down to the beach you will discover this great cavern into the back of which a high waterfall tumbles. Its special appeal lies in its naturalness and its position on one of the finest sections of coastline in Britain. Many people, however, prefer the show caves. The best known are those around the Cheddar area in Somerset, although the

Dan yr Ogof show caves. Visitors are not expected to be quite this active *(Dan yr Ogof Show Caves)*

largest cave complex, not just in Britain but in the whole of Western Europe, is that of Dan-yr-Ogof, north of Abercraf, Powys. You can even find show caves in the unlikely surroundings of Torquay. Kent's Cavern can be found at Wellswood, a district of Torbay, where visitors are given a guided tour of the labyrinthine passages and illuminated grottoes. People come to such caves to admire the stalactites and stalagmites, which can achieve fantastic forms. They are the stuff of fantasy and legend, and if we see trolls and petrified witches, so much the better. It is a more interesting explanation than an unvarnished account of accumulations of calcium carbonate built up over the aeons by water dripping through limestone. (Those who have trouble remembering which name applies to which formation should note that a stalaCtite Comes down and a stalaGmite Grows up.)

Such caves as these are undoubtedly very beautiful and are certainly very popular, although for me the appeal is limited. One grotto seems much like another, so that having seen one lovely show cave I feel no great urge to dash off to another, unless it has something to set it apart, and that something is usually human interest. In fact, many caves were once inhabited, even if not very recently. Kent's Cavern, for example, was occupied tens of thousands of years ago, a span of time that all but defies understanding. Man lived here during the Ice Age and you can see some of the finds of the area at the Torquay museum – remains from the time when the land was occupied by the bear and the sabre-toothed tiger. The museum also has a crude hand axe of stone, probably about 300,000 years old and one of the oldest man-made implements ever found in Britain. Little of this, however, is reflected in Kent's Cavern today, which is rather more concerned with the attractions of strange formations.

Those who prefer more adventurous excursions could visit the St Clement's Caves on the slopes of West Hill, Hastings, a tremendous system that covers 4 acres and allegedly the haunt of smugglers. Everyone, I suppose, imagines that a big cave near the sea must have been a smugglers' hide-out, and if there is any cave anywhere where reality and romantic fiction are likely to meet, then it is in this corner of England. Rudyard Kipling knew the area well, for he lived a few miles north of Hastings at Batemans, near Burwash (a house, by the way, well worth visiting) and he wrote perhaps the best-known lines ever penned on the subject of smugglers. The ominous note sounded in the last line was no more than an accurate comment on the dangers of seeing too much in those violent days:

> Five and twenty ponies,
> Trotting through the dark –
> Brandy for the Parson,
> 'Baccy for the Clerk:
> Laces for a lady, letters for a spy
> Watch the wall, my darling, while the Gentlemen go by!

Smoo Cave, a seaside
cavern near Durness
(Anthony Burton)

Whether smugglers, in fact, ever trusted valuable contraband to anything
as open as a cave seems somewhat unlikely, but the thought adds a
piquancy to a visit – although the hope of finding an abandoned brandy
barrel are, to say the least, remote.

Other caves have more mundane associations, but are not necessarily
any the less interesting. The limestone hills of Derbyshire are a great
hunting ground for would-be underground explorers. There are natural
caves galore and those who want a gentle introduction should visit Buxton
Country Park, where they can combine a pleasant stroll through the
woodland with a visit to Poole's Cavern. This is known as the 'first wonder
of the Peak' and is certainly a fine natural cave, typical of the district. It was
inhabited in Neolithic times, and the finds of archaeological excavations
are on show. But the great centre for cave exploration is Castleton. Caves
here have always been something more than just holes in the ground, for
within their depths man has found minerals that he could exploit for profit.
Each of the great caverns that is open to the public in this area has been put
to use in one way or another.

One mineral in particular is found in profusion in the area – Blue John, a
fluorspar which has been used for ornaments since at least Roman times.
The obvious starting point for following this local story is the Blue John
Cavern, on the A625 west of Castleton, opposite the shapely hill of Mam Tor

– and with such a name the actual shape of the hill should require no further description. The cavern itself was formed by water erosion, and the cave system extends for over ¼ mile (400m), the largest chambers rising some 200ft (60m) above the old stream bed. From here a series of Blue John veins – more than half of those discovered in the whole region – extend outwards, all of which have been worked during previous centuries. Another equally rich, if not richer, source of Blue John was found at the nearby Treak Cliff Cavern. Why should such caves seem more interesting than others where the natural order has remained undisturbed? I can only give an entirely subjective answer. The Treak Cliff Cavern and Dan-yr-Ogof have much in common, because they boast similar, and equally attractive, features in their caves and pinnacles; yet I find the fact that man has worked so extensively in the one, hacking away through the long hours of a lightless day, provides a special fascination. I identify in imagination with those troglodytic workers fumbling through the dark.

The Speedwell Cavern, in the same area, was exploited for lead. A visit down this mine, however, is unlike any other, for as it is permanently waterlogged, access is by boat down a mile-long underground canal. Originally, boats were hauled along by fixed chains, but nowadays an outboard motor provides an easier, if noisier, means of transport. The end of the line is a vast cavern with a 'bottomless' lake, and a complex of old workings. The story of these workings is explained in an exhibition, which includes photographs of mining days. One feels that it is now too easy to get down there, with an engine doing all the work, but once you are there the special atmosphere of the subterranean lake, deep and mysterious, exerts its influence. You do feel that you are indeed at the heart of a mountain and have entered another world. It is very easy to see this as a place inhabited by creatures out of Tolkien: dwarfs digging for mineral wealth, or more sinister orcs and even the wretched Gollum might be glimpsed emerging from the dark depths.

Nearby Peak Cavern is nothing like as creepy, although not a jot less spectacular. Peak Cavern is the largest natural cave in a district of big caves, and it was the space it offered rather than mineral wealth that provided the lure for entrepreneurs. This was the work-place of the Marrison family for more than two hundred years, and for others who came to the caves before them. There was nothing especially romantic about their efforts, but they were undeniably useful. They made ropes: everything from thick haulage ropes to sash cords for windows. The manufacture of ropes involves the twisting of twine together, traditionally by a man walking backwards down a rope-walk adding the necessary twist as he went. It was an activity that required space, which the cavern supplied. The end product may not have been as beautiful as a Blue John rose, but it was in great demand, and it was only the rapid spread of synthetic fibres that brought the business to a close. Work has ended, but the cave itself is as splendid as ever, and visitors can explore walkways that lead ½ mile (800m) into the hill.

The business of tunnelling underground for mineral wealth has a very long history, and it is only comparatively recently that this hidden world has been opened up to the general public. One can start right back in the Neolithic or New Stone Age. The name 'Stone Age' derives from the use of a special kind of stone, flint, which has one particular property that makes it valuable – it can be knapped. When flint nodules are hit with a hammer, and when it is done with skill, flakes of stone break off. In this way the flint can be shaped and polished to produce a very serviceable axe-head, or to make knives and arrow- or spear-heads. But Neolithic man discovered that some flints were better than others, and the very best often lay deep underground. At Grimes Graves near Weeting in Norfolk is an area that looks like a World War I battleground covered with shell holes. The shell holes are, in fact, collapsed pits from which Neolithic man dug out his flint. Some pits have now been excavated and one has been opened up to the public. Visitors clamber down a vertical ladder to the bottom of a wide pit that has been cut through the chalk, from the foot of which a series of long, low passageways lead off. The flint itself appears as a dark band at floor level, and it was comparatively easy to remove the soft chalk with a pick-axe fashioned from a deer antler and then to lever out large pieces of flint.

It is perhaps unfair to whet the reader's appetite when that appetite cannot be satisfied. Where now you can only peer down the lit galleries, once you could crawl. It is not hard to see why the practice was stopped: there was an element of danger and more than an element of dirt, for there are places where you can only wriggle on your belly through the wet chalk. But when you do visit one of the 'unimproved' pits, you feel much closer to the miners of four thousand years ago, and you can peer into old workings that have remained undisturbed since work finished. Heaps of broken chalk and flint, and even the remains of abandoned antler picks can still be seen. It is a somewhat eerie sensation to stare into this ancient world, but even more eerie if, as happened to me, your light goes out and you are plunged into total darkness. But if visitors can no longer explore that particular, undisturbed world, there is compensation in the shape of the excellent small museum on the surface, where the workings of the old mine system are explained.

The Stone Age gave way to the Bronze Age, the Bronze Age to the Iron Age. They have been digging iron from the ground in the Forest of Dean for well over three thousand years. The Phoenicians brought their boats up the Severn and traded for iron bars with the men of the forest. These are the men who began a long tradition, the tradition of the Free Miners of the Forest, which continues to this day. They decided their own affairs, meeting at the Speech Place in the forest centre. A hunting lodge was built on the spot in the seventeenth century; it later became a hotel but carries the name Speech House, and the foresters still meet there. The ancient mines also remain, and one group, the Clearwell Caves, has been opened up. This is a series of inter-connected chambers, some of great antiquity, some comparatively modern. There is the Bat Passage, winter home to a variety of snoozing bats, and Chain Ladder Cave, where an old metal ladder leads down into an apparently impenetrable void. Something of the workings of the old mines can also be seen. A blackened roof tells of fire setting, a technique used in the days before the invention of explosives. A fire was lit against the rock and when the rock was red-hot, water was dashed against it. The sudden cooling cracked the stone, but it also filled the cavern with smoke and steam, making life very unpleasant for the miners. The smoke has gone, but the blackened roof remains. The caves can be explored along lit passages, but there is also another form of exploration for special parties, who are taken down into the lower depths of the mine. I went with a party of young children who loved every minute of it, and who found it considerably easier to get through some of the narrower gaps than I did. It was most definitely not a route for anyone overweight to follow, but I ranked it as an outstanding underground visit, and I was fascinated by the thought that each level we traversed represented a different level in a history that stretched back over so many centuries.

Moving forward in time and sideways across the country, we come to the Romans and Wales, more especially to the little town of Pumpsaint in Dyfed and the gold mines of Dolaucothi (p163). Britain is not, perhaps, the first country that comes to mind when one thinks about gold mining, but it was once an important part of the national economy. And gold has a great advantage over, say, tin or iron, because only a little is needed to create a great deal of wealth. The importance laid on the local reserves by the Romans is apparent from the huge expenditure of effort and cash that went into the enterprise. The first step in a Roman gold-mining operation was known as 'hushing' – torrents of water were sent pouring down the hillside, washing away the soil to reveal the ore in the rocks beneath. The water came from the Rivers Cothi and Annel. The trouble was that the gold was high up the hillside and the rivers were down in the valley. Aqueducts up to 7 miles (11km) long had to be built to carry the water to the mine. The watercourses can still be traced today. Once the vein of ore was revealed, the miners followed it into the hillside, and the narrow passageways they cut can be explored. Much of what we now see, however, is of a more recent date, representing a reworking of the old veins that began in Victorian times. The exploration of these workings may not have the obvious glamour of following in the footsteps of the Roman miners – or, to be more exact, their Celtic underlings – but they do reach far deeper into the mountain. Inside, a three-dimensional maze appears: ladders lead up and down and passageways point in all directions. Visitors are guided by experts, for without their help one might walk this subterranean world forever. Here, one feels, is an introduction to the real world of mining: no

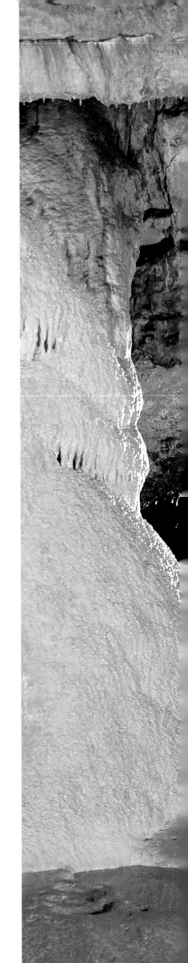

The fantastic formations and underground river of Wookey Hole in Somerset *(Wookey Hole Caves)*

pre-set lighting, no laid-out pedestrian walks, just a complex of routes that was formed by men who followed the gold wherever it led them.

There is an extraordinary variety of mines in Wales in which are found many different minerals. If the principality has never experienced a gold rush, it did have its own silver rush in the middle of the nineteenth century. At that time the Llywernog Silver-Lead Mine was a hub of activity, but even at its peak it was still producing over 8,000 tons of lead for every ton of silver that was extracted. Today, the old mine has been brought back to life. You can walk into the hillside to the workings, where streaks of ore can be seen in the tunnel roof and the Blue Pool – not a fairy grotto but a prospecting pit sunk nearly two hundred years ago – can be viewed. But the underground exploration is only a part of the story; the main emphasis is on the surface remains: the offices, the giant water-wheels that powered pumps to keep the mine dry, machinery for crushing and processing the ore, and a collection of exhibits that tell the story of mining. Visitors learn that mines were more than just holes in the ground: one does not just dig a hole, climb into it, hack out a lump of silver and go home a rich man. The different processes are laid out as a miners' trail: there are over twenty places to pause along the way, either to see things work or to be told how they worked a century ago. There is one odd little building, which looks like an outsize beehive built of stone. This is the gunpowder magazine which is set, not unreasonably, a long way from the rest of the buildings.

The Carnglaze Slate Caverns at St Neot in Cornwall (John L. Rapson)

Big Pit. The underground world of the coal mine, now open to visitors *(Big Pit)*

Hopping briefly across into England and over to the Yorkshire Dales, one can find what must be one of the most attractive gunpowder stores in Britain. This was another great area for lead-mining and over in Arkengarthdale they built a hexagonal stone powder house, which looks for all the world like a small roadside chapel.

Wales had two great mining industries: slate and coal. In Snowdonia, entire mountainsides are carved away in terraces, that rise hundreds of feet above the valley floor. The slate capital is undeniably to be found at Blaenau Ffestiniog. You cannot escape the slate: it is everywhere, shattered mountains of the stuff surround the town. Once the slate was used to roof the houses of Britain. Now composites do the job instead and all that remain are the vast spoil heaps and the old workings. They are now open to tourists and certainly offer the chance of spectacular underground visits. The Llechwedd Slate Caverns can be explored by electric railway or on foot, but the dominating mine of the region is Gloddfa Ganol, in its day the biggest slate mine in the world. It is like a visit to the Hall of the Mountain King, for the hillside is a complex of tunnels and caverns; the visitor has the odd experience of visiting underground workings where you lose not only a sense of direction in terms of left and right, but also in the ups and downs, so that you can see light from the outside world and find yourself emerging high up the hill looking down on to the town. Gloddfa Ganol is more than a mine museum, it is the story of a community that both lived and worked on the mountain. What makes slate mines special is the sheer volume of material that is removed, so that great caves are left behind, as grand as the most popular of natural cave systems.

The Chwarel Wynne Mine in Glyn Ceiriog near Llangollen has a surprising setting, with peacocks strutting around a verdant hill which at first sight seems never to have been disturbed by man. But it too has underground pathways and soaring caverns. It also has a ghost – a man who drowned while checking water levels deep underground. Brian James, owner and mine guide, was telling this story to a party of visitors when a bearded man, caked in mud, emerged from a hole and ran, seemingly naked down a gallery. A longer look revealed that he was wearing somewhat unghostly underpants. He was, in fact, a member of a pot-holing team exploring the old workings who had found a passage through which he could only squeeze by removing his clothes. Brian James says that this is the nearest he has come to seeing an apparition.

There are other slate mines in Wales, and still more in Cornwall, but it would be tedious to list them all, so let us turn from the great industry of North Wales to that of the valleys to the south – coal mining. Until recently, the underground world of the miner was as mysterious to the average person as the Amazon forests or the polar ice-cap. Now, as with slate, a shrinking industry has caused mines to close and to be opened up to visitors. No one should believe that in visiting a mining museum one is experiencing the reality of mining. I remember after a day underground in a working colliery in the English Midlands, telling a miner that I was still blowing coal dust down my nose days later, to which he wryly commented: 'It's what you don't blow out you have to worry about.' Equally, one is amazed by the cramped conditions of some mines. It was another old miner who told me of the first trip underground with his decidedly well-girthed father. They were to work in a seam less than 3ft (1m) high, and he could not understand how his father would manage. 'But,' he said, 'he just chucked his belly up and climbed in after it.' Visitors to mining museums are not required to follow his example, but they do get at least a notion of life in the perpetual velvet blackness of a coal mine. The Big Pit at Blaenavon was a working colliery until 1980 and visitors must still conform to colliery rules – full safety equipment, no matches and nothing to cause a flame. Visitors are dropped by the cage at what seems literally break-neck speed down a 300ft (91m) deep shaft. There are other similar colliery museums elsewhere, each offering something a little different. At Caphouse Colliery, near Wakefield, for example, visitors can see the pit ponies enjoying a new life above ground in the sunlight and fresh air.

Metals of all kind and coal have been extracted from the ground, and there is now a chance to see examples of various workings, as well as some more esoteric substances. At Coalport on the River Severn near Ironbridge, a tar tunnel is just what its name suggests – a tunnel for extracting tar. In Scotland, you can take the preserved Bo'ness and Kinneil Steam Railway to visit the Birkhill Clay Mine. Most gardeners will no doubt feel that they have no need to go down a mine to find clay, but the mine at Birkhill produces special fire clay.

Visitors to the gold mine at Dolaucothi, first worked by the Romans *(Martin Trelawney/National Trust)*

This conjunction of underground visits and transport brings us to the one form of underground exploration we all know – travelling through tunnels. Even here, however, there are some odd things to discover, some of which have already been discussed in Chapter 8, but I will conclude this chapter with a curiosity associated with the great name of Brunel.

In London there is a tunnel that now holds a railway, although it was not built to carry one, along which you can travel for the modest expenditure of the price of a journey from one stop on the London Underground to the next. It runs from Wapping on the north bank of the Thames under the river

to Rotherhithe, and was the first tunnel under the Thames, indeed, the first tunnel under any river. The engineer responsible for this feat was Brunel – not Isambard of railway and bridge fame, but his father Marc. Not that young Isambard was absent from the work, for in fact, it nearly marked the end of his career. When the workings flooded during construction, he came very close to drowning. Constructing the tunnel was a long and costly undertaking, but it proved a triumph for Marc Brunel's revolutionary techniques – even if it was not successful as a roadway. Originally it was intended that a long spiral ramp would carry carriages down to the tunnel, but the money men baulked at funding this idea and the tunnel satisfied the more modest needs of pedestrians until the railways came. However, if you descend the spiral staircase at Wapping Underground, you can see the tunnel with its double-mouthed portals much as it was a hundred years ago, and London Transport have provided excellent explanatory panels. At the far end, the Brunel Exhibition Project has found a home in the building that stands over the old access shaft, and inside the steam engine is being restored. It is good to see the memory of Marc Brunel being honoured, for he was, if not quite the genius that his son proved to be, an engineer of exceptional ingenuity and skill.

Entertain-ments and Diversions

THIS chapter is not about entertaining activities as such, but rather a look at some of the more interesting and unusual places where people go for amusement and pleasure. The theatre has a long history that stretches back into antiquity, and the oldest theatre in Britain is Verulamium, modern St Albans. There were, of course, amphitheatres for games, and one at least has a very long history indeed. Maumbury Rings on the edge of Dorchester began as a henge, a circular bank standing over 10ft (3m) high with a ditch inside, constructed in the new Stone Age. A couple of thousand of years or so later, the Romans used it for games and less edifying spectacles. After the Romans, the Rings had a somewhat chequered fate, and later still the site was used as a gun emplacement during the English Civil War. In 1766, it was the site of one last, brutal ritual. Mary Channing was found guilty of poisoning her husband, and she was taken to the Rings, where, before a large crowd, she was strangled and her body burned.

After that bloodthirsty beginning, perhaps it is time to turn to theatres where ladies who are strangled turn up again to take a bow at the end of the last act. We all know what ancient theatres look like, in the Roman empire or Greece: great tiers of seats rising up above a stage, and all open to the elements. Paradoxically, the nearest thing that Britain can boast to a theatre of this type is the Minack, near Porthcurno in Cornwall. A twentieth-century creation, it was the brainchild of Miss Rowena Cade. Set half-way down the cliffs, the seats rise in a semicircle from the stage, which has been created in a natural dip in the rocks. The stage area is flat with a spectacular back drop, for there is a steep fall down to the sea which beats a regular accompaniment at the bottom of the cliffs to whatever is being

An arena used for Stone Age rites, Roman entertainments – and a public execution: Maumbury Rings, Dorchester *(Anthony Burton)*

played above. As anyone who has played at the Minack or come to a performance can testify, it combines the unique atmosphere of an open-air theatre with superb acoustics. It is also prey to the rigours of a British summer.

During the 1960s, there was a memorable performance of *Macbeth* at the Minack. Not one, but two, separate storms could be seen raging out over the sea. Their timing was immaculate: no sooner had a witch appeared mumbling about eye of newt and other delicacies, than thunder would crash and lightning would streak the sky! But the weather saved its most dramatic effect for the end. The producer had arranged for a small army of extras, clutching sizeable clumps of trees to approach the stage along one of the narrow cliff paths. They were none too keen at the best of times, but on this occasion they were half-way to the stage when man-made electric supplies lost the battle with the electrical storms above, and the lights went out all over the tip of Cornwall. The petrified stage army was helped to safety by members of the audience who had sensibly brought their own flashlights. The performance, sadly, was at an end, and one began to see why so many open-air theatres were built around the Mediterranean and so few in Britain.

The Georgian Theatre in Richmond, Yorkshire, has had almost as varied a career as the Maumbury Rings. Built by the actor-manager, Samuel Butler, in 1788, the Butler family ran the theatre until 1830. Then it went into decline and was used for various activities: as wine vaults, an auction room, a corn chandler's and finally as a salvage depot. Restoration work began in 1960 and now it is a perfect jewel – intimate, highly decorated and full of atmosphere. The Georgian period was an age which favoured elegant restraint; the same could scarcely be said of the Victorians who followed later. The great Victorian theatres are masterpieces of over-the-top opulence. Many cities can boast of the splendour of their Victorian theatres: Leeds, for example, has the sumptuous Grand and the lively City of Varieties, but it is Newcastle upon Tyne which can make the strongest claim to own something really special.

The Theatre Royal, which was opened in 1788, closed and then reopened on a new site in the elegant Grey Street in 1837. It was destroyed by fire after a performance of *Macbeth* – yet another disaster associated with that ill-famed play – in 1899 and was rebuilt by one of the great names in theatre architecture, Frank Matcham. The exterior of the building was preserved, but inside a new auditorium in a sumptuous French Renaissance style was built. In the 1980s it was restored and enlarged in a way that has added modern facilities but kept the old atmosphere and style – and, even, one can reasonably say, improved them. The Theatre Royal is a work of grandeur, but its old rival the Tyne Theatre and Opera House has something which even the Royal cannot match: a full complement of original stage machinery, restored to its condition when it was installed in the theatre in 1867. It was this machinery that enabled the theatre to stage spectacular effects. Scenery can come up through the stage on lifts, be rolled in from the wings or descend more conventionally from the flies. What spectacles they were! In 1888 *Pleasure* featured an earthquake; the next year *The Armada* had 32 tons of scenery that needed nine railway wagons to bring it to the theatre, and had a grand finale in which a Spanish galleon was sunk by English fire-ships. But the finest show of all must have been *The Prodigal Daughter* of 1887 in which the Grand National was featured. Turf was laid, a water jump created on stage and the starring role was taken by 'Voluptuary', a genuine National winner. Spectacular transformation scenes are still staged at The Tyne – but I doubt if they will ever run the National again. But what a joy the old machinery is; it includes the thunder-roll, a sloping metal tube with kinks in it, down which cannon balls are rolled to create the sound of thunder. The balls are now contained in the run by iron hoops, following a tragedy in 1887 when one fell out and killed a carpenter on the stage below.

The Bristol Hippodrome may not be able to match the Tyne Theatre for stage machinery, but it does have a most intriguing ventilation system. All regular theatre-goers know how stifling a summer evening can become, as hundreds of bodies begin gently to glow in the heat. Modern air-conditioning could be the answer, but why not simply let out all the hot air during the interval? At the top of the Bristol Hippodrome is a dome which is not quite as solid as it appears. It is, in fact, lightweight and can be winched away to open up a large hole in the roof through which the hot air escapes. A similar device might profitably be introduced into the House of Commons.

Hambledon, Hampshire The Bat and Ball Inn is a reminder of the famous Hambledon Cricket Club.

Kinloch, Isle of Rhum Kinloch Castle, an Edwardian mock castle in the grandest of styles; it is now a hotel.

Norwich, Norfolk The Maddermarket Theatre is a replica of an Elizabethan playhouse.

Phillack, Cornwall The Bucket of Blood pub received its name from a gruesome story. The landlord drew the blood from his well after a headless corpse had been dumped there.

Soham, Cambridgeshire A steelyard can be seen at the rear of the Fountain Inn.

Tinsley Green, West Sussex Home to the marbles rink where the national championship is held.

Welford-on-Avon, Warwickshire The Four-All pub has a four-all, not a four-ale bar. The stained glass window shows 'Fight All, Pray All, Rule All, Pay All'.

The Minack theatre, carved out of the Cornish cliffs (Anthony Burton)

An alternative design for keeping the audience comfortable can be seen not in a theatre, but in a concert hall, one of the grandest in the country – St George's Hall in Liverpool. A competition was held in 1839 for designs for two new concert halls to be housed in one building, which had to be in the classical style. The winner, Harvey Lonsdale Elmes, had also won a competition for designing new assize courts, so he simply designed the courts and concert halls together in one huge Corinthian temple. The main concert hall is stunning: giant Doric columns, a frieze with devices borrowed from the Elgin marbles, colourful tiles by Minton and ten chandeliers, each of which now holds over a hundred light bulbs. Dominating everything is the massive organ. What is not so obvious is the ingenious 'air conditioning system'. Hollow tiles in the floor and outlets hidden in ceiling panels allowed air to be blown in by steam-powered fans. In winter, the air was passed over hot-water pipes, in summer it was drawn in from the streets, cooled by fountains.

Some theatres in use today began as buildings of a very different

character. In the days when Manchester was the cotton-trading capital of the world, the Manchester Exchange had eleven thousand members and twice a week they packed the Great Hall to deal or simply exchange notes on the state of trade. It was so crowded that there was a coded system for rendezvous: the pillars around the hall have either numbers or letters. They were used as map references by traders who would arrange to meet at C6, a point on the floor where an imaginary line drawn out from column C met one from column 6. As trade faltered, the Exchange dwindled and eventually closed. It was an important building, but how could it be used without destroying what was there? The extraordinary solution was a theatre, looking exactly like an oversized spaceship, a steel monster that squats in the middle of High Victorian splendour. Other changes of use elsewhere have not been quite so dramatic. One of the famous landmarks of Glasgow is the Tron Steeple, a tall tower that stands isolated in the middle of the street. It was built in 1637 and survived the fire of 1793 which removed the church to which it was once attached. A new Tron church was built, which is now a theatre, a conversion which has kept much of the character of the old building intact. The same cannot be said of the Little Theatre at Chipping Norton in Oxfordshire, which was once the Salvation Army Citadel. 'Little' is certainly the operative word, for the theatre has a tiny stage and a small auditorium – which does not prevent the staging of ambitious productions, even if, for example, *Don Giovanni* has an 'orchestra' reduced to one player. The original occupants of the theatre might just about have tolerated the sounds of Mozart – he did, after all, compose some remarkably stirring tunes and the wicked Don ends up descending to the Inferno – but what would they think of a bar in the old Citadel? The Little Theatre is small but not the smallest theatre in Britain. That title is claimed by the Mull Little Theatre. Housed in what looks remarkably like an overgrown garden shed, an audience of thirty-six represents a full house. The total company – administration, direction, acting, stage management – amounts to two people.

Many theatres went into decline once the cinema began to gain in popularity, just as the cinema in its turn suffered from the advent of television. So, just as old theatres have been restored, so too the oldest cinemas are re-emerging. The Electric Palace in Harwich was purpose-built as a cinema in 1911, so that it can now proudly claim to be the oldest unaltered cinema in Britain. It is appropriate that it should be in Harwich, home of the pioneer of cinematography, William Friese-Green, who built the first practical movie camera in 1889. Oxford's Electra Cinema was opened in 1913, and it had a peculiar rule that members of the university would only be admitted to the most expensive seats – whether this was to preserve delicate undergraduates from contamination by the brutish lower orders, to keep the sober citizens clear of rowdy undergraduates, or simply to ensure a larger profit is now uncertain. In any case, the cinema no longer exists, but the city does possess two splendidly idiosyncratic cinemas. *The Last Picture Show* became something of a cult movie in the seventies, but

A pair of legs can-cans out over the entrance to Oxford's Not the Moulin Rouge cinema
(Anthony Burton)

Oxford took a step further back to provide its citizens with The Penultimate Picture Palace. It announces its presence to the world by the best known attributes of Al Jolson – a pair of white gloved hands that are spread out, no doubt to Mammy, sprout from the entrance. Inside there is a conventional cinema – conventional, that is, excepting the fact that the owner does not clutter the screen with endless adverts and pleas to patrons to eat the popcorn. There is, however, one good joke at the expense of the best known of cinema advertisers : the 'Ladies' and 'Gents' signs on either side of the screen are labelled, respectively, Pearl and Dean. The same company took over a second cinema, the Moulin Rouge, which had a somewhat seedy reputation and was largely frequented by shady gentlemen in long raincoats. To announce its change of ownership and policy the cinema was given a new name: 'Not the Moulin Rouge'. Not much problem here about deciding on a symbol – two fetchingly gartered legs can-can their way out of the façade. Another curious fact about the cinema also poses an interesting problem should the management ever employ a female projectionist – the only entrance to the projection box is through the Gents!

The three-dimensional sign has a long history. In medieval times, every tradesman had his own identifying symbol, but the practice was only kept on by a very few. The chemist's shop may still have its pestle and mortar, the clock- and watchmaker his timepiece, and at Dyson's of Leeds Old Father Time himself looks down from above an ornate clock. Then there is the barber's pole, striped red and white to signify the blood and bandages of the barber-surgeons. But one group of signs proliferates still in tremendous variety: the pub sign. It is so well known that it can easily be ignored, yet many are fascinating, colourful and have their own stories to tell. So, here is a selection of pubs, their names and their signs.

One should, logically, start with the oldest pub in Britain – but which is it? Does one mean the oldest building which is now a pub, or the building that has been a pub the longest? How does one deal with the pub that has been changed so much over the centuries that little, if anything, of the original remains?

The Fighting Cocks at St Albans has probably existed since the eighth century, but not always as a pub. It was, according to the local stories, rebuilt after 'The Flood' though they conspicuously fail to mention which flood. In fact, it was originally used as the abbey dovecote and was not

Pub signs can tell a story. The City Arms, Minera in North Wales recalls the nearby City Mine *(Anthony Burton)*

even built on its present site. It became an inn at the dissolution of the monasteries, when it was renamed The Round House, although it is actually octagonal. The shape, however, made it ideal for cock-fighting, hence its present name. The Trip to Jerusalem in Nottingham, on the other hand, is a relative upstart from the twelfth century, but a good deal of the original building does remain, including the cellars that are carved out of the rock on which the castle stands. There are three good reasons for paying it a visit: it is very old, it has a good deal of its old character left, and it sells decent ale. Then there is The Royal Standard of England at Forty Green in Buckinghamshire. Apart from its claim to old age, there is the curious fact that it was originally called The Ship and still boasts ships' timbers and furnishings. But what on earth is a Ship doing in the middle of rural Buckinghamshire? At least there is no argument over which is the smallest pub in Britain. The Smith's Arms at Godmanstone in Dorset was originally, as the name suggests, a smithy. The story goes that Charles II stopped there to have his horse shod and demanded a beer while he was waiting. The smith explained that he had no licence to sell ale, at which point the king demonstrated one of the advantages of royalty by promptly granting a licence and getting his ale. Perhaps we should follow that with the pub with the shortest name: a pub sign in Garstang simply bears the letters 'XL', but its name is really the Excel, so it does not count. In East Anglia, the pleasant town of Whittlesey has a hostelry named simply the letter 'B'. It once had companions 'A', 'C' and 'D' but they have gone leaving only B behind. No one appears to have any explanation for this curious licensed lexicon, other than paucity of imagination.

The days of really impressive inn signs are sadly gone. The White Hart at Scole in Norfolk still stands, and very pleasant it is too, but its sign has long since gone. How sad that is, for it stretched right across the road, it showed the hunting of a hart and featured twenty-five life-sized figures. It was said to have cost the landlord the equivalent of a hundred thousand pints of ale. Such massive signs were known as 'gallows signs' – a morbid nomenclature, but sadly too apt. In 1718 the sheer weight of one inn sign pulled down the whole wall and crushed two passers-by to death. The grandest survivor from the age of grand signs, which still stretches across the road, can be seen at The George at Stamford.

Signs, as well as being impressive, can also tell stories, and here are just a few, in no particular order. The fascination lies, often enough, in a certain ambiguity. Is, for example, the famous Elephant and Castle of London really anything to do with Cockneys not knowing their jumbos from their infantas or is it simply a link with a guild insignia, the mark of the cutlers? Sometimes, one just does not want to know any more, simply because what little one knows is so gloriously improbable. The Baladud Arms is, according to *The Good Beer Guide*, named after 'a local swineherd and prince who cured himself and his pigs of leprosy'. The Drunken Duck at Barngates has an amusing, if improbable, story to account for its name. Many years ago a landlady came out of her door to find all her ducks inexplicably dead. A lady of frugal habits, she was not one to turn sentimental, so she vigorously set about plucking them. The last feather had just about floated to the floor, when feeble quacks were heard. A search revealed a leaking barrel: the landlady's ducks were not dead, but merely drunk. Overcome by remorse at the sight of the naked quackers, she knitted them all little jackets to keep them warm until their feathers grew again – and the pub was given a new name.

The Flying Monk of Malmesbury was a man possessed, it is said, of such strong faith that he believed he could fly and he launched himself into space from the upper storeys of the abbey. Gravity proved stronger than faith, though whether it was the force of gravity as discovered by Isaac Newton or the gravity of the ale in the pub is a matter of debate, and now the monk flies only across the sign of the pub named after him.

Other signs have simpler, but no less interesting, stories to tell, often providing an insight into local history. Visitors to The City Arms at Minera in North Wales might wonder what such an isolated spot has to do with any city – in fact the city referred to is the old City Lead Mine, long since defunct. The memory of those working days, however, is kept alive in the pub's splendid bas-relief sign. The City Arms has a fine collection of these

A candidate for the title of Britain's oldest pub: the Trip to Jerusalem in Nottingham *(City of Nottingham)*

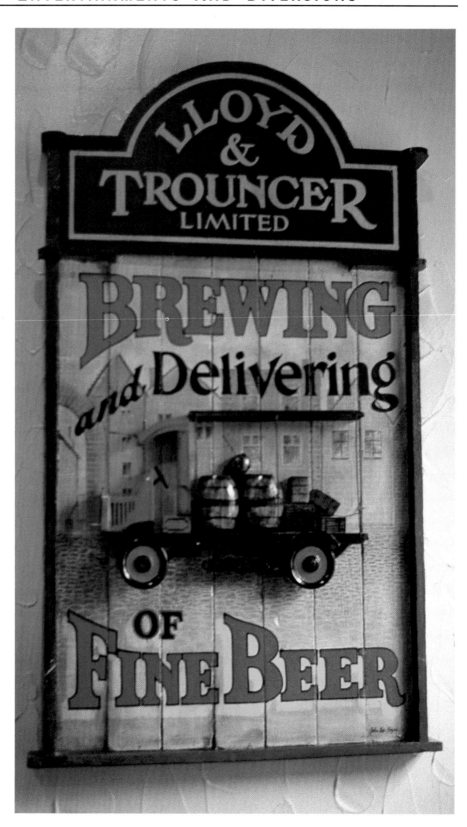

At their best, pub and
brewery signs can be works
of art *(Anthony Burton)*

signs and, add to that the pub's very own brewery, and you end up with a spot very well worth visiting. Other pubs have similar tales to tell of the vanished past. The Railway Inn at Abingdon stands near the site of the old station, which is now disused, and when the last train ran in 1984 the tracks were taken as well. The pub sign shows the railway in its heyday as part of the Great Western Railway empire, when trains ran on the broad-gauge track, with rails set 7ft apart instead of the standard 4ft 8½in of today. So, the past is preserved in paint if not in reality. The Old Station Inn at Blackmoor Gate scarcely needs its sign, for it is not standing close to the site of the old station – it *is* the old station. Once serving the passengers of one of the country's most delightful little railways, the Lynton & Barnstaple, it now serves beer. Sometimes the railway connection is by no means obvious. The North Star at Steventon takes its name from a famous Great Western Railway locomotive that is painted on the sign, but there is a little more to the explanation than that. This traditional country pub, with its high-backed settles that line the tiny bar rooms, was once the waiting place for travellers to and from Oxford, before the railway reached that city. It is easy still to imagine a roomful of disgruntled dons complaining that no coach was on hand to meet the 7.18 from Swindon.

The canal world, too, has its share of old associations. Nottingham has a comparatively new pub – near the very old Trip to Jerusalem – called Fellows, Morton & Clayton. FMC, as they were always known to the canal world, were famous carriers, with one of the biggest fleets of canal boats in Britain. The pub is, in fact, a converted warehouse which, by carrying through the canal theme from name to decoration, has helped to keep an old tradition alive. The Old Bell and Steelyard at Woodbridge in Suffolk needs no sign to advertise itself, for the steelyard, which resembles a great gallows, constructed from solid, sturdy timbers, rises to the full height of the building. It is, in fact, a machine for weighing waggons, on the principle whereby a weight was moved along the arm until it balanced.

Occasionally one stumbles across a good story by accident. Travelling on the Shrewsbury–Wrexham road, I spotted a sign to Myddle. There is a splendid book, written by Richard Gough around 1700, called *The History of Myddle*, a sort of seventeenth-century equivalent of 'The Archers', full of the minutiae of everyday life. I knew the book, but had never seen the village, so I turned off the main road to take lunch in the village pub. I remarked to the landlord that I did not imagine the pub could be in the book – but it was. It seemed that one villager was first an inefficient carpenter, then an equally unsuccessful carrier, and for his third trade as a builder, he pulled down a barn and rebuilt it as a house, 'and there he sold ale'. Look at the pub today and you can still see that the part next to the road is a timber-framed building with a separate stone building added on later. To divert slightly, this business of moving buildings around seems to have been quite common in Myddle, and still goes on elsewhere today. When, for example, Coventry lost so many ancient buildings during the bombing raids of World War II, it was decided to collect many of the surviving structures and to make Spon Street into a 'new' medieval street.

Everyone has their favourite pubs and pub signs, and one could produce pages full of examples, but here is a small personal selection. The first is The Philharmonic in Liverpool. It was built between 1898 and 1900, and the architect gave out the job of decorating the place to students from the local art school. They went at their task with a will. Art nouveau was all the rage at the time, so the arch over the entrance is decorated with all kinds of writhing shapes and forms, including, inevitably, at least one liver bird. The interior matches the entrance with no surface left undecorated. Panelling and tiles, pillars and glass all get the full treatment – and nowhere escapes. The Gents is justly famous for its palatial porcelain. It is

What is odd about the Olde Leathern Bottle at Goring? Nothing it seems, until you notice the life-sized figure sitting cross-legged above the window *(Anthony Burton)*

The extravagant art nouveau entrance to Liverpool's Philharmonic pub *(Anthony Burton)*

tempting to digress at this point, since there is a strong natural connection between pubs and loos, but I shall do no more than to recommend the streets of Birmingham to devotees of the decorative cast-iron urinal. The Olde Leathern Bottle by the Thames at Goring has just one really good quirky detail. Passers-by tend to do a double take when they see a gentleman in old-fashioned dress sat cross-legged on a flat roof. However, it is not the pub ghost – simply a very convincing three-dimensional pub sign.

One cannot leave the subject of pubs without mentioning at least one haunted inn. The Ring o' Bells in Halifax stands, as the name suggests, next to the parish church. It is a pleasant, unassuming inn where one is likely to take stories of ghostly visitations with more than a little solid Yorkshire scepticism. But landlord and landlady were equally insistent that they, too, had been sceptics, until the ghost – who goes by the improbable name of 'Wally' – started to play tricks on them. For those who are still not convinced, scepticism tends to fade if they visit the old stone flagged cellar, for there, let into the wall among the other plain slabs, is a gravestone. Whose it is or how it came to be in a pub cellar remains an intriguing mystery.

At the beginning of this chapter, it was said that this would not be a

Comrie in Scotland is a town of excellent, hand-painted signs. The delights of the local toy shop are displayed by a sign, showing the doll's house on one side, and its crowded rooms on the other
(Anthony Burton)

discussion of entertaining pastimes as such, but about objects. So although to the non-initiate, cricket might seem the most curious of pastimes, there will be no mention here of the sport other than to record that the village of Hambledon, where the rules were first formalised, has a fine crop of cricketing inn signs. But it is impossible to resist mentioning the emergence – or re-emergence – of one of the most bizarre of all pub games, dwyle flunking. It is either a new invention by a modern idiot or a very old invention by an ancient idiot, for idiotic it certainly is. There are rules, although few seem to know them, and as any game involves the consumption of vast quantities of ale, those who knew them at the beginning of the game can seldom remember them at the end. In essence, dwyle flunking involves one team dancing around a member of the opposite side, who holds a beer-soaked sponge at the end of a broom handle. The sponge is flicked at the dancing team and points are scored according to the part of the anatomy that has been hit. Any thrower failing to score a hit must down a large quantity of ale, usually from a chamber pot. It is not unknown for both teams to end the evening insensible – which goes down in the books as an honourable draw. Few other results have ever been recorded.

Finally, to show that games have not always been a frivolous occupation, let us look at a sport that was designed to foster the skills of the cavalryman: tilting at the quintain. There is only one surviving quintain in Britain, and it stands on the village green at Offham in Kent. It consists of a high wooden post, on top of which is pivoted a board, one end of which is marked with five rows of dots and from the other end of which is suspended a heavy bag of sand. The object was for the horseman to gallop at full speed and attempt to strike the dotted end of the board. He was jeered at if he missed the board, but his troubles were not over if he did hit it, for unless he was agile the board would swing around and the sandbag knock him off his horse. Tilting the quintain thus provided a splendid training in both attack and defence, and kept everyone amused at the same time. The quintain is an unlikely survivor from a former age, and it is still used on May Day, although the sandbag has been replaced by a bucket of water. This is only one of many May Day customs, and other equally strange customs are still continued in other places and on other days.

Calendar of Curiosities

Alciston, East Sussex
Locals skip on the ancient barrows each Good Friday.

Alnwick, Northumberland
Shrovetide football is played starting with a procession from Alnwick Castle.

Atherstone, Warwickshire
Shrovetide football is played on Shrove Tuesday afternoon along the main street.

Bacup, Lancashire The Coconut Dancers clog dance in bizarre apparel.

Derby Easter eggs are rolled on Bunker's Hill.

Edinburgh Arthur's Seat is the scene of egg rolling at Easter.

Hallaton, Leicestershire On Easter Monday a hare pie is shared out followed by a game of bottle kicking.

Hinton St George, Somerset Punkie Night on the last Thursday in October is the occasion for a parade of turnip lanterns.

FOLK customs are themselves somewhat curious things; curious because they survive long after their original significance has been lost. Up and down the country, at summer fairs, on special occasions and at informal events, apparently sane men, and rather less frequently women, dress up in white, tie bells to their legs and leap up and down waving handkerchiefs. Most of us are now fairly used to Morris dancers but just try explaining their cavortings to a foreign visitor. Why do Morris men do it? One assumes that they are not serious believers in pagan rituals. There is a definite wish in some people, it seems, to keep a tradition going, simply because it is a tradition, and particularly if it is a local tradition. There are more rational explanations available: Morris dancing is good exercise, a bit like aerobics with better music; or, to take a different view, it provides a fine excuse for downing several pints of beer afterwards – the Morris seems to have particularly strong connections with licensed premises! The most telling reason, however, seems to be that it is simply good fun, bringing colour and a touch of welcome eccentricity to the community. So, even if no one seriously believes that there are evil spirits to drive away or gods to placate, old customs survive, each with its own special time and place. So here is a calendar of selected customs to take us through the year.

We could start on 6 January at Haxey on Humberside, although to the locals this is not towards the end of the first week of a new year, but Christmas Day of the last one. The people of Haxey have simply ignored the 'new' calendar of 1752, and kept the old one so that they can play the ancient Hood Game. The ceremony starts with a Fool accompanied by twelve boggars – this makes up the official 'team'. The Fool is allowed to kiss any woman he meets while the boggars are busy getting bruised and muddied, suggesting that although he may be a Fool, he is certainly no fool. He does, however, have to suffer in the cause as well, since before the game begins, he has to make a speech to the crowd, reminding them of the

May morning Morris
dancers outside the
Radcliffe Camera, Oxford
(Oxford Mail)

Jedburgh Jethart Ba', the traditional ball game is played on Candlemas Day and Shrove Tuesday, the latter a movable feast.
Olney, Buckinghamshire A pancake race is held here every Shrove Tuesday.
Penrith, Cumbria Easter eggs are rolled in the castle moat.
Preston, Lancashire Egg rolling takes place every Easter at Avenham Park.
St Columb Major, Cornwall 'Hurling', a hand ball-game is played on Shrove Tuesday.
St Ives, Cambridgeshire Each Whitsun local children dice for bibles on the church steps.
Sedgefield, Durham Communal football is played on Shrove Tuesday.
Stonehouse, Grampian A fireball parade is held on New Year's Eve.
Tissington, Derbyshire On Ascension Day, well dressing of five wells in the town takes place. Tissington has the longest tradition of well dressing, but other Derbyshire towns have followed the tradition.
Welford-on-Avon, Warwickshire has a 70ft (21m) striped maypole.
Workington, Cumbria A communal game of football is played on Good Friday and on the following Tuesday and Saturday.

simple rules of play, which amount to little more than 'every man for himself' and if anyone gets in your way knock him over. While the Fool delivers this speech, a fire is lit behind him, but suitably damped down so that he is soon enveloped in smoke. In former times he was actually suspended over the fire by a rope. The game can now begin.

The hoods are not hoods at all, but bundles of canvas, or, in the case of the main hood for the main game, a piece of thick rope bound in leather. The object of the game is to get the hood to one of the goals – in this case, pubs. As the hood cannot be kicked or thrown forward, the huge, heaving crowd tries to go in several directions at the same time. Eventually, they reach one of the pubs and that hostelry then holds the prize for a year. Many theories have been put forward to explain the origins of this strange pastime, but no one now remembers why the game is played every year.

Old Calendar Christmas Day is followed on 11 January by Old Calendar New Year's Eve, which brings us to Burghead in Grampian and the Burning of the Clavie. The Clavie itself is similar to a great torch, which is prepared and lit according to rigid rules. The basic holder is made up of a barrel bottom nailed to a long pole. Strict rules are applied in making the holder: the pole or spoke must be a salmon fisherman's stake; the nail is specially forged for the occasion and hammered into place with a stone instead of the conventional hammer. The container is strengthened by the addition of parts of a herring barrel, and the clavie is filled with wood from the same barrel that forms the firebasket. The whole assembly is controlled by a Clavie King, who has the responsibility of ensuring that everything follows the correct pattern. When evening comes burning peat is brought out from one of the cottages, the clavie is lit and then smothered in tar so that flames shoot up to the sky. It is carried in procession to a headland where it is set on a special stone pillar. After it has burned for a while, the clavie is smashed into pieces, at which there is a mad rush for the smouldering fragments which are supposed to bring good luck. It might be thought of as a ceremony to bless the New Year, but originally it marked an end, not a beginning – the end of the old year.

A far more famous ceremony marks the end of Yule in the Shetland Islands – Up-Helly-Aa, which falls on twenty-fourth night, now reckoned as the last Tuesday in January. It is another of the festivals which attracts national attention, although mostly through television coverage. Early summer visitors might swell the crowds for the Maytime celebrations in Cornwall, but fewer people are prepared to make a winter excursion to the Shetlands. The festival has changed a good deal over the centuries but in its present form it emphasises the islands' connections with the Norsemen who settled here more than a thousand years ago. The model of a Viking long boat, some 30ft (9m) long, is constructed and dragged through the streets by torch bearers in Viking costume. At the climax of the ceremony, the torches are hurled into the boat and the result of a year's work goes up in flames. As the boat burns, the crowd sings a Norse song, and then the next stage of the proceedings begins – dancing, singing and a fair bit of drinking. So the old year ends and continuity with the Norse past is retained.

Shrove Tuesday was the traditional time for football matches, in the days when football was an activity in which the whole community took part, in a general free-for-all. Games were played all over the country; there was seldom any limit to the number of players, frequently no time limit set for the playing, and few rules for anyone to worry about. The only certainty was that there should be a ball and some goals. The most energetic of the surviving games must be that played at Ashbourne in Derbyshire, between the Up'ards and the Down'ards. The dividing line between the two teams is a brook, and as you live either to the north or to the south of it, so you have the two teams. The goals are mills, set 3 miles (5km) apart and at 2 o'clock in the afternoon the game gets under way. It continues through the afternoon and frequently into the evening as the players splash their way through the brook and other streams until they eventually reach one of the goals. It is all such good fun that they come out and do it all over again the next day.

Some places have rather more peaceful Shrovetide occupations. The people of Scarborough have the pleasant notion that the best way to celebrate the occasion is to go down on to the shore and skip. At noon, a bell is rung and everyone meanders down, in their own good time, for a little skipping practice. There was a time when skipping had a magical, ritual meaning and skippers would travel to particular sites, often very ancient ones, such as burial mounds. It is not difficult to see the connection between the traditional magic circles and an activity which involves making great circles in the air through which the participant must jump.

The first day of March brings us to Lanark and Whuppity Stourie or Scourie. The bells of the local parish church are rung, and the local children, armed with home-made weapons of paper balls on strings, pursue each other three times around the church, beating each other over the head as they go. That completed, the town officials, who have been watching the proceedings from the safety of a raised platform, throw down handfuls of pennies and the children all dive in for what they can grab. Once the weapons were rather more potent – screwed-up hats and caps – while the participants were also a good deal larger. The grand finale is a battle between the lads of Lanark and those of New Lanark, but because New Lanark was only built in the eighteenth century, and the custom goes back further than that, there must have been earlier 'battles' fought between other factions.

Good Friday, at the other end of the Lenten fast from Shrove Tuesday, has many games associated with it. It also marks the end of the marbles season. Those who think of marbles as a game for small children have clearly never been to Tinsley Green in West Sussex on Championship Day. Good Friday sees teams from all over the country competing not just for the local nor even the national championship, but for what is generally regarded as the world marbles championship. The centre of activity is the circular rink where the coloured glass balls are propelled towards their targets. It is a very serious matter.

The week after Easter, on the two days following Low Sunday, once saw some of the year's most boisterous feasting. This was Hocktide, which is all but forgotten now, but still an important time in the affairs of Hungerford in Berkshire. Hungerford is one of those towns which, instead of being run by a mayor and a corporation, is controlled by a sheriff or constable and court. The officials are always elected at a Hocktide Court, in a proper and solemn ceremony, while elsewhere in the town other activities are carried out which, if they are not improper, are at least a good deal less solemn. Two Tutti-men and an Orange Scrambler set off on a tour of the city. The Tutti-men were the old town wardens who kept watch throughout the year and collected their dues of a penny per head at Hocktide. They each carry staffs decorated with ribbons and flowers and topped with an orange. Fully arrayed, they set off to claim their dues, although the women of the house have the right to offer a kiss instead of a penny. If the kiss is accepted, an orange is offered in return. The Orange Scrambler has the busy task of sticking new oranges on the staffs. Kisses are also demanded of non-Hungerfordians who happen to take the Tutti-men's fancy. The morning ends with a luncheon at the Three Swans, presided over by the newly elected Constable, at the end of which the Tutti-men and the Scrambler shower down the remaining oranges on a waiting crowd of children. An initiation ceremony also takes place, but it is strictly reserved for Hungerford men and those who are about to join the community. Like all the best ceremonies, Hocktide at Hungerford still retains significance for the local community and it has not degenerated into a mere show.

May Day is one of the great festival days in the calendar. There are many May Day customs which are peculiar to particular places, but perhaps the most common is that of dancing around the maypole. Nowadays, it is regarded as a charming entertainment, as often as not performed by the children of the local primary school. The maypole is usually a manufactured one that is brought out every year and festooned with ribbons. The children dance, the May Queen and her attendants look on, while proud parents clap enthusiastically and try to understand why that ghastly Mary, who isn't even pretty, was chosen as queen instead of their Jane! This is quite different from earlier May Days when a tree, cut especially that morning, was trimmed and brought to the green for the dancing that celebrated the arrival of spring. It was such an obviously pagan ritual that it inevitably attracted the displeasure of the Puritans who, whenever they had the opportunity, banned the practice. Some communities had permanent maypoles, and many of these were destroyed. Of course, they came back eventually, but there are now few places where the maypole can be seen all the year round. This is rather a shame, because they were often very impressive and brightly coloured. Visitors to Barwick-in-Elmet in West Yorkshire can see the country's tallest

maypole at 86ft (26m), rising high above the village square. The locals who decorate it each year need a good head for heights.

We may have long since given up the pagan beliefs which are at the heart of May Day celebrations, but down in the West Country at least they still act as if it all matters. The best known and most popular of all the May Day ceremonies takes place at Padstow in Cornwall. The ceremony starts on the eve of May Day, when the Mayers go from house to house throughout the town, serenading the inhabitants – flattering the lady of the house with a traditional song of good fortune and inviting her to join the celebration of the coming of summer:

> Rise up, Mrs – all in your gown of green,
> For Summer is i-comin' in today.
> You are as fair a lady as waits upon the Queen,
> In the merry month of May.

The male members of the household have a similar song sung for their benefit, similar except that the words of the third line are changed to a clear hint that they are expected to dip their hands into their pockets to pay for the compliments to their ladies:

> You've a shilling in your pocket, and I wish it were in mine.

Any suggestions that the references to coinage should be decimalised have so far been resisted and one hopes that we shall never hear 'You've five pee in your pocket' being sung in the streets of Padstow. There are many verses and many variations, but all contain that essential reference to the merry month which heralds the coming of summer.

The following morning sees the arrival of the Hobby Horse. The man who acts the part of the horse must be fit and especially strong in stamina. His costume consists of a large hoop, about 6ft (2m) in diameter, which is covered by a tarpaulin, on the front of which is a horse's head. The man inside is almost invisible, his face being covered by a mask while a tall hat crowns his head. Accompanied by another strange figure, the Club Man, who wears a variety of strange clothes and carries a special soft club, the Hobby Horse sets off in the early morning for his dance around Padstow.

The horse whirls and gyrates through the streets, occasionally pausing to submerge a young woman under its voluminous skirt. The young ladies who are enveloped in this way are assured of a husband or, if they are already married, children. From time to time, the horse drops down as though it is dead, and a dirge is sung over it, but when the May song is resumed, he leaps back to life and the dancing continues. Apart from providing a welcome respite for the horse, it is an obvious symbol of the annual cycle of death and renewal. The Hobby Horse, with its great crowd of followers, dances through the morning and into the afternoon, when the day ends at the brightly decorated maypole in the market square. A similar

custom takes place at Minehead in Somerset, where the Hobby Horse is known as the Sailor's Horse and lives by the sea.

The Padstow Horse is now a popular tourist attraction, and people might believe that it is the Hobby Horse's popularity that ensures the survival of the custom. But, as anyone who has been to Padstow on May Day can tell you, there is another explanation. Although tourists line the route to watch, the ceremony itself is not for them; they are always spectators, never participants. The Hobby Horse is Padstow's Hobby Horse, and one has the feeling that they would go on just as they always have, even if not one tourist turned up – in fact, they might well prefer it that way.

The same is true of another famous Cornish celebration, held not on May Day itself, but on 8 May, the feast day of St Michael the Archangel, patron of the local parish church. Helston's Furry Dance is unlike the Padstow celebrations, however, because the dance involves the whole community. It is not strictly accurate to speak of the Furry Dance, for there are several dances. At 7 o'clock in the morning, the young people dance through the town; later come the children, dressed in white and wearing or carrying lilies-of-the-valley. There is then one main dance when, led by the mayor in full regalia, all the people of Helston join in. The couples are very formally attired, the men traditionally in morning coats and top hats, the women in their best dresses. The couples dance through the streets and on through gardens, shops and houses, bringing good fortune wherever they go. And all the time the band plays the traditional Furry Dance music. At the end of the day any visitors may join in, but for the main dance they must remain as spectators while the natives of Helston perform their own rituals.

Music as well as dance has always been associated with the celebration of May Day. The best known, and certainly the most attractive of May Day musical celebrations, is that of Oxford. You have to be up early in the morning to hear it, but every year thousands are present. The ceremony takes place at 6am prompt at Magdalen College. The college choristers climb to the top of Magdalen tower to sing the hymn *Te Deum Patrem Colimus.* After that the bells ring and Morris dancers, including one of the most famous of all groups, the Headington Men, dance their way down the street. This is the signal for general music-making to begin, with everyone from folk groups to, in recent years, rock bands contributing to a very festive morning. The actual music to be heard on an Oxford May Day morning may not always be traditional, but the idea that everyone can join in the music-making has been part of the Oxford celebrations for a very long time.

Ascension Day, which occurs fifty days after Easter, is one of those fixed

Padstow's May Day: the locals are dressed in their whites, while the two 'osses dance in competition. It is a rare event when the two appear together *(Gill Scott)*

The horn blower announces the planting of Whitby's Penny hedge *(Whitby Archives)*

points in the ecclesiastical year which once had special significance for the community as a whole, but which now go largely unmarked. It is, however, celebrated in Whitby, where on every Ascension Eve the Penny Hedge is planted out as it has been since, it is said, the twelfth century. It was originally a ceremony which ensured that certain tenants of Whitby Abbey could continue in their tenancy. The ceremony originated with a dastardly deed, when three huntsmen chased a boar into a hermit's chapel. The hermit closed the door behind it, at which the infuriated huntsmen beat the old hermit to death. This early and extreme example of the clash between huntsmen and their opponents had long-term effects. Before the hermit died, he forgave his assailants but insisted that, in future, they should hold their lands only as tenants of the abbey, and they would have to reaffirm their rights in an annual ceremony. The pact was sealed, the hermit died and ever since the hedge has been planted on Ascension Eve. A complicating factor is that the hedge must be planted on the shore below high-water mark, and must stand for three tides. When the hedge is completed the Manor bailiff blows a horn and shouts, 'Out upon ye! Out upon ye!', which is said to recall the original incident.

Whit Monday is another occasion for games, although many old

customs have now died, just as Whit Monday itself has gone, to be replaced by the new, dull Spring Bank Holiday. However, some traditional games have survived to be played on the new date, including the most spectacular of them all, cheese rolling on Cooper's Hill at Brockworth in Gloucestershire. The hill is very steep, and the object is to chase after a cheese that has been rolled down the hill, which tends to involve rather more tumbling and rolling than actual running. Surprisingly, serious injuries are rare.

The Arbor Tree ceremony dates back to the ancient British religion of tree worship. Very little of that old cult survives, although it turns up again with Christmas holly and, more especially, the mistletoe bough. At Aston-

The Abbot's Bromley Horn Dance *(British Tourist Authority)*

on-Clun in Shropshire, a tall poplar in the centre of the village is decked out in flags on Arbor Day, 29 May, and the flags remain throughout the year. No one is sure why this is done, but it is generally said locally that it commemorates an eighteenth-century wedding. It most certainly goes back further to tree worship, and the more modern story simply provides a rationale for the custom. It is, after all, somewhat unlikely that there should be many active tree worshippers in twentieth-century Aston.

At least one can make a reasonable assumption about the origin of the Arbor tree, but once a year, on the Saturday nearest to St Bartholomew's Day, the folk of West Witton in Wensleydale burn an effigy of a character known as 'Bartle' – and no one seems to have the least notion of just who the original Bartle was. Nevertheless, the figure is carried around the village and displayed to everyone along the way. A splendidly enigmatic verse is then declaimed, describing a series of calamities that befell Bartle, starting at Pen Hill where he 'tore his rags' and finishing with 'At Grassgill End he made his end', having broken his knee and his neck along the way. And at Grassgill he does indeed make his end, on the bonfire.

The strangest of all August rituals takes place on the day before the Ferry Fair at South Queensferry in Lothian. This is, in fact, one of the strangest and most mysterious of all old British customs, and it is very satisfying to find it carried out in the shadow of one of the great monuments to Victorian rational thought, the railway bridge across the Firth of Forth. Each year on this day one man is dressed in a white flannel costume, with just his eyes visible, and burrs are then stuck all over the material, so that he resembles a moving bush. In his outstretched hands he carries two staves, which are decked with flowers, and he wears a headpiece made of roses. The strange creature makes his slow progress around the town, with two attendants who help to take the weight of the staves. He walks for 7 miles (11km) with his arms outstretched all the time, stopping at each house but never speaking. People come out to give him gifts, but the Burryman merely stands there. The origins of this ceremony have long been lost, but they are clearly ancient, and one can only marvel at the persistence of such strange rituals which have lasted down through the centuries.

Jersey in August sees a comparatively modern custom, but one which is already well established with a permanent place in the island's calendar. The Battle of the Flowers is, in fact, a competition between floats that are decorated entirely with flowers. And they are no simple flower arrangements – not even artistic compositions à la Constance Fry – but flowers built up to form giant sculptures. The massive figures can be surprisingly realistic or totally fantastic, but they are always wonderfully colourful.

The Battle of Flowers,
Jersey's annual competition
for floral floats *(Jersey
Tourism Committee)*

September sees another, almost equally strange, custom – the Abbot's Bromley Horn Dance. The dance takes place on the Monday after the first Sunday after 4 September, and it begins outside the vicarage at 8 o'clock in the morning. Six sets of reindeer antlers are handed out from the church, the largest having a spread of 2ft (60cm) and being given to the chief dancer. The six dancers wear a form of Tudor costume, and they carry the antlers in such a way that they appear to belong to the human figures. The dancers are joined by the Fool, hobby horse, bowman, a man dressed in woman's clothing and known as Maid Marian, and two musicians. Such dances are ancient and can be seen depicted in cave paintings, although some of the attendants may have been added over the years. Why Tudor dress is worn is uncertain. It is possible that the earliest dancers were nude, and that Tudor dress was the first costume worn; thus the tradition has been kept ever since.

The period around Hallowe'en featured particularly in old customs, but generally it is not connected with any one place. It is a time when everyone can join in the activities and a time for ghosts and spirits, when mischief is abroad in the land. Nowadays the spirits tend to be no more frightening than children in masks and turnip lanterns. The degree of mischief involved is also variable. Children in Yorkshire celebrate 4 November as the night for making mischief. The following day is, of course, associated with Guy Fawkes, with bonfires and fireworks. But other strange ceremonies take place on 5 November. At Ottery St Mary in Devon, the

Firing the Fenny Poppers
(Milton Keynes Gazette)

Comrie's procession of flaming torches, burning out the old year and lighting the new *(British Tourist Authority)*

bonfire is enlivened by the addition of tar barrels. The barrels are lit, then rolled or carried through the streets and burned on the fire. Not far away in Shebbear they turn the Devil's Boulder because once again, the Devil has been littering the landscape with rocks. One particular example stands outside the churchyard and, because of its Satanic associations, the annual ritual has to be performed to keep evil at bay. What form the diabolic association takes is unclear. One story relates that the boulder was dropped by the Devil on his flight from heaven to hell. Another tells that the stone was quarried locally for rebuilding a church, but was returned to this spot every night after it had been moved during the day. The Devil, not wanting to see the church completed, was in fact, the culprit. In

either case, the Devil must be kept at bay by ringing a discordant peal on the church bells, while two men with crowbars turn the boulder over.

November, with its fireworks and discordant chimes, is then an unusually noisy month. There is a further eruption of noise on the 11th at Fenny Stratford in Buckinghamshire, when the Fenny Poppers are fired. These are six miniature cannon which are fired three times during that day, which is the feast day of St Martin. St Martin is the patron saint of the local church which was built largely through the efforts and benevolence of Dr Browne Willis. When he died in 1760, the firing of cannon was introduced in his memory and has continued ever since.

December brings Christmas and the familiar traditions, but few which have any local peculiarities. Some old traditions are continued, such as the mummers' play which is performed on Christmas Eve at Marshfield in Avon, but the season is celebrated mainly by families in their own homes. For end-of-year celebrations there is only one place to be – Scotland, where, apart from drinking out the old year they also burn it out. There are many variations on this old practice of lighting fires to mark the end of winter and darkness and the coming of light, spring and renewal. At Biggar they light a giant bonfire. At Comrie in Tayside the citizens dress up in various costumes and parade through the streets carrying flaming torches. But for the most spectacular end to the year, and to this look at the year's customs, one should travel to Stonehouse in Grampian for the fireball parade. The balls are made of cloth soaked in tar, which are held in a wire cage at the end of a long wire. The balls are lit and the young men in the procession whirl them around their heads. It looks both spectacular and alarming, but is actually safer than it appears. It is intended to keep the evil spirits at bay and to send them scurrying back to the graveyard where they belong, which seems as good a way as any to bring the year to a close.

Useful and Decorative

THE object of this chapter is to prove that the commonplace need not be boring; that usefulness need not be equated with dullness, and that our own age seems to have woken up to the notion that a little decoration and a bit of fun do no harm to a building. This is not a lesson our ancestors needed to learn. To take one example: what could be more prosaic than a drainpipe? But on the sea-front at Lyme Regis there is an attractive two-bayed house with a thatched roof. It still has its late seventeenth-century lead drainpipes and they are beautifully ornate: even a bracket holding a pipe to the wall can be graced by a pair of moulded swans, while the rain-water tub is a work of art.

Water supply in the old days was usually dependent on natural sources, and wells and springs were vital to the life of a village. At Fulking, under the lee of the South Downs, a perpetual spring gushes out through an ornate ceramic surround, inscribed with improving biblical texts. In the last century, literally thousands of sheep were brought down from the hills to be washed in this spring. But this is a modest affair compared with the well at Hartwell House in Buckinghamshire. This is known as the Egyptian Spring and was designed by that well-known lover of all things Egyptian, Joseph Bonomi Junior, brother to the equally Egyptian-influenced architect, Ignatius Bonomi. Here, instead of biblical texts, there are messages in hieroglyphics of dubious authenticity. But the strangest well must be the one at Stoke Row in Oxfordshire. It was presented to the village in 1864 by the Maharajah of Benares, and has a very strong Oriental look to it, which makes it seem quite a bizarre addition to a peaceful rural scene. The actual winding mechanism is, however, very much home produced, and was built at nearby Wallingford. The well was in the care of a keeper, who lived in his own little octagonal cottage which was graced by a tall chimney springing up from the centre of the roof. This must have made it look not unlike the conduit at Walsingham in Norfolk, except that here the local worthies decided that it was a shame to waste a perfectly good building on just one function. So it sprouts a column from the roof that held

Chester, Cheshire, has an ornate jubilee clock, Eastgate.

Cirencester, Gloucestershire The lock-up in Trinity Road has now been opened as a museum telling the not unrelated stories of lock-ups and workhouses.

Deeping St James, Lincolnshire Village lock-up, circular with a little spire. The stone walls are lined with brick with three niches into which prisoners were squeezed.

Disley, Cheshire Lyme Cage is a hunting lodge in Lyme Park which was also used as a prison (NT).

Elsdon, Northumberland (2½ miles (4km) south-east of village on the Newcastle road) A replica gibbet stands here although why a replica gibbet is wanted is a mystery.

Harpsden, Oxfordshire Opposite the church is a barn with walls made up of old printing blocks.

Harrold, Bedfordshire A small stone lock-up near the market house still has its original giant padlock.

Leicester An extravagantly ornate clock tower, like a miniature Albert Memorial, in the city centre.

Western Avenue, Greenford, London A multi-coloured factory in the Art Deco style built for Hoover.

up a beacon, and the little building at the base became the village lock-up. There are similar lock-ups all over the country, and all have similar characteristics. They are dark, airless, uncomfortable places, but they are often built in rather curious shapes.

At Shenley in Hertfordshire, the lock-up is unusual in that it actually contains windows, although they are very small and heavily barred. The building is shaped like a beehive and admission is through a doorway with a pointed arch. The prisoner, brooding either over the heinous nature of his crimes or his misfortune at being caught, has suitable inscriptions to consider on all sides. 'Do well' and 'Fear not' they exhort, while others entreat the reader to 'Be sober' and 'Be vigilant'. Such inscriptions clearly come too late for the prisoner, but as they are on the outside of the building they were presumably intended to keep the rest of the population out of the lock-up rather than reform those already inside.

The majority of lock-ups are what one would now describe as unisex, in that all offenders were simply shoved inside the single cell. The lock-up at Barmouth in Gwynedd, however, is an exception. The round lock-up by the harbour had its busiest time when sailors returned from their voyages and celebrated in style and preferably in company. The company, it seems, frequently finished up as drunk and as unruly as the sailors, so Barmouth's lock-up has a division inside and two separate doors, although it says something for the behaviour of the women that their portion is smaller than that set aside for the men.

An alternative to being locked up indoors was being locked up outdoors in the stocks or pillory. Local citizens could then come along and join in the jolly sport of pelting the malefactors with rotten fruit. The authorities of Colne in Lancashire decided this system was unfair. Too many citizens were unable to get to the site to enjoy the fun, so they decided to bring the stocks to the people and had a three-seater set of stocks mounted on a trolley which could be wheeled all round the town. They are still preserved – but not used.

One step up – or down, depending on how you look at it – from the lock-up, is the gaol. Of all utilitarian structures, one would expect prisons to be the least adorned, the grimmest of establishments. Yet divorce a prison from its function, and it may appear a surprisingly handsome building. The Old Gaol in Abingdon is a stone hexagon with two wings that stands close by the bridge over the Thames. Its dark days are done, and no one thinks it the least bit odd to spend their spare hours in a former prison, for it is now the town's leisure centre. Across the road, however, is a grim reminder of the building's grim past: the Broad Face pub is supposed to have got its curious name from the grimaces of the condemned man on the scaffold. It is not a thought to make for cheery drinking.

Few of us care to visit prisons at all – certainly not for a long stay, but it is fascinating to see one old prison that is now a museum. Before visiting Beaumaris Gaol you should be aware that this was a 'model' prison built in 1829 to the new humanitarian standards set by the Gaol Act of 1823. Its

Colne's movable stocks
(Lancashire Library)

designer was Joseph Hansom, better known for the horse-drawn cab which bears his name. At the end of a visit you are left wondering what, if this is the best, the worst gaols must have been like. Here you can see the rough cells, and the even rougher punishment cells, where bread and water was the only diet. You can still see the workrooms where men carved their initials on the floor, and women had ropes beside their work-places which they pulled in order to rock the cradles in which their babies slept on the floor above. The treadmill on which the 'hard labour' prisoners marched up and down for hours every day is on display and, most macabre of all, you can follow the walk from the condemned cell to the scaffold.

Following this macabre thread brings us to two other grim memorials. There is an old rhyme:

> From Hull, hell and Halifax
> Good Lord deliver me.

The Halifax associations are said to derive from the local practice of executing cloth thieves in Yorkshire's own early version of the guillotine, a

The ornate Jubilee clock stands above the city walls at Chester *(Anthony Burton)*

replica of which can be seen in the town. Any criminal, however, who was nimble enough to pull his head out from under the blade, leap from the scaffold and cross the river at the foot of the hill before being caught was pardoned. A more likely fate that awaited prisoners was to be hung in chains from the gibbet. One of these macabre devices survives at Steng Cross in a suitably lonely stretch of country near Otterburn in Northumberland. It is said by some to be a local attraction.

One of the pleasantest ways of passing the time is looking at ways of measuring the passing of time, and now we return to the watery themes with which we began. A very fine multi-purpose sundial, the work of John Nash, can be seen at Blaise Hamlet. The sundial is mounted on a high column, on top of which is a weather-vane, and at the bottom a pump. The pump's pipe emerges through a carved lion's head, so that it appears that the beast is sticking out its tongue and spitting. At least this has not suffered the fate of an equally elegant, if older, sundial, the so-called Countess Pillar which was erected in memory of Lady Anne Clifford at Brougham in Cumbria. It has lost the gnomon from the south face, thus rendering the monument timeless.

The most elaborate of the high-perched dials is atop a column at Barrington Court in Somerset. The column ends in grand style with an heraldic lion rampant at the very pinnacle. An elaborate dial in a different sense is to be seen over the doorway of Eyam church in Derbyshire. As well as telling the local time, it also informs passers-by of the local times in other spots as far apart as South America and India, although what use the inhabitants of this delightful village are supposed to make of the information is far from clear.

An extraordinary Elizabethan sundial can be seen at Madeley Court in Shropshire, although it is in a sad state of repair. Holes cut in the stone block were used to make astronomical calculations, such as the positions of the planets. The sundial is too heavily damaged to be of any practical value, even if one could work out how it was used in the first place.

Sundials suffer from one incurable defect: they only work when the sun shines. Sailors at sea, however, must know the time with accuracy if they are to practise the ancient skills of solar and astro navigation, so they need to be able to check their chronometers. In 1812 the Admiralty built a signal station at Deal for sending semaphore messages to ships, but in 1855 it was converted into a Time-Ball Tower. At precisely 12.55 Greenwich Mean Time each day, a 14ft (4m) diameter copper ball is raised half-way up a mast on top of the tower; at 12.58 it rises to the top and at 13.00 it drops, giving mariners their time check. Nowadays the tower houses a museum of maritime communication.

Activity on the hour every hour is a feature of many clocks: figures emerge and strike bells and perform various antics, but for pure, unadulterated fantasy the twentieth century can take a bow. And the settings for these timely displays are as unlikely as the event – modern shopping centres. The Victoria Centre in Nottingham has, at its heart, a

Hampstead, London NW3 11 Cannon Place, Hampstead: grilles in the wall show the position of the old lock-up.

Milton Keynes, Buckinghamshire The Neath Hill shopping centre has a somewhat surprising Chinese-style clock.

Old Brampton, Derbyshire (4 miles (6.4km) west of Chesterfield) The church clock is divided into 63 minutes.

Pevensey, East Sussex has the oldest and the smallest town hall in Britain, incorporating a lock-up with two tiny cells.

Shrewton, Wiltshire A massive village lock-up stands beside the bridge.

Weymouth, Dorset Splendidly ornate clock tower on sea front.

Wheatley, Oxfordshire has a pyramidal stone lock-up.

clock tower and fountain that were designed by that brilliant cartoonist and inventor of improbable machines, Roland Emett. On the hour, various fantastical beasts, birds and butterflies fly out on metal stalks to circle the skeletal clock tower. Swansea's shopping precinct runs Nottingham a good second. Here, they change the clock from time to time, but whatever goes in always displays an ingenious mechanical movement. On my last visit, the clock was a water-mill: when the clock struck, the wheel turned and the miller busied himself at the rotating grindstones, while his colleague looked out on a sack being hoisted up from a cart.

Anything that provides variety in shopping centres must be welcome, and most still have a long way to go before they can match the exuberance of the best covered markets. Kirkgate market in Leeds is an example of the best of the nineteenth century, combining the engineering principles of a railway station with the typical Victorian love of decoration. The engineering was the work of the city engineer, Thomas Hewson, who provided an iron frame and glass roof, with colonnades carrying an

The Halifax gibbet still stands, but fortunately is no longer used *(Leeds Central Library)*

Madeley Court sundial – but how does it work? *(Shropshire Libraries)*

elaborate system of domes. The decoration was presumably rather more the responsibility of the architects, Leeming and Leeming, who made the most of their chances, providing red and gold lions to watch over the shoppers. The centre-piece is a commemorative clock that records the fact that Marks & Spencer set up their first shop in this market. Newcastle's Grainger Market, however, still has a Marks & Spencer penny bazaar among its stalls. This is, in fact, a market that really looks like a railway station with stalls: it comes as no surprise to find that the architect John Dobson was also the designer of Newcastle's station. If anything, the station is the more elegantly dramatic, for although it has a similar style, of glazed roof on iron columns, it has the extra visual appeal of being built on a curve. No station in Britain has a finer approach than that provided by Newcastle for travellers from the south crossing the Tyne. Part of the appeal of the Grainger Market lies in this obvious sense of belonging specifically to one place. The latest generation of shopping centres – successors to the old markets – seem to be striving for similar identification. In Glasgow this means borrowing devices from the city's greatest architect and designer, John Rennie Mackintosh; in Stoke-on-Trent the market has been embellished with a magnificent giant teapot – the biggest in the world.

Sometimes objects attract one's attention simply because their function is now so far removed from everyday experience that they become instantly, if oddly, attractive. Down by the harbour at Falmouth is a stepped brick chimney, rising in four tiers from a stone base. It might, perhaps, lay claim to being the world's largest pipe and is, in fact, known as 'The King's Pipe'. It was here that customs men brought contraband tobacco to be burned, and the fumes were carried away to bother no one but disconsolate smugglers and the seagulls. Staying in the West Country and moving around the coast brings us to the very picturesque village of Clovelly, famous for sledges. There is nothing very odd about sledges, but we normally think of them in terms of winter snow; in Clovelly, however, sledges are used all year round. The popularity of the village has been aided by its amazingly steep cobbled streets, and the sledges are no more than a practical help to the locals for their everyday shopping. They seem strange but they also act as a useful reminder that however picturesque a spot might be, it still has to provide for the practical needs of those who live there.

The Kent coast near Greatstone-on-Sea has what could easily pass as modern sculpture on a grand scale. A wall, about 200ft (60m) long and 30ft (8m) high, curves around towards two shapely dishes that appear to be standing on their rims. It gives the appearance of a strangely petrified radar station – which is not, in fact, far from the truth, although it predates radar. This is a giant listening station, in which the wall and dishes were supposed to concentrate the sound waves sent out from distant aircraft, focusing them just as light waves are focused by curved mirrors and lenses. Fortunately for Britain, radar was invented shortly afterwards, for the giant

A witty mural on a house in Bedminster, Bristol
(Anthony Burton)

A rare example of whole-hearted art nouveau decoration on a former printing works in Bristol
(Anthony Burton)

ear-trumpet was a decided failure. It has certainly, however, left the seashore with one of its most striking monuments.

A monument of a different kind can be seen at Holme Fen in Cambridge-shire. Whatever one might anticipate finding in the Fens it is surely not a cast-iron pillar from the Crystal Palace. It was driven into the ground at Whittlesey Mere in 1851 just before drainage work began. As the water was pumped away, so too the peat contracted and the ground level steadily lowered. Each year, more and more of the slender fluted column became visible: by 1957 guy ropes were needed to keep it upright and a second, less artistic, post was added to measure the continuing shrinkage. The Crystal Palace column now stands a full 13ft (4m) high, a monument to the folly of starting 'beneficial' schemes without thinking through all the problems. The drainage scheme was designed to clear the land for farming, but now all that the shrinking peat will support is scrub and birch.

Columns of a very different kind grace the commercial heart of Bristol. Corn Street became the banking centre for the city in the eighteenth century, when the Exchange was established there. Outside are four short bronze round-topped columns around which traders would meet to make their deals. The columns became known as 'The Nails' and the many cash transactions that took place gave rise to the phrase 'pay on the nail'. This is a good area to explore highly decorative commercial buildings. Traders who wanted a more relaxed atmosphere than that provided by the hagglers round The Nails could retire to the Commercial Rooms of 1811 whose classical pediment was supported by statues representing the city, commerce and navigation. The grandest building in the area, however, is Lloyds Bank, inspired by a building in another trading city, Sansovino's Library in Venice. It has an impressive ornate façade that was designed to reassure would-be investors that this establishment at least had cash in plenty to spare. The country still has a wealth of such impressive commercial buildings, but often the decoration is no more than that – bits tacked on to give a sense of opulence. The very best, such as the Lloyds Bank building in Halifax, extend their grandeur right through the building, which becomes a Temple of Mammon. However, the most interesting of all decorative details are those which have something to say, and few are more interesting than the old Thomas Cook offices in Leicester.

Thomas Cook began his travel business early in the Railway Age. On 5 July 1841 he packed 570 sober citizens into open trucks, sent them off to a temperance meeting at Loughborough and brought them home again to Leicester at the cost of just one shilling. It was the start of one of the most famous travel agencies in the world. If you look up at the old building, you can see the temperance excursion carved in stone, followed by other highlights from the company's history. An excursion train steams to the Crystal Palace with passengers for the Great Exhibition; Thomas Cook excursionists cross the newly opened Forth rail bridge and the extension of the business to ever more exotic locations is commemorated by a paddle-steamer on the Nile. It is a history of Cook's, and a history of the

development of the Victorian travel business, all preserved in stone.

It is surprising how much there is to see in city streets, once one gets into the habit of looking up above ground-floor level. A recent visit to Plymouth, for example, produced a wealth of material in the most unlikely places and in all kinds of forms. Sir Francis Drake, of course, features everywhere: a ceramic Armada is to be seen being colourfully destroyed over the entrance to the New Palace Theatre; and a galleon 'sails' from a cinema wall. But much more surprising is Barclays Bank near the Civic Centre. There are two different sets of figures. The first stays with traditional Plymouth themes: at one corner an Elizabethan sea captain and bollard, and at the other a duffle-coated sailor looks sternly from his bridge. But around the rest of the building are some incongruous figures, very much in the style of the thirties, representing industry. For some reason they have all been given Grecian drapes, including a miner with a pick-axe and safety lamp who looks understandably reluctant to go down the pit, and a gentleman holding a stiff zig-zag of lightning to represent electrical power. The older part of the city, the Barbican, also has some delightful curiosities. Here, in a little garden, a lovingly carved Elizabethan ship sails across a doorway, but just when one is getting used to stepping back in time, one is brought right back to the present day. A local artist, R. O. Lenkiewicz, has a studio and gallery in a converted warehouse, and rather than hang out a conventional sign he painted a mural across the whole of the gable end. The faces of modern Plymouth look out on the old streets of the past. It is just one example of what seems to be a renewed enthusiasm for the very old art of mural painting, which has brought new excitement and colour to many towns and cities. Some are meant to inform, others merely to

Swansea shopping centre clock. On the hour everything begins to work *(Anthony Burton)*

Thomas Cook excursions rumble on in stone across the façade of the company's old Leicester offices *(Anthony Burton)*

Dundee's industrial history
on display on a gable end
(Anthony Burton)

entertain, but all the best add genuine colour and a touch of much-needed fun to towns and cities.

No city has taken this movement more to heart than Dundee, where the local authority began by looking at the decidedly run down and dingy area of the city known as Blackness – which by then was all too appropriate a name – and decided that what it needed was cheering up. Artists were commissioned to produce a variety of works on different themes and in different media. An entire house-end in St Peter Street was painted to tell part of the Dundee story. At the top, fishermen chase the famous Tay whale, while below is the story of jute and printing, together with the construction of iron ships and the great railway bridge. At the bottom, citizens read the local paper which has refused to follow *The Times* down the slippery slope of modernism, so that its front page is still entirely devoted to small advertisements. All that is lacking is a verse or two from that best of all bad poets, William McGonagall, who celebrated both the Tay whale and, most memorably, the disastrous collapse of the first Tay railway bridge:

> Beautiful Railway Bridge of the Silv'ry Tay!
> Alas, I am very sorry to say
> That ninety lives have been taken away
> On the last Sabbath day of 1879,
> Which will be remember'd for a very long time.

The best part of the Dundee mural is its connection with the local community. This is true of much public art. Passengers coming into Hull by train pass newly built terraces where gables have been decorated by incorporating designs into the actual brickwork. All have local themes, and a city that has two professional Rugby League teams had to have at least one player up there. With his ball tucked under his arm, he heads for the line, but which of the teams he represents has been left tactfully uncertain. But art can be both local and exotic. This is certainly true of Manchester's Chinatown. It is obvious when you have arrived in the area, for street signs are duplicated in Chinese. The proper way to enter is through the triumphal arch, which was designed and built in traditional style by craftsmen brought over from China. There is also an immense mural of junks tossing on a stormy sea. The Chinese do keep in touch with local traditions as well: Manchester has the only Chinese restaurant I have ever visited which has tripe on the menu. It is not, one has to say, the easiest food to eat with chopsticks.

After such exotica it is perhaps time to return to usefulness: to a monument to usefulness and a monument of usefulness. Edward Jenner of Berkeley, Gloucestershire, achieved lasting and well-earned fame when he discovered that exposing people to the harmless cow pox made them immune from the deadly smallpox. No one can calculate how many lives have been saved by inoculation. The house in which he lived is preserved as a museum, but the memorial to Jenner and his discovery in his home town is no great public monument, but a simple rustic summer-house with a thatched roof. All that is grand about it is its name – the Temple of Vaccinia.

Finally, there is a tower on the coast near Kingswear in Devon. It is octagonal, raised on eight pointed arches to a height of 82ft (25m). It has no doors, no windows, no stairs; it might be a lighthouse but it has no light. It would seem to be the perfect folly, and it is certainly a local landmark. In fact, that is precisely what it is – a prominent mark set up on land to enable sailors at sea to take their bearings.

Landmarks

THERE are many organisations and individuals who have made it their goal to preserve old, interesting and very unusual buildings. Some people restore and preserve buildings for their own benefit, others open up their treasures to the general public, allowing them in to see and enjoy what is on display. But there is one organisation which has a unique policy: they restore as meticulously as any other conservation body, but they neither keep the results to themselves nor do they charge visitors for a brief wander round or a guided tour. Instead they let them out as holiday homes, and for a few days or longer anyone can enjoy the privilege of living in some extraordinarily interesting buildings. They can stay in castles and 'pineapples', prospect towers and follies and buildings whose only claim to fame is their antiquity. It is a personal experience, so I hope readers will forgive a personal introduction.

One of my delights has, for many years, been travelling by canal. A famous landmark as you come down the Staffs and Worcester Canal towards its junction with the Trent and Mersey is a magnificent Tudor building. If it were not for the arch that runs through it one would take it for a minor stately home, yet in fact it was no more than a gate-house – the great house itself has long gone, and the gate-house itself almost disappeared. Until comparatively recently it was reduced to a mere shell – no floor, no roof, no windows, just a beautiful shelter for cattle. Tixall Gate-house is now restored to its former splendour and the news that it was available as a holiday home seemed incredible. I wrote for details, and received not just the details of Tixall but those of an array of equally astounding buildings. In the event I opted for a very different choice, a converted Cornish engine-house in the Tamar Valley near Calstock. Our arrival set a pattern that has been repeated over and over again, for it begins with the sheer delight of discovering the property which, if only for a short while, is to be your home.

We drove into Calstock and followed the Tamar down to a small wooded valley with a road that was little better than a track. Anyone who has spent any time in Cornwall becomes accustomed to the gaunt ruins of the old engine-houses that stand above long-abandoned tin and copper mines. We drove right past yet another before we realised this was *our* mine. Danescombe Mine, which is set back from the track and reached by a little bridge across a stream is so quiet and secluded that I came out one morning to find a heron fishing off the doorstep. The engine-house has been converted to a delightful and comfortable holiday home, but the monumental quality of the building itself has not been sacrificed. We went inside and were stopped in our tracks by the sheer size and wonder of it all. This first encounter is always special, but then comes the period of exploration, of getting to know the building, of living with it. In the case of the Danescombe mine, this meant endless poking about trying to reconstruct in our imaginations how the building fitted in to the pattern of the working mine, without any curatorial voice warning us off. Other properties offer different experiences, such as sitting by candlelight in a medieval house while huge logs flame – with luck – in the grate, or retiring to bed via a walk across battlements. But whatever the property, it is the special nature of actually living there that is unique. I knew by the end of the first day that I was hopelessly and completely hooked on the experience. Many years and many lettings later, I still am.

The Landmark Trust was started in 1965 with the simple aim of rescuing buildings which would otherwise fall into total decay or simply be demolished. A grand house might well be taken over by the National Trust and opened up to visitors, but there is a range of buildings which do not fit that mould, but may be too dilapidated, or too inconvenient or too large to attract a private buyer. Then the Landmark Trust steps in, and begins the long, often tedious and not always successful, process of negotiation. After that comes restoration, a subject fraught with problems. We all know medieval churches where heavy-handed Victorian restoration has removed all the building's original character. Equally, a house can be restored to a pristine condition which leaves it looking more like a pastiche than the real thing. There is a delicate balance to be reached between restoring a building to make it safe and habitable while maintaining the patina of age. A building that has been lived in develops rough edges and idiosyncrasies; clear all those away and you may have a show house – you will never have a home. The same philosophy applies to furnishing. Landmark properties are not filled with expensive antiques that must be carefully guarded against every stain and scratch. Their houses remind one of those country houses where the labrador is always the first to settle down on the best armchair – good quality, but a little shabby, always interesting but with a decidedly lived-in look. Landmark homes have furniture that belongs, just as the books on the shelves and the pictures on the wall belong with the house. All this costs money, and although there is a small contribution from grants and income from lettings, most of the cash comes from the charitable trust. In their 1988 handbook, the Landmark Trust recorded that they had worked on 173 buildings in Britain, but new projects are being started all the time.

Some Landmark Trust restorations have already been mentioned (see pp72-3), but that gives no notion of the extraordinary variety of delights on offer. Most people who glance at the property handbook find their attention

held by the bizarre and the strange, the follies and the prospect towers. One building, in particular, can fairly lay claim to be one of the most eccentric buildings in Britain. In 1761 the Earl of Dunmore decided that his garden required a summer-house. It was conventional enough to begin with – a small octagonal tower flanked by single-storey wings. The ogee arches over the doors and windows are decidedly individual, but higher up the building becomes unique. Stone, spiky leaves begin to sprout from the tops of columns and the little tower is transformed into a giant, perfectly formed pineapple. It is a glorious, fruity eccentricity which anyone who visits Dunmore, near Stirling, can go and see, if only a few can enjoy the privilege of announcing that they have just had a holiday in a pineapple.

A house of almost equally eccentric appearance can be found at the opposite end of the country, in the centre of Penzance. Like Marshall's flax mill in Leeds, Egyptian House in Chapel Street was built in the Egyptian style which enjoyed a brief flourish of popularity after Napoleon's Egyptian campaign at the end of the eighteenth century. It was not originally intended as a dwelling. It was to be a museum and geological storehouse, for the beaches of the area were and are full of fascinating pebbles, stones and crystals. The style of the building certainly gives no idea of its use, for it is Egyptian at its most flamboyant, not to say absurd. The doorway is flanked by lotus columns and above are two sphinx-like ladies, staring out at the world. Above them is a rather more domestic motif in the shape of the lion and the unicorn. Apart from this oddly British note, the rest of the façade is extravagantly Egyptian and colourfully so at that, for it has been restored to its full polychrome glory.

The follies of Stowe have already been mentioned, but the Gothic Temple is generally recognised as the grandest, if not the loveliest, of them all. Designed by James Gibbs around 1740, it sounds as if it ought to have a classical eighteenth-century unity. The plan is based on a triangle and circles. There are towers with circular rooms at the three corners and a circular room in the centre of the triangle. However, the building's design is far from well-balanced: the towers are of uneven height and sprout an apparently random array of turrets, pinnacles and battlements. It is, in fact, a rather ugly building, but it has been carried out with such panache and bravado that it defies criticism. At the top of the staircase is a belvedere from which to view the rest of the estate.

The Landmark Trust also has on offer some excellent prospect towers. Luttrell's Tower at Eaglehurst near Southampton was built by Temple Simon Luttrell in about 1780, and was probably designed by James Wyatt. Whoever was responsible for the construction, it is certainly a fine piece of work. The house has a castellated base, with many fine features including an oriel window, and from this base a circular tower arises. From the top of the tower one has a perfect view right across the Solent, over the busy river traffic going to and from Southampton. However, tradition has it that the tower was built for a much more sinister purpose than the idle watching of ships. Under the tower are exceptionally large cellars and from these an

The Château, Gate Burton, Lincolnshire is an exceptionally grand weekend cottage, built in 1747 as a retreat for a busy lawyer *(Dave Bower/ Landmark Trust)*

underground passage ran down to the beach. Luttrell's Tower was said to be the headquarters of the local smugglers. Why else, so the argument goes, should a simple prospect tower require such a huge cellar? There is, however, an answer to that question, for Luttrell was a good friend of the Prince of Wales and entertained him at the tower. Anyone who expected to entertain Prinny on a regular basis would certainly have needed a large cellar.

Although many stories exist regarding the construction of prospect towers, there are few which go on accumulating stories after they are built. Luttrell's Tower is, however, an exception. It has a curious monument, for example, in the shape of a pair of black granite feet mounted on a plinth. They were brought to the tower by Lord Cavan, Luttrell's son-in-law, who became the tower's second owner. He had commanded the British forces in Egypt from 1801, and the feet are said to belong to a statue of Rameses II. Why he should have wanted Rameses' feet is not known, nor is it known if there were other pieces of Rameses lying around for the taking, though it would seem logical to suppose that the feet were the sole remains (no pun intended)! The tower passed out of the hands of the Luttrell family and at one time was almost purchased by Queen Victoria when she considered buying Eaglehurst House, although eventually she settled for Osborne instead. Marconi used the tower for radio experiments at the beginning of this century, and he laid a cable for mains electricity. Clough Williams-Ellis, of Portmeirion fame, came here and built a pair of magnificent monumental gates at the top of a staircase from the tower to the beach.

The Culloden Tower, overlooking Richmond in Yorkshire, was built in 1746 by an enthusiastic Hanoverian, John Yorke. Externally it would hardly qualify as one of the great folly towers, but the best is kept for the interior. Inside the tower are two octagonal rooms with beautiful rococo decoration. Looking at the tower today, one can only guess at the skill that went into restoring the rooms to their former glory. The architects worked from old photographs to reassemble the jigsaw of ruined plasterwork and carvings. Laughton Place, near Lewes in Sussex, appears to be another prospect tower, handsome but unusual, being built of brick and terracotta (see p52). It is, in fact, even more interesting than it appears. Laughton Place was originally built in 1534 as the manor house of the Pelham family, but they found their new home damp and cold and moved away. Slowly the buildings crumbled, leaving only the central tower. Then, in the eighteenth century, Henry Pelham took pity on this last fragment of the ancestral home and built a new Gothic farmhouse around it. The scheme was never finished and the building was sold in the 1920s. But misfortune continued to dog the old building. The new owner abandoned it; the Gothic farmhouse crumbled and once again the tower was left in stately, if by now somewhat unsteady, isolation. Now that the tower has been restored, it is difficult to imagine how anyone could have abandoned such a lovely building.

The Nicolle Tower on Jersey has an equally strange history, which dates back to prehistoric times. It seems that there was once a menhir, or standing stone, on the cliffs, which served as a navigation mark for generations of sailors. A large boulder can now be seen under the tower, and the rock is carved with a date, 1644, and a compass rose. Was this boulder the menhir? It is not certain, but a look-out tower was certainly built here, which was extended in 1821 by Philippe Nicolle to make a fully fledged prospect tower, with Gothic embellishments. But this is not the end of the story. During the last war, Jersey was occupied by the Germans who wanted to restore the tower to its old function of look-out post. However, they also wanted to keep their activities secret, so they simply lifted the roof, added another storey to the tower, and put the lid back on again. The Gothic tower now comes complete with a 'letter-box' viewing slit and ranging marks on the top storey ceiling. Another tower which is not quite what it seems is to be found at Lympstone at the mouth of the River Exe. William Peters built a colourful clock tower here in 1885 as a memorial to his wife. Now an ornate iron spiral staircase takes holiday-makers up from kitchen to bathroom to living-room to bedroom – and the clock still works.

Sham castles are almost as common as towers in any list of follies. Some are no more than preludes to a greater design. Shute Barton near Axminster, is a fine, but not noticeably odd, medieval house that was much altered in Tudor times and to which a splendid gate-house was added in the late sixteenth century. There is a central block above the actual gateway, from which battlements lead out to flanking towers. It js a splendid place to stay, although visitors staying in one of the towers have a draughty walk to the main block, where all the facilities, including the lavatories, are situated. During the restoration of Shute Barton, the Landmark Trust was offered a superb seventeenth-century plaster ceiling from Barnstaple. It fitted the house perfectly, with plaster to spare, so that now an occasional errant dolphin can be found decorating the bathroom.

A sham castle which is no mere gate-house can be found in Wales. Clytha Castle was built not just as a folly but as a memorial. An inscription informs callers that it was built in 1790 by William Jones, 'for the purpose of relieving a mind sincerely afflicted by the loss of a most excellent Wife whose Remains were deposited in Lanarth Church Yard A.D: 1787 and to the Memory of whose virtues this Tablet is dedicated.' It is a building to set alongside the Ashton memorial in Lancaster, as Britain's answer to the Taj Mahal. It is, perhaps, unfair to describe it as a sham castle, for it is in fact a complete original. The design is superficially similar to that of Shute Barton, except that the battlements sweep upwards to a pinnacled crest in a style unknown to military science. Perhaps one should say that Clytha Castle is not a sham castle at all, but a pure invention.

The Landmark Trust's activities are by no means restricted to preserving follies and imitations: they restore the genuine article as well. Those who feel that staying in a sham castle is not quite the thing can always head north for a fortress which, even if a little late for Macbeth, certainly has an atmosphere that recalls such warlike times. Saddell Castle on the Kintyre Peninsula was built in 1508, and was described by contemporaries as 'a fayre pyle, and a stronge'. So it is, a typical building of its time, not quite castle, not quite house, a fortified tower of forbidding aspect. It has all the trappings of the feudal past, including a removable section of floor just inside the main door, so that unwelcome guests step straight over the threshold to plummet to the dungeon. It is a building of uncompromising, barbaric splendour.

One of the most unusual houses in Britain: the Egyptian House, Penzance *(Derek Pratt)*

Woodsford Castle, in Dorset, on the other hand, was built in the fourteenth century at a time when thoughts of comfort in this part of England were becoming as important as the needs of defence. What has survived is just one side of the old quadrilateral castle, long since domesticated, but even the domestication is on a monumental scale. The

The castellated gatehouse at Shute *(Anthony Burton)*

old towers and battlements may have disappeared beneath a thatched roof, but that roof is, in places, as much as 6ft (2m) thick. The castle lies in the heart of Thomas Hardy's Wessex, and Hardy himself came here as apprentice to a local architect to work·on the building.

The warlike aspect of Woodsford Castle has softened over the years, but the fortifications built up in the nineteenth century as a response to the threats from France are uncompromisingly and grimly solid affairs. During the Napoleonic Wars, 103 martello towers were built on the coast of south-east England from Sussex to Suffolk. They were named after the Torre della Martella in Corsica which successfully withstood a British onslaught. They are mostly plain brick towers, with room for a small garrison and a gun emplacement on the roof. The most northerly of the chain, at Aldeburgh, is more elaborate: it is quatrefoil in plan and able to mount four guns, although it is no less stark than any of the other 102 towers. Oddly, perhaps, this is one of the most popular of all Landmark properties. Perhaps their customers are *literati* who have in mind another martello tower near Dublin, from which 'Stately, plump Buck Milligan' emerges to start the 24-hour journeyings of James Joyce's Ulysses. But one of the grandest of all the fortifications is Fort Clonque on Alderney. Built in 1847 as part of a programme of reinforcement of the Channel Islands, it proved insufficient to meet a later threat. When the Germans occupied the islands, they made Fort Clonque into an even sterner fortress than it had been a century before. It is still massively impressive, a fort on an island off the main island, approached by a causeway that vanishes beneath the higher of the high tides. Revellers at local hostelries are advised to watch the tide-

Aldeburgh's martello tower: once a fortress, now a holiday home *(Landmark Trust)*

The Landmark Trust at work. Gibside Chapel, before and after restoration *(Turners/Landmark Trust)*

The startlingly ornate mock-medievalism of Clytha Castle, near Monmouth *(Richard Hayman/Landmark Trust)*

table if they want to sleep in a bed in the fort rather than spend a night on the cliff-top. Fort Clonque must be one of the most dramatic of holiday homes in Britain and on my week on the island it turned out to be more dramatic than I had bargained for. The unthinkable happened. Alderney was swept by blizzards, the sea beside the causeway froze and Clonque became a truly isolated fortress.

Occasionally, one stumbles upon a Landmark property almost by accident. It was while walking along a disused railway line between Consett and Newcastle upon Tyne, now known as the Derwent Walk, that I saw first of all a towering monument, the Column of British Liberty, then came across a splendid Palladian mausoleum, the Gibside Chapel and the ruins of Gibside Hall. All this grandeur was paid for from the profits of coal mining, but it was mining that brought so much of the great estate crashing down again, when the ground subsided. Subsidence was almost the

undoing of the Gothic banqueting hall, which was built around 1750 to a design by Daniel Garrett. It has lost its spire, but otherwise this beautiful little building has survived remarkably well, and restoration has brought out all its finer elements. It can be compared with the Gothic temple at Stowe, for it displays the same mixture of pinnacles and castellations, quatrefoils and ogee arches, but in the hall all the elements seem to come together into a convincing, coherent whole. The building seems to sit literally as a crown on the landscape.

There is an element of the folly in Gibside, as in most of the other buildings described so far. This seems to add to their popularity, but almost equally popular are the holiday homes which began their lives with different personae. Warden Abbey in Bedfordshire, for example, is yet another of those buildings which has gone through quite an array of transformations. As the name suggests, it began as a Norman abbey, built for the Cistercians in 1135. Then, at the dissolution, it suffered the fate of many monastic institutions: it was pulled down and rebuilt as a grand house. Over the years, the house, too, fell on hard times, until only a part was left standing. It looks like a fragment of a greater whole, almost entirely dominated by a tall, barley-stick chimney. Yet some of the past has survived in this one building, which was part monastery, part manor – although it is more a house than a monastery.

The Old Hall at Croscombe in Somerset reversed the Norman progression: domestic first, ecclesiastic afterwards. It began life as the great hall of a manor house, but fitted easily into its new role of Baptist chapel which it was for 250 years. Apart from its ecclesiastical windows, it is obvious that you are in a great medieval hall. The conversion to chapel did, however, remove one necessity for a comfortable life. Presumably the medieval owners enjoyed a roaring log fire in a massive fireplace. In its place there is now a Gurney stove, a cast-iron monster of a type normally used to heat cathedrals. It positively eats fuel and when it is well stoked up actually begins to glow bright red in an alarming manner.

Another building with religious connections can be found near Bolton Abbey in the Yorkshire Dales. Beamsley Hospital was founded in 1593 by Margaret, Countess of Cumberland. From the road one sees only conventional almshouses – terraced houses that spread out on either side of a central arch – that are to be homes for retired Landmark Trust employees. Beyond the arch, however, a path leads to the hospital itself, a circular stone building with a conical roof topped by a lantern which is encircled by tall stone chimneys. The interior of the building is even more remarkable. Around the perimeter are seven rooms for seven almswomen, who were not allowed to forget their religious duties, for each room opens directly into the central chapel. There was nowhere they could go, whether it was outside or simply to visit a neighbouring room, without passing through the chapel. The rooms have been altered, but the chapel remains in the centre, with its plain wooden pews and pulpit and an original Beamsley Bible. It is a very strong-willed visitor who can resist giving at

least one pull on the chapel bell to see if it still clangs – it does.

Everyone, no doubt, has a private fantasy about the sort of building they would like to convert to create a family home. Few people achieve their ambition, but thanks to the Landmark Trust they can at least find temporary homes. The engine-house in Cornwall was my first choice, but a railway station was a strong contender. Alton Station, on the North Staffordshire Railway is something of an oddity. The railway company generally favoured a Jacobean style, but here an Italianate design was ultimately chosen – perhaps a well-mannered nod in the direction of neighbouring Alton Towers. The station is surprisingly grand, but just a little sad, for the platform stretches out waiting for the crowds to disembark from one of the many excursion trains that ran from the Potteries: now they will never come.

Landmark Trust properties come in all shapes, sizes, styles and periods. There are some which are amazingly grand, such as Wortham Manor, a magnificent medieval house in Devon: it is grand on the outside and even grander on the inside, with its rich panellings and mouldings. Other houses owe their appeal to their delightful intimacy. Purton Green is a typical timber-framed Suffolk hall house – all that remains of a deserted village. Modern roads no longer go there, so modern visitors have to wheel their belongings to the house across a ford, using a barrow provided by a thoughtful management. Sometimes, the appeal of a property is simply the bizarre associations with its original use. The House of Correction at

(Opposite) Warden Abbey was pulled down to build the house, then the house fell down and this is all that remains *(Landmark Trust)*

The circular almshouses of Beamsley Hospital *(Alwyne Gardner/Landmark Trust)*

Folkingham in Lincolnshire, for example, was a prison, but now only the grand classical entrance survives and it could pass muster as a charming summer-house. So the list can be extended, but for me few buildings are more appealing than those which keep their secrets tucked away, waiting to be discovered. Margells at Branscombe in Devon seems just one among many picturesque stone-built, thatched houses. Once inside, however, you find medieval panelling, medieval wall paintings and, visitors frequently report, a medieval ghost. During a New Year stay, one of our party announced that he was going for an early morning walk – a remark greeted with some scepticism. But I was woken by footsteps on the stairs, a door opening and closing. I went back to sleep, content to leave Jim to his exercise. But at breakfast, I was told that no one had been out – but someone had certainly walked the old house that night.

But if I had to pick just one house to explain the special Landmark quality, I think it would be Plas Uchaf near Corwen in Wales. It has that special appeal – the gasp factor. From the outside it is a pleasant, very solid, stone farmhouse, but hardly remarkable. However, step inside, and you stop at the threshold and gasp in amazement, for you are faced with an echoing medieval hall, rising the full height from stone-flagged floor to the elaborate timbers of the roof. You step back in time, not just for a few moments, but for every day when you are privileged to live in this great building.

A full list of Landmark Trust properties is obtainable from The Landmark Trust, Shottesbrooke, Maidenhead, Berkshire SL6 3SW.

The Amazing Finale

THIS book is based on the premise that people enjoy the unusual, the bizarre and the puzzling, and this last chapter will look at just two variations on this theme: the strange, artificially created microcosm of the grotto, and the often vexatious, always intriguing world of the maze. The essence of the grotto is an artificial cave, either excavated into the ground or built up artificially above ground. It is then given an elaborate treatment, studded with seashells and pebbles, decorated with statues and figures of Neptune and mermaids and, in the very grandest, provided with fountains. The earliest versions, however, were simply rooms encrusted with shells. There is a charming example in the gate-house of Skipton Castle in Yorkshire, said to be the work of the indefatigable Lady Anne Clifford, dating from the seventeenth century. The principal feature is a mother-of-pearl figure of Neptune, although he is not the conventional bearded figure that is normally portrayed, but rather he is a reclining figure looking like a smug tom-cat. Another seventeenth-century grotto, at Woburn Abbey, is on altogether a grander scale. The room itself is vaulted and every surface covered with shells, some forming strict geometric patterns, the rest providing attractive tableaux. Neptune looks down benevolently on cavorting nymphs and cupids who are pulled across the water on scallop shells drawn by dolphins. For all their splendour, shell rooms had to wait for the next century and the dawn of the picturesque movement and Romanticism before they found any imitators.

The vogue for grottoes during the eighteenth century began with Alexander Pope, a poet who liked to mock the pretensions of others, but who was clearly possessed of a taste for the bizarre and the extravagant. He bought a house in Twickenham, the garden of which was divided by a main road. He decided to unite the two halves by means of a tunnel, and, in the words of Samuel Johnson, who did not greatly approve of such frivolities, 'he extracted an ornament from an inconvenience, and variety produced a grotto where necessity enforced a passage'. Pope himself left a far more poetic description:

Coleford, Gloucestershire Lower Perrygrove Farm on the B4228 has a curious mixture: old Roman iron mines and a wood laid out with puzzle paths.
Durgan, Cornwall (4 miles (6.4km) south-west of Falmouth) Beautiful maze in the grounds of Glendurgan House (NT).
Edenbridge, Kent A yew maze in the grounds of Hever Castle.
Esher, Surrey Claremont Park, 1 mile (1.6km) south of Esher, one of the earliest landscape gardens complete with pavilion, grotto and turf amphitheatre (NT).
Gateshead, Tyne and Wear A recently restored hedge maze in Saltwell Park.
Hatfield, Hertfordshire There is a maze in the grounds of Hatfield House.
St Agnes, Isles of Scilly A stone maze which was made in 1726.
St Martin's, Isles of Scilly A modern maze constructed to amuse the tourists.
Kelso, Borders Floors Castle has a modern beech maze, using heraldic and chess symbolism.
Machynlleth, Powys The Centre for Alternative Technology has a labyrinth full of dead ends symbolising government decision-taking.
Newquay, Cornwall A dragon-shaped maze at the zoo.

I found there a spring of the clearest water, which falls in a perpetual rill, that echoes through the cavern night and day. From the river Thames you see through an ivy arch, up a walk of the wilderness, to a kind of temple wholly composed of shells in the rustic manner; and from the distance, under the temple, you look down through a sloping arcade of trees, and see the sails on the river passing suddenly and vanishing, as through a perspective glass. When you shut the door of this grotto, it becomes in the instant, from a luminous room, a camera obscura, on the walls of which all the objects of the river, hills, woods, and boats, are forming a moving picture, in their visible radiations: and when you have a mind to light it less, it affords you a very different scene. It is finished with shells, interspersed with looking glass in regular forms, and in the ceiling is a star of the same material, at which when a lamp of an obicular figure of thin alabaster is hung in the middle, a thousand pointed rays glitter, and are reflected over the place. There are connected to this grotto, by a narrow passage, two porches; one towards the river of smooth stones, full of light and open, the other towards the garden, shadowed with trees, rough with shells, flints and iron ore.

The bottom is paved with simple pebbles, as is also the adjoining walk up the wilderness to the temple, in the natural taste, agreeing not ill with the little dipping murmur, and the aquatic idea of the whole place.

Curiously, Pope's house has gone but the grotto has survived. Sadly, however, it fails to live up to the description, for it has not been well kept, and it remains now simply as a place of interest, the starting point from which others set off to build grottoes of their own.

One notable grotto continues the Alexander Pope connection. The gardens at Stourhead in Wiltshire are justly famous, and contain a remarkable collection of ornaments and monuments, including a vaulted grotto over one of the sources of the River Stour. Among the reclining statuary is an inscription, translated from the original Latin by Pope:

Nymph of the Grot these sacred springs I keep
And to the murmur of these waters sleep.
Ah! spare my slumbers, gentle tread the cave,
And drink in silence or in silence lave.

The title of 'largest and most beautiful in the world' was given to the grotto at Goldney House, Clifton, by, of all people, John Wesley, a gentleman whom one would not normally associate with being a keen judge of such matters. On this occasion, however, one has to say that his judgement is impeccable. If ever a grotto seemed to be a perfect evocation of the home of the god of the sea this is it: watery, grotesque and just a touch sinister as though there might actually be a supernatural being lurking inside. It was built by a wealthy Bristol industrialist and banker, Thomas Goldney, who by 1737 had recorded the completion of a subterranean passage to his grotto but was not able to announce the completion of the grotto itself until 1764. It was an immense effort and

The grotto at Goldney
House *(Rob Scott)*

A twentieth-century grotto at Dinmore Manor, Herefordshire *(Anthony Burton)*

produced a suitably grand result. The entrance is down a long, dark, sinister passage towards the dimly lit grotto where the waters roar. Four encrusted pillars mark the entrance to the cave itself, a miniature wonderland of exotic rocks and shells. At the end of the cave, in the inner sanctum, is Neptune himself, a ghostly figure of marble resting casually on an urn from which the water empties to make a grand cascade. What differentiates Goldney from all other grottoes is the completeness of the vision. One does not think of it as a fashionable conceit, a typical piece of Georgian whimsy: Goldney seems a genuine temple to the gods which the ancients themselves would have been proud to own.

Perhaps the only grotto which can challenge Goldney is at Ascot Place in Berkshire. This is an elaborate concoction which begins with rocks piled high and a cavernous entrance across a lake. Inside one finds not just one grotto, but a group linked by passageways. There are pools and stalactites and fantastic rocks and exotic shells, coloured lights and little seats for visitors to pause and enjoy the fantasy. It is doubtful if anything on this scale will ever be built again, but the art of grotto building did survive into the present century at a house which, in itself, has more than a touch of the curious about it. Dinmore Manor in Herefordshire has a serious claim to fame, for it was the headquarters of the Knights Hospitallers of St John of Jerusalem, the company whose emblem is still well known today through the St John Ambulance Brigade. Here is the chapel that dates from the twelfth century, and in it are recorded the names of all the early commanders of Dinmore. The roll ends with the lines:

> The Knights are dust
> Their swords are rust,
> Their souls are with the Saints we trust.

Dinmore is a delightful place, but it would never have been included in this book if the manor had not been bought in 1927 by Richard Hollins Murray, an ingenious gentleman who made a fortune by inventing cat's eyes which blink down the middle of so many roads. He showed equal ingenuity in transforming Dinmore Manor. He built a splendid music room in imitation of a medieval hall, complete with gallery and a pipe organ, which can be played in the conventional manner or mechanically by organ rolls. He also built cloisters along one side of the garden, and it was here that he created his grotto. Where Goldney's workers struggled for years with intractable rock and stone, Murray took a more modern approach. Concrete was pressed through fine mesh wire and coloured with earth colours. There are two small pools, but the grotto's glory is the stained-glass window which floods the area with light. The design shows an exotic landscape of palm trees, water and distant mountains, and has been carefully positioned so that the horizon on the glass landscape coincides exactly with the actual horizon outside.

Grottoes are artifices with no purpose other than to give pleasure: the same is not true of mazes. In the ancient world, the maze had important religious and mythical overtones. The best known story concerns the Minotaur, half-man, half-bull that lived in the heart of the labyrinth. Each year the beast extracted a penalty, imposed by King Minos of Knossos, of seven youths and seven maidens. The Minotaur was slain by Theseus, who, in his passage into the labyrinth, had laid a fine thread which he was able to follow back to safety. In time, the labyrinth came to be associated also with the other great Cretan city of Troy, so that the appearance of the name 'Troy' even now alerts one to expect a maze: Troy Town at St Agnes in the Scilly Isles for example, or the City of Troy at Brandsby in Yorkshire. The latter is built to the traditional seven-ring pattern of the Cretan maze. But there are far older mazes than this, carved in the rocks of the Rocky Valley near Tintagel in Cornwall. They have been dated to the early Bronze Age, perhaps as early as 1800BC. The carvings also show the Cretan labyrinth, and the date coincides with a period when the Phoenicians, those great navigators of the ancient world, were expanding their trade from the Mediterranean. There is a strong local tradition that they came to Cornwall to trade for tin. Did they bring with them the symbols of the Cretan

Pennard, Gower Peninsula, West Glamorgan A Cretan labyrinth on the beach.
Saffron Walden, Essex Bridge End gardens have a restored hedge maze and a turf maze can be seen on the common.
Somerleyton, Suffolk Somerleyton Hall has a yew-hedge maze leading to a pagoda.
Symonds Yat, Hereford and Worcester There is a maze with a temple at the centre and a maze museum.
Wardour Castle, Wiltshire (2 miles (3.2km) south-west of Tisbury) An eighteenth-century grotto.
Ware, Hertfordshire Beside 28 Scott's Road is the entrance to Scott's Grotto, built by a Quaker family in the eighteenth century.
Warminster, Wiltshire Longleat House numbers among its attractions a complex hedge maze given a third dimension by the use of bridges.
Whitley Bay, Tyne and Wear Springfield Park, Forest Hall, has a Stephenson *Rocket* maze.
Winchester, Hampshire Square turf maze, St Catherine's Hill.
Woburn Abbey, Bedfordshire The house and grounds have a fine collection of oddities, including a grotto and shell room, a Chinese dairy and a timber pagoda in a hedged garden maze.

The grotto in the cliffs at Hawkstone *(Royal Commission on the Historical Monuments of England)*

labyrinth? Were they the work of Mediterranean sailors whiling away the time while their ship was loaded for the voyage home? Or is there a connection with the 'cup and ring' markings carved on rocks in Scotland? One carved slab, also from the Bronze Age, is kept at Cardoness House, Gatehouse of Fleet, and shows a pattern of seven concentric rings, but instead of a maze, a 'passage' leads straight to the heart. Whether there is a connection or not, there seems to be something in these patterns of rings which has a powerful appeal.

The true maze, the Minotaur labyrinth, regularly occurs in Roman mosaics, either in the traditional ring form or squared off. In the squared version, however, the basic pattern, angular instead of curved, is repeated in each of the four quadrants of the square, but still preserving the image of Theseus and the Minotaur at the centre. It may not be immediately apparent at first glance, but the traditional Cretan maze is built up from a cross; this motif was taken up by the early Christians. Similar designs began to appear in churches in Europe as part of the pavement of naves as early as the twelfth century, but were comparatively rare in Britain. One early survivor can be seen high up in the roof of the beautiful church of St Mary Redcliffe in Bristol. One of the bosses has an eleven-ring maze in gold and black, in which the cruciform pattern, formed by the connecting links between the circles, is very plain. A similar design was re-created nearby in Victoria Park, some five centuries later in 1984, as a water maze.

Some mazes may have originated from the culture of the invaders who overran so much of southern England in the Dark Ages: the Vikings, the Angles and the Saxons. It is only appropriate that those who try to follow the history of mazes find themselves in as complicated a system as those who try to trace a route through the mazes themselves. The name 'maze' shares a common root with the word 'amaze' and both have obscure early English origins; they give rise to another delightful name, 'mizmaze', which is only used in southern England. This name is applied to a particular type of maze which again is limited to southern England, the turf maze where the pathways are cut as gullies through the grass. These do seem to have a connection with pagan rites. Another name for them is 'maiden's bower' and legends tell of youths pursuing the maidens up and down the pathways: those girls who reached the centre before they were caught went cheerfully on their way; those who did not were spared the fate of the young girls sent to the Minotaur, but suffered what Victorian moralists would have described as 'a fate worse than death'. But all this is thrown into confusion by the existing turf mazes which sometimes look to Crete with their 'Troy' names and sometimes have unmistakable cruciform patterns in the Christian tradition. The turf maze at Wing in Leicestershire, for example, is found in a village whose origin can be traced back to the Norse Vengi, but has a turf maze of unknown antiquity with a cruciform pattern. A similar maze at Hilton in Cambridgeshire has a pillar in the centre, informing visitors that it was constructed in 1660 by William Sparrow, but whether the maze itself was new at that date or just Sparrow's pillar is uncertain.

This maze in Bristol is based on the one shown in a roof boss at nearby St Mary Redcliffe church
(Anthony Burton)

(Left) The Bicton maze, designed for children, is made up of upright logs, and forms the shape of a giant footstep *(Minotaur Designs)*

In time, the religious significance of the maze became lost to sight. There have, nevertheless, been returns to religious themes. There is a maze at the rectory in Wyck Rissington in Gloucestershire. It is a hedge maze which was begun by the rector in 1944 as the result of a dream. It was finally completed and fully planted in 1950 and every year the local children are brought to wend their way through the maze. It is still good fun, but the maze represents something more than that. It also acts as a symbol for the journey through life, starting with birth at the entrance and, if you follow the right path, ending in Paradise at the centre. Each wrong turn represents a sin that leads away from the goal, and as you penetrate deeper, travel further along the path, so the maze becomes more complex, mirroring the increasing complexity of life as one gets older. This symbolic journey has a good deal in common, one suspects, with the ancient mazes. An even more elaborately symbolic maze was built at Grey's Court in Oxfordshire in 1981, designed by Minotaur Designs, of whom more later. It had its origins in Dr Robert Runcie's enthronement address when he became Archbishop of Canterbury.

> I had a dream of a maze. There were some people very close to the centre, but they could not find a way through. Just outside the maze others were standing. They were further away from the heart of the maze but they would be there sooner than the party that fretted and fumed inside.

And the archbishop got his maze, full of symbolism, which can be threaded for ¼ mile (400m) to the centre where a sundial rises up on a column standing on a cross.

All this may seem a long way from the image most of us have of a maze, a series of bewildering passages between tall hedges that keep the wanderer from having any view of the final goal, the centre of the maze. The hedge maze, or puzzle maze, has no significant purpose other than to provide amusement. The oldest and most famous maze in Britain is at Hampton Court, designed in 1690. In spite of its fame, it is comparatively small, but its pathways are so convoluted, doubling back on themselves so frequently, that the total length of pathways extends for ½ mile (800m). It appears, at first, to be a simple enough business to win through the maze to the centre and out again. Readers of Jerome K. Jerome's classic story of a trip up the Thames, *Three Men in a Boat,* will remember Harris's valiant but doomed attempt to lead a party through. Eventually, in despair, they called for a keeper, who attempted to direct their progress from the top of a ladder. When that, too, failed, he went in to collect them:

> He was a young keeper, as luck would have it, and new to the business; and when he got in, he couldn't get to them, and then *he* got lost. They caught sight of him, every now and then, rushing about the other side of the hedge, and he would see them, and rush to get to them, and they would wait for about five minutes, and then he would reappear again in exactly the same spot and ask them where they had been.

(Above) A traditional hedge maze at Hever Castle
(Minotaur Designs)

They had to wait until one of the old keepers came back from his dinner before they got out.

Harris said he thought it was a very fine maze . . .

One can easily understand why mazes became popular. A device that will amuse and, if necessary, lose one's guests has a good deal to be said for it. In truth, the Hampton Court maze puzzle is not too difficult to solve. All you need to do is – but I shall not spoil everyone's fun by giving the secret away, other than to say that it is entirely logical.

One of the great attractions of the maze is that, unlike so many other 'follies' its popularity has never died. The 1930s produced a maze in what was the then unlikely setting of a municipal park – Hazelhead Park in Aberdeen. The Lord Provost in the early thirties was Sir Henry Alexander who, rather than follow hallowed tradition by presenting the city with a dull statue or portrait, gave it this delightful and cunningly devised maze. It covers the best part of an acre and the path to the centre – marked by an infuriatingly visible but seemingly unapproachable flagpole – is over ¼ mile (400m) long. He is a clever visitor who reaches the centre of the maze without walking a good deal further than that.

It is only in recent years, however, that the maze has really made a comeback, and no one has done more to foster this admirable movement than Minotaur Designs who are almost certainly the only company in the world specialising in maze design. The Lappa Valley Railway in Cornwall is a narrow-gauge steam railway with all kinds of other attractions offered as well, including a maze. But this is no ordinary maze. The pattern it traces on the ground is one that is entirely appropriate both to the railway and to Cornwall, for it shows the world's first successful steam locomotive, built by the great Cornish engineer, Richard Trevithick. It was a curious engine, with a piston stuck out in front like a giant trombone slide, an unwieldy array of cogs and a great fly-wheel. But the complexity that made it unsatisfactory as a machine makes it into the splendid basis for a maze. To add to the fun, hidden in the maze are the date of the first successful run, 1804, in Roman numerals, Trevithick's initials and EWR for the East Wheal Rose mine alongside the maze: what this maze does do is to show the Minotaur philosophy at work.

Making a successful maze is not just a matter of creating a complicated path. It must have an intrinsic logic and it must be satisfying. But Minotaur Designs believe that is not enough by itself. The right materials must be used to fit the surroundings, and Minotaur believe that the cost is not important: 'The Daedalus of today will only build your maze for a four-century survival. Settle for that, it is probably the longest term investment you are ever likely to make.' To make a really good maze seems to require the combined skills of the best graphic designer and the finest landscape gardener, with a touch of the art of the mystic. Here are just three examples of Minotaur's art.

The first is pure fun, built for a children's playground at Bicton Park in

Devon. It takes the shape of a giant's footstep in which the paths are separated by wooden posts. Children who follow the logical step of simply always turning in the same direction will find that they will have made a tour of the entire foot, with visits to all five toes, before finishing up precisely where they started.

A very different maze can be seen at Kentwell Hall, Long Melford in Suffolk. It was built in the courtyard in 1985 to celebrate the 500th anniversary of the Battle of Bosworth which ended the Wars of the Roses and established the Tudor dynasty. Only one design was possible: the Tudor rose which combines the white rose of York with the red rose of Lancaster. The immense rose maze used 27,000 paving bricks. There are five different pathways, starting from the five pointed thorns on the outside. It has the qualities of the very best mazes: it is both a good puzzle and a work of beauty.

The finest maze is also the most elaborate. Planted at Leeds Castle in Kent in 1986, it is difficult to imagine anything more fitting to end this catalogue of absurd but, one hopes, always delightful constructions. The castle itself in its lake setting is one of the most romantic in Britain, and the maze draws its theme from that. The maze forms a topiary castle, with hedges shaped into towers and battlements, surrounding a central mound; it is, in fact, a motte and bailey. Visitors cross a bridge over a dry moat to enter through a topiary gateway, and once inside they are faced by a bewildering pattern, with circles inside the basic square. But the effort of reaching the centre is amply rewarded. From the motte they can view their green castle, but they do not have to retrace their steps. A secret entrance leads down to a lovely grotto, with a fountain and a grotesque giant's face. Beneath is a tiny hermit's cell from which a secret passage leads out of this strangest of strange castles. So many fantastic elements come together here that it would surely be the envy of the great folly builders in the past.

I began by quoting my own words, from a book I completed in 1981: 'someone somewhere is perhaps providing a new wonder . . . constructing a maze.' I had no notion then of how gloriously true these words would prove to be. So may I raise my glass to the maze builders of Minotaur Designs and to all who continue to make wonders which have no use other than to give delight and no purpose other than to make a sometimes dull world a great deal brighter. Long may they thrive.

The Tudor Rose maze at
Kentwell Hall is believed to
be the world's largest brick
pavement maze
(Minotaur Designs)

Further Reading

Barton, Stuart, *Monumental Follies: An Exposition on the Eccentric Edifices of Britain* (Lyle Publications, 1972)

Bland, John, *Odd and Unusual England: An Illustrated History of Curious Things* (Spur Books, 1974)

Bord, Janet, *Mazes and Labyrinths of the World* (Latimer New Dimensions, 1976)

Bord, Janet and Colin, *A Guide to Ancient Sites in Britain* (Latimer New Dimensions, 1978)

——*The Secret Country: Interpretation of the Folklore of Ancient Sites in the British Isles* (Paul Elek, 1976)

Burton, Anthony, *Opening Time, A Pubgoer's Companion* (Unwin Hyman, 1987)

Clayton, Peter, *Archaeological Sites of Britain* (Batsford, 2nd edition 1985)

Coate, Randall, Fisher, Adrian and Burgess, Graham, *A Celebration of Mazes* (Minotaur Designs, 1986 (4th edition))

Darley, Gillian, *Villages of Vision* (Architectural Press, 1975)

Edwards, Paul, *English Garden Ornament* (G. Bell, 1965)

Gaunt, Arthur, *Tourists' England: A Kaleidoscope of Oddities and Strange Places* (F. Graham, 1969)

Grigson, Geoffrey, *The Shell Country Alphabet* (Michael Joseph and Rainbird, 1966)

Hawkes, Jacquetta, *The Shell Guide to British Archaeology* (Michael Joseph, 1986)

Herbert, A. P., *Sundials Old and New* (Methuen, 1967)

Headley, Gwyn and Meulenkamp, Wim, *Follies: A National Trust Guide* (Jonathan Cape, 1986)

Hitching, Francis, *Earth Magic* (Cassell, 1976)

Hogg, Garry, *Facets of the English Scene* (David & Charles, 1973)

——*Odd Aspects of England* (David & Charles, 1969)

——*The Shell Book of Exploring Britain* (John Baker, 1971)

Hole, Christina, *A Dictionary of British Folk Customs* (Hutchinson, 1976)

Hunt, John Dixon, and Willis, Peter, *The Genius of the Place: The English Landscape Garden* (Paul Elek, 1975)

Jones, Barbara, *Follies and Grottoes* (Constable, 1974)

Lea, Raymond, *Country Curiosities: The Rare, Odd and Unusual in the English Countryside* (Spur Books, 1973)

Lindley, Kenneth, *Of Graves and Epitaphs* (Hutchinson, 1965)

Timpson, John, *Timpson's England* (Jarrold, 1987)

Vince, John, *Village Style* (Ian Allen, 1974)

Warren, Geoffrey, *Vanishing Street Furniture* (David & Charles, 1978)

Whitelaw, Jeffrey W., *Follies* (Shire Publications, 1982)

Index